The Virtuous Spiral

List of Figures, Tables and Boxes

Figures

Tables

Boxes

Contents

To Allan and Sue,
for opening a gate to new horizons

First published in the UK and USA in 2000
by Earthscan Publications Ltd

Copyright © Alan Fowler, 2000

A catalogue record for this book is available from the British Library

ISBN: 1 85383 610 9

Typesetting by PCS Mapping & DTP, Newcastle upon Tyne
Printed and bound by Redwood Books Ltd., UK
Cover design by Richard Reid

For a full list of publications please contact:

Earthscan Publications Ltd
120 Pentonville Road, London, N1 9JN, UK
Tel: +44 (0)20 7278 0433
Fax: +44 (0)20 7278 1142
Email: earthinfo@earthscan.co.uk
http://www.earthscan.co.uk

22883 Quicksilver Drive, Sterling, VA 20166–2012, USA

Earthscan is an editorially independent subsidiary of Kogan Page Ltd and publishes in association
with WWF-UK and the International Institute for Environment and Development

This book is printed on elemental chlorine-free paper

The Virtuous Spiral

A Guide to Sustainability for Non-Governmental Organisations in International Development

Alan Fowler

Earthscan Publications Ltd, London and Sterling, VA

Acronyms and Abbreviations

ABONG	Association of Brazilian Non-governmental Organisations
ACORD	Agency for Co-operation and Research in Development
ACP	Association of Craft Producers, Nepal
AfDB	African Development Bank
AFRODAD	African Network on Debt and Development
AKF	Aga Khan Foundation
AKRSP	Aga Khan Rural Support Programme
ALOP	Association of Latin American non-governmental organisations
AMREF	African Medical and Research Foundation
ANC	African National Congress
ANGOC	Asian Non-governmental Organisation Consortium
APPC	Asia Pacific Philanthropy Consortium
ASAPU	Association de Soutien a l'Autopromotion Sanitaire et Urbane, Côte d'Ivoire
AsDB	Asian Development Bank
Asia-DHRRA	Asian Development of Human Resources in Rural Areas
BAIF	Bhartiya Agro Industries Foundation, India
BEST	business expenses and saving training
BRAC	Bangladesh Rural Advancement Committee
CAF	Charities Aid Foundation
CASES	Centre d'Animation Sanitaire et d'Etudes Sociales, Côte d'Ivoire
CBO	community-based organisation
CCF	Christian Children's Fund
CCR	Centre for Conflict Resolution, South Africa
CDF	comprehensive development framework
CDRA	Community Development Resource Association, South Africa
CECADE	Centro de Capatación para el Desarrollo, Costa Rica
CEDEP	Centre for the Development of People, Ghana
CEDI	Ecumenical Centre for Documentation and Information, Brazil
CEFRAR	Centre de formation et de Recherche en Animation Rurale, Côte d'Ivoire
CENCOSAD	Centre for Community Organisation and Social Action for Development, Ghana
CETEC	Corporación Para Estudios Interdisciplinarios y Asesoria Tecnica, Colombia
CIDA	Canadian International Development Agency
CINDE	Centro Internacional de Education y Desarrollo, Colombia
CIP	Côte d'Ivoire de Prosperite
CIVICUS	World Alliance for Citizen Participation

CODE-NGO	Caucus of Development Non-Government Organisation Networks, Philippines
CONAIE	Confederation of Indigenous Nationalities of Ecuador
COPE	Community Organising for People's Enterprise, Philippines
CPAR	Congress for People's Agrarian Reform, Philippines
CPS	Centre for Policy Studies, South Africa
CREN	Centre de Recuperação Nutricional, Brazil
CRS	Catholic Relief Services
CRY	Child Relief and You, India
CSO	civil society organisation
CVEI	Composite Village Empowerment Index
CWIN	Child Workers in Nepal Concerned Centre
CYDF	Chinese Youth Development Foundation
DAG	Development Action Group, South Africa
DESCO	Centro de Estudios y Promoción del Desarrollo, Peru
DFID	Department for International Development, United Kingdom
DMC	developing member country
DSA	Development Studies Association, UK and Ireland
ESCUELA	Escuela para el Desarrollo, Peru
EU	European Union
FAO	Food and Agriculture Organization, United Nations
FAVDO	Forum for African Voluntary Development Organisations
FES	Friedrich Ebert Stiftung, Germany
FFES	Fundaçion FES, Colombia
FLO	foundation-like organisation
FMO	Netherlands Development Bank
FONCAP	Social Capital Fiduciary Fund, Argentina
FPE	Foundation for Philippine Environment
FS	Fundación Social, Colombia
FSSP	Foundation for Sustainable Society Philippines
GDP	gross domestic product
GRO	grassroots organisation
GTZ	German Agency for Technical Cooperation
HASIK	Harnessing Self-Reliant Initiatives and Knowledge, Philippines
IADB	Inter-American Development Bank
ICNL	International Centre for Nonprofit Law, US
ID	institutional development
IDA	International Development Assistance Fund
IDB	Inter-American Development Bank
IFCB	International Forum for Capacity Building
IMF	International Monetary Fund
INTRAC	International NGO Training and Research Centre, United Kingdom
IPG	Institute of Politics and Governance, Philippines
ISA	Instituto Socioambiental, Brazil
ISEA	Institute for Social and Ethical Accountability
ISODEC	Integrated Social Development Centre, Ghana
IWGCB	International Working Group on Capacity Building

MST	Landless Rural Workers Movement, Brazil
MWENGO	Mwelekeo wa NGO, Zimbabwe
MYRADA	Mysore Relief and Development Agency
NEF	New Economics Foundation, UK
NGDO	non-governmental development organisation
NGO	non-governmental organisation
NOVIB	Netherlands Organisation for International Development Cooperation
ODA	overseas development assistance
OECD	Organisation for Economic Cooperation and Development
OELF	Organizaço de Aduda Fraterna, Brazil
ORAP	Organisation of Rural Associations for Progress
PBSP	Philippines Business for Social Progress
PHILDHRRA	Philippine Partnership for the Development of Human Resources in Rural Areas
POLIS	Assessoria, Formação e Estudos em Politicas Sociais, Brazil
PRIA	Society for Participatory Research in Asia
PRRM	Philippine Rural Reconstruction Movement
SAPRI	Structural Adjustment Participatory Review Initiative
SASE	Servicios para el Desarrollo, Peru
SDC	Swiss Development Cooperation
SIAD	Sustainable Integrated Area Development, Philippines
SIF	Social Investment Fund
SSM	Sarvodaya Shramadana Movement, Sri Lanka
TANGO	Tanzania Association of Non-Governmental Organisations
TEWA	Women's Support Organisation, Nepal
TNC	transnational corporation
TTO	Triple Trust Organisation, South Africa
TVO	Trust for Voluntary Organisations, Pakistan.
TWN	Third World Network
UK	United Kingdom
US	United States of America
UNDAF	United Nations Development Assistance Framework
UNHCR	United Nations High Commission for Refugees
USAID	United States Agency for International Development
USN	Urban Sector Network, South Africa
VAT	value added tax
VDRC	Village Development Resource Centre, Nepal
WB	World Bank
WCED	World Commission on Environment and Development
WTO	World Trade Organisation
WVI	World Vision International
WWF	World Wide Fund For Nature

Acknowledgements

This book has been made possible by support from the following non-governmental development organisations (NGDOs): the Aga Khan Foundation–Canada, the Bangladesh Rural Advancement Committee, DanChurchAid, Novib, World Vision UK and World Vision International. In addition to finance, they endorsed a proposal that royalties resulting from the book would benefit MWENGO, an African NGDO. To them, my thanks for the trust they have shown in supporting this initiative – it is an expression of their interest in learning from and sharing experience about issues of importance to the NGDO community.

In addition to financial assistance, a number of individuals have helped make this publication possible. Some, such as Nandy Aldaba, Al Alegre, Maria Christina Garcia, Andres Falconer, Willi Haan, Caroline Hartnell, Roger Hodgson, Carmen Malena, James Sarpei, James Taylor and Zane Dangor helped set up country interviews. Others, such as Mariano Valderrama have done this too, as well as providing written contributions. And, in less direct ways, through conversations and sharing materials, I am indebted to John Batten, David Bonbright, Mike Edwards, Leslie Fox, Liz Goold, Richard Holloway, Rick James, Lars Jorgensen, Allan Kaplan, Chris Purdy, Dunham Rowley, Ian Smillie and Roger Young.

I must also thank Fazle Abed, Dr Salehuddin Ahmed and Dr Mushtaque Chowdhury for the opportunity to work with BRAC in developing its approach to sustainability thinking and practice. It was an important spur to further investigation and writing about the topic.

This book draws on ideas and insights about NGDOs and sustainability put forward by Leslie Fox, Bruce Schearer and Richard Holloway. It also applies obervations on learning and adaptability from the corporate sector by, among others, Chris Argyris, Donald Schon, Peter Senge, Shona Brown, Kathleen Eisenhardt and Margaret Wheatley.

This publication has also benefited from critical reviews of *Striking a Balance*, especially in terms of density of material and layout. I appreciate this and other helpful feedback from, amongst others, David Lewis and Brian Pratt. These and other observations have been incorporated into this volume, hopefully improving its accessibility.

Thanks are also due to the staff of NGDOs, too numerous to name, who gave their time to be interviewed. Inevitably, I remain responsible for translating their opinions, experiences and insights into the pages that follow.

Finally, the encouragement and support of my partner, Wendy Crane, has helped me cope with the frustrating pleasures of a concentrated period of writing. As well as being expressed in other ways, my appreciation needs to be put on paper too.

Introduction

As part of a process of internal reform, in early 1999 the Asian Development Bank organised a regional workshop.[1] It brought together officials from borrower governments, staff of non-government development organisations (NGDOs), members of community-based organisations (CBOs), staff of bi- and multilateral donor agencies and the local media.[2] By way of introduction, participants were asked to 'vote' on the importance for them of four contemporary development concepts: gender, participation, empowerment and sustainability. An overwhelming majority voted for sustainability. This outcome was rather unfortunate because the workshop was dedicated to enhancing participation in the Bank's business practices. Nevertheless, the participants' response illustrates that the topic of this book is a common and predominant interest of actors across the aid system.

The importance of sustainability is reflected more widely and in many other ways as well. It can be seen, for example, in the numerous international conferences devoted to ensuring a viable future for the planet: in the rapidly growing number of academic publications, newspaper and other popular articles with the 'S-word' somewhere in the title: in the inclusion of 'environmental sustainability' perspectives and conditions for new investments and growing acceptance of the need for a 'triple bottom line' of social acceptability, ecological soundness and economic viability:[3] in the evolution of trading in emission permits for carbon dioxide and other greenhouse gases: in new sustainability-oriented legislation and emission control limits and standards, and in the design criteria for development projects and initiatives. In addition, it can be seen in a virtual industry that is trying to identify and design sustainability indicators and measures at all levels of environmental, economic and social processes.[4] The following pages relate to these and other endeavours, but with a particular origin, focus and purpose.

The initiative to write this book has its beginnings in *Striking a Balance*, a previous publication that, consequently, is referred to quite often and with which the reader's familiarity would be an advantage as its detail is not repeated or summarised. *Striking a Balance* sought to answer the question, 'what makes NGDOs effective?' In the course of interviews with NGDO leaders and staff, they often posed another question: 'what are NGDOs doing about sustainability?' At that time, the task was not to look systematically at this feature of organisational life. However, if *Striking a Balance* proved useful, I undertook to find the resources to look for answers to this specific, urgent concern.[5] The subsequent search took me to interviews with NGDOs in Africa, Asia and Latin America. The selection of organisations was based on referrals by individuals familiar with the NGDO community in a country. Some NGDOs were small, others were large: some young, some old. Some had a national perspective and spread, others were local. Together, the process involved interviews with staff in over a hundred organisations, as well as gathering literature from numerous sources, much of it unpublished.

The Virtuous Spiral differs from *Striking a Balance* in a number of ways. First, the previous book filled a gap in terms of providing comprehensive material on NGDO management and organisation.[6] This volume seeks to complement the growing amount of detailed material already available. But existing material is seldom combined into one integrated story. For example, attention to sustainable impact – typically through writing about monitoring and evaluation – seldom links to issues of organisational capacity and reputation and, hence, ability to raise funds. On the other hand, fund-raising manuals seldom highlight the other direction to the relationship between fund-raising choices and actual work and enduring change on the ground, or in organisational life cycles and regenerative processes.[7]

A second difference is that rather than acting as a detailed technical 'handbook', this volume concentrates on the strategic level in order to convey two major messages or ideas. One of the two ideas, and hence the title, derives from the previous paragraph, that is, different dimensions of sustainability need to be recognised and woven into each other as a comprehensive, mutually reinforcing strategy. This requirement is captured in the following quotation:

> 'Although the greater access to funding for their work undeniably helps such groups to be effective and have greater impact, few would deny that superior organisational capacities and successful execution of their programmes are the starting point. The finances come as a result.
>
> The lesson is profound: without a vital, relevant mission and strong organisational capacity, financial resources are not likely to be forthcoming no matter how worthy a group's intentions. And, even more important, financial resources alone do not generate the extent of programme results or the impact that could be achieved if an organisation's management, planning and ability to evaluate its role and work are as well developed as they can be.'[8]

Until now, no publication brings these aspects together in a balanced treatment or explores in detail the linkages between them.[9] By doing so, this volume complements and ties together other works on NGDOs in a particular and important way.

The other major message is that, in the final analysis, sustainability is not about techniques or measurement. For NGDOs, sustainability is all about a particular type of organisational capacity, identified as *'insightful agility'*. In an increasingly unstable, unpredictable and chaotic world, with NGDOs as very modest dependent actors, sustainability will only be realised if they can continually adapt and adjust in a purposeful, not random, way. This is an unconventional approach to the issue of sustainability. But it is one that is sometimes articulated in conversations with perceptive NGDO leaders and managers. Moreover, this view is more fundamental than a reliance on new technologies and skills to diversify a resource base. To this extent, many publications on NGDOs and sustainability are missing the essential point – the essence of sustainability in unstable environments.

Hopefully, the reader will see that the two messages are allied with each other. The concept of a virtual spiral ties the three parts of the book together – each containing a common theme of increasing both organisational insight and agility in terms of adapting to an ever-changing world.[10]

Complementing a growing amount of ongoing work requires care not to simply duplicate or summarise information and the many case studies to be found elsewhere. Additional information gathered through interviews is therefore used primarily to illustrate points and issues. Overall, the approach, especially in Part II, is to concentrate at the level of strategic options and choices. The intention throughout is to make the text less dense and more accessible, providing references and readings to more elaborate material. Given my tendency to see linkages and explore minutiae, I have found it difficult to maintain focus on two big messages without feeling that the resulting text is superficial. The reader must judge whether or not this is the case.

The content is both broad and narrow. It is broad because, conceptually, the topic is wide-ranging and multifaceted. However, its breadth has been narrowed in a number of ways. First, the sources of information and primary audience for the work are NGDOs: that is, non-profit organisations dedicated to ending poverty and injustice in developing countries. In addition, even more narrowly, it draws primarily on the experience of NGDOs indigenous to these countries that, in one way or another, are linked to the system of international development and aid.

Further, the study concentrates on organisational dimensions of NGDOs, complementing the more technical and sectoral treatment to be found in many other development publications. In other words, it tries to look through the eyes, experiences and intuition of NGDO leaders, managers and staff, rather than through the 'technologies' of international development practice.

The book's main objectives are straightforward. One is to provide a usable analysis and explanation of what NGDOs across the world are thinking and doing in terms of sustainability – in other words, to share experience and learning from within the NGDO community. In addition, the intention is to bring a better mix and balance into what is happening in the NGDO hunt for sustainability. For reasons explained in Part II, the NGDO perspective on sustainability is dominated by the search for more stable and secure funding – there is a strong perception that financing from the aid system cannot be relied on in the long term. The natural response, therefore, is to equate sustainability with reducing dependency on foreign aid in the quest for organisational survival. However, this reply to vulnerability is too limited. It will not ensure organisational longevity.

More complex responses are needed in terms of a 'virtuous spiral' that links three types or dimensions of sustainability: of external impact; of human and financial resources; and of the 'invisible' features that keep an organisation healthy, relevant and viable. The types have been identified through interviews, from many years of working with and for NGDOs, and from existing written material.[11] They reflect three common 'lenses' that effective and aware NGDOs look through when focusing on the tasks they face in translating sustainability into practice. Hence, the book is structured around the idea of multiple dimensions to sustainability.

Part I addresses sustainability from the perspective of development impact and enduring change. Parts II and III shift the story to the issue of sustainability of NGDOs themselves in terms, respectively, of resource mobilisation and the adaptive viability of organisations. Each part starts with an overview of important issues and the content of related chapters. As long as the two major messages – insightful agility and a virtuous spiral – are borne in mind, each part can be read on its own. In addition, it is intended that the content serve as material for study programmes, training courses and internal reflections that help the NGDO community and those who study it. For this reason, readings are suggested for important topics and an extensive set of references is provided.

Challenging as it is, my hope is that this publication proves useful for practitioners, for those with a more academic interest and for the donor community concerned with the issues involved. I trust this proves to be the case. As part of my own learning, critical and other feedback is always welcome.

Part I

Change that Endures – Sustaining Development Impact

'Sustainability is the shadow side of unsustainable development.'

(Allan Kaplan, CDRA)

Sustainable progress is supposed to be the guiding light and intention of all development endeavours. The paradox is that what is currently termed progress, or development, is causing greater instability and uncertainty allied to a growing certainty that the present path cannot endure ecologically or socially. The clarion call for development to be sustainable can be seen as a response to a contradiction between the intentions and effects of human action.

Within this paradox, NGDO interventions are meant to make a difference in that their achievements are maintained without them. However, the results of an array of assessments of their impact show that sustainability is a major weakness in performance.[1] There is little evidence to suggest that NGDOs are any better at generating enduring change than official aid agencies, where sustainability is estimated to occur in about 15 per cent of interventions.[2] Part I examines why this is the case for NGDOs and suggests what can be done to improve the situation.

Chapter 1 sets the scene by unpacking the concept of sustainability in relation to the 'big picture' of global change and the many 'little pictures' of NGDO interventions. The basic argument is that sustainability is a condition of three overlapping systems, but that these systems are unstable. Moreover, NGDOs are minor and highly dependent actors in terms of change. They control a little, they can influence some things but, in the main, they can only appreciate and respond to the actions of others with more power. Consequently, their approach to sustainability should be both integrative and, more importantly, must focus on building the capacity of communities and themselves to continuously adapt. This is the only approach to sustainability that makes sense in unstable, dependent situations. Sustainability is not to be found in new technologies or policies but in the ability to be agile.

Chapter 2 takes this perspective forward in relation to how NGDOs can intervene with communities and policy makers. It describes three components that need to be present and complementary and that define the content. Allied to content is the importance of the process adopted. Significant aspects of an intervention process relate to participation, linking with and embedding into other processes, and the eventual orderly withdrawal. These two aspects are common areas of NGDO weakness. Limitation stems from the inadequacy of projects as a way of thinking and as a development tool, coupled with problems of organisational psychology that create difficulties in moving from community dependency to independence. NGDOs too seldom have a development practice that serves this purpose, which is necessary if people are to be empowered towards the organisation, not just towards others like the government.

A common problem for NGDOs is to know where they are in a process with communities and others. Typically, monitoring and evaluation are the means to find out. However, Chapter 3 stresses that sustainability requires a new way of thinking about indicators. Rather than measuring achievement against a baseline and towards a (project) goal, NGDOs need signs that predict what will happen once the intervention ends. The chapter describes the real life indicators used as proxies for prediction. It also describes how NGDOs use stages and progressive measures to increase the probability of sustained impact.

Chapter 1

What Does Sustainable Development Mean for NGDOs?

'*... in contexts marked by poverty and gross inequalities, the whole notion of sustainability has little meaning.*' (Peter Oakley, INTRAC)[3]

Bringing about sustainable change is context dependent. The context in question – from local to global – is characterised by forces that create or reinforce instability and unpredictability, economically, socially and environmentally. Two important forces are market capitalism as a wealth-creating system and the search for and assertion of personal and group identity within and across existing political boundaries. This chapter reviews these forces as a way of locating NGDOs in the 'big and small pictures' of their operational contexts. It argues that their highly dependent position requires a perspective of sustainable development that, at its core, enhances people's capacity to cope with instability, not simply reactively, but in a directed way. However, NGDOs face constraints in pursuing this approach, three of which are described.

NGDOs and the 'Big Picture'

'*UN Report warns of Earth's unsustainable future*'. This headline captioned a newspaper article about *GEO-2000*, an end of millennium report on the state of the global environment and a remedial programme of action proposed by the United Nation's Environment Programme (UNEP).[4] The caption reflects the biggest scale and the most fundamental feature to which the concept of sustainability is being applied. Its perspective is the condition of the natural world in relation to mankind. The report is founded on a systems view of the world. It is a system embracing everything, everyone and every human activity. Global sustainability can be seen as a condition of a 'system of systems'.[5] This system of systems is a set of complex and dynamic interrelationships. It is composed of subsystems that horizontally link the smallest scales of individual choice and collective action. In turn, they interact with other subsystems that aggregate vertically to the global level in terms of their intended and unintended effects on other people and on the planet. In short, global sustainability – the 'big picture' – is the top or outermost shell or expression of multiple lower layers of processes, interactions and consequences that feed backwards and forwards on each other.

No one institution controls the process by which the world works and changes. At best, through the United Nations system there is a forum for negotiating – but seldom enforcing – what should be done to stop what is unwanted and reinforce what is desired. But, if the *GEO-2000* report is to be believed, this institutional arrangement is not up to the task. For example, modest progress in implementing some aspects of an international agreement intended to redress global warming – known as the Kyoto Protocol – is being outpaced by the negative impacts of population and economic growth. But, in turn, these factors are driven by, on the one hand, basic survival of those who are poor and, on the other, by limitless expectations of the better off about what politics, economics and technology should deliver in terms of personal satisfaction, freedom and a contented life.

The head of UNEP attributes the cause of continuing environmental degradation to two primary forces: '...the continued poverty of the majority of the planet's inhabitants and excessive consumption by the well-off minority'.[6] Addressing these causes lies at the heart of much of what NGDOs do. Most undertake direct interventions to improve the circumstances of people who are poor. In addition, through campaigns, information and development education they seek to modify the behaviour of those who are rich as well as heightening their sense of interdependence with and obligation to those living in poverty. In other words, in ways not always easy to see or trace, many NGDOs are intimately connected to the 'big picture' causes of unsustainability.

The choices NGDOs make in terms of 'big picture' advocacy are typically informed by structural constraints to improving the 'small picture' lives of people who are poor or in distress. Their pressure for reform is commonly directed towards the policies and practices of powerful political and economic institutions. For example, recent proposals by

Western governments to accelerate and ease debt relief for heavily indebted countries can be attributed to the continued advocacy pressure from NGDOs grouped together as Jubilee 2000. NGDO campaigns also contribute to changes in corporate behaviour that cause insecurity and instability. One recent example is the announcement by De Beers – a virtual monopoly in the world trade in diamonds – that it will not, even indirectly, purchase diamonds from Angola. The war-stricken population of this unfortunate country may see an end to conflict if a major source of funds for buying arms dries up. Meanwhile, pushed by non-profit organisations such as the Rockefeller Foundation and Greenpeace, Monsanto – a food commodities giant promoting genetic modification of crops – has publicly stated that it will no longer pursue the introduction of a 'terminator' gene designed to stop farmers from reusing seed.

NGDO advocacy and lobbying in the 'big picture' can bring indirect change by altering global political or economic structures, business behaviour and public policies. Their influence can affect large numbers of people, both rich and poor. But figures for such impact are impossible to measure or even guess. However, the purpose of this book is not to describe or explore the vast array of paths that link widely diverse NGDOs into the scale of the 'big picture'. The goal is more limited. The purpose is to use a sustainability perspective to examine organisations that take this requirement seriously in their grassroots work, with a view to enhancing their ability to do so.

To be meaningful, NGDO achievements in high-level policy reform must be translated into real and enduring benefits for the poor. Two problems stand in the way. First, the 'linear' model of policy making as an objective process of analysis and choice of options separated from implementation is an inadequate under-standing of what actually happens. Instead, policy and policy implementation are best understood as a 'chaos of purposes and accidents'.[7] In other words, predictability of a policy's effects cannot be assumed, nor can the policy process itself.

Second, in terms of both policy formu-lation and implementation NGDOs are far from in control of how they occur. The potentially 'big-picture' impact of policy influence rests on real commitment, coher-ent decision-making and capabilities of others. It requires decisions to be taken and applied through multiple linkages in world processes and within and between institu-tions that produce change in the intended way. But unintended effects are numerous, if not the norm. For example, the adoption of a Convention on Children's Rights is not meant to make families destitute if their labouring child can no longer work. Aid conditions are not meant to create depen-dency, or disempower and create perverse incentives for recipient governments that lead to 'fungibility' and devious relocation of external funds – but they too often do so.[8] In other words, there is much that can go wrong before the effects of lobbying and campaigns are positively felt by the poor. This has an important lesson and implica-tion for a core approach to sustainability described below.

NGDOs and Many 'Little Pictures'

How NGDOs, individually and collectively, go about their disparate, geographically spread tasks is explained in detail in *Striking a Balance* and in numerous other publications.[9] In brief, their approach typi-cally involves localised, small-scale direct interventions with communities and disad-vantaged groups. As described above, the many thousands of 'small picture' direct grassroots projects are increasingly being complemented by higher levels of national and international advocacy and lobbying. But we need to retain a sense of proportion and learn about an important consequence coming from the roots of NGDO develop-ment work.

Within the 'big picture', through their many 'little pictures', NGDOs probably directly reach or touch some 15 to 20 per cent of the population in the developing world that are classed as poor and margin-alised.[10] In other words, the scale of their direct outreach and impact on local sustainability is modest at best. Moreover, they are operating in 'little pictures' that suffer from a high degree of dependency on and vulnerability to the dynamics of the context – they control a little, influence a few bigger things, but can only appreciate most factors shaping their operational environment.

Together, modest direct outreach and heavy reliance on how others implement policy or corporate reform provide a very important lesson when approaching the issue of sustainability. The lesson is that, in both the 'big and little pictures', NGDOs are essentially dependent on other factors in the various systems that reduce or enhance the prospects for sustainability at any level. The significant consequence of this reality is that the lasting, fundamental contribution to sustainability of NGDO work lies not in technologies and social, economic or political reform. The heart of sustainability in development work lies in increasing the capability of people, and of NGDOs themselves, to respond to forces they do not yet control in a particular, insightful, way.

The fundamental challenge is to enhance local 'response-ability' directed towards sustainable outcomes in the new and rapidly changing circumstance that poor people and organisations continually find themselves facing.[11] Put another way, no condition is permanent or controllable. The core task in sustainability is creating conditions so that benefits endure under changing conditions – in other words to engender adaptability based on an understanding of what sustainability demands at any particular place or moment. This lesson can be summed up in the words of one NGDO leader: 'Sustainable impact is about creating a continuous ability to adapt.'[12]

This book argues that an NGDO's continued ability to do and improve on this central task depends on a number of things. First, it calls for generating an external development impact that is itself socially valued and enduring. Second,

NGDOs must assure continuity in the resources they need in order to work. Third, they must stay relevant by regenerating the 'life force' that drives and repositions them in an ever-changing context.[13] They must learn that tomorrow must be present in today's behaviour. In sum, they must be insightful and agile.

Within this perspective, this chapter explores the notion of sustainable development in terms of its concept and essential system components. The next chapter examines the elements that must be present in interventions that aim for sustainable impact. It concludes with a framework NGDOs can use to locate the elements of a sustainable systems approach to their work. Chapter 3 takes the framework forward in terms of an integrated and phased development practice. It describes the proxy indicators or signs managers use when reading what is going on and how change is likely to endure.

Sustainable Development – Concept and Content

International development is a system designed to direct and accelerate changes in society that should bring about improvement in the living circumstances of those in poverty or facing other forms of avoidable disadvantage. The criterion that change induced by international assistance must be sustainable has been part of the development agenda for many years. This chapter looks at what we have learned about the concept and content of sustainable change. The starting point is a reflection on the notion of sustainability and definitions of what sustainable development is thought to mean. From here, a systems framework is developed that NGDOs need to be aware of and work consciously towards.

The Notion of Sustainability – A Question of Scales and Balances

Sustainability is not a 'thing' that can be found or held. It is a condition or a property of complicated systems linking human behaviour to the natural environment. The system can be very small, localised and simple, or very large and complex. But, 'local' or 'simple' appearances are usually deceptive, because in the real world boundaries between systems are seldom, if ever, completely closed. In one way or another, systems interact with each other horizontally and vertically.[14] In other words, what is local is also global and vice versa.

For example, I have a piece of land in a semi-arid area on a mountain slope through which a small stream flows. A friend owns the catchment feeding the stream. Our agreement is that, to protect the integrity of the stream, we will not take more than 50 per cent of its flow for our domestic needs. But, cutting down the trees on the land below the major catchment area will negatively impact on the formation of clouds that condense on the mountain, which is the source of the springs that feed the stream. This way of providing for our energy needs effectively negates the intentions of our water agreement – 50 per cent of nothing is nothing. Moreover, our localised choices have impacts not only on our microclimate but on the potential for rainfall on the other side of the mountain where neighbours graze their livestock. In addition, my work involves much international travel on aeroplanes that contribute to global warming and climate change that indirectly affect the rainfall on the land we have, again potentially negating a decision about the stream. So one personal decision becomes tied to another and to effects elsewhere and at other levels.[15]

Therefore, any attempt at inducing a change that is meant to improve the prospect of sustainability must always take horizontal and vertical linkages into account. This frustrating fact is one reason why, in the past decade, the horizon of many NGDOs has been raised from local to higher levels of power and decision making that co-determine local achievements. It also implies that NGDOs need to be clear about the scale on which sustainability is being pursued. They must also be aware of boundary conditions that can only be appreciated or influenced, but not controlled. In other words, they must make a broad 'reading' of the local situation with which they are becoming involved.[16]

In addition, the notion of sustainability is intimately tied to the idea of an enduring balance. Put another way, sustainability implies that a given situation is stable in a particular way, for example that resources are not being used or degraded beyond the rate that they are being regenerated or upgraded. In addition, it implies that people are sufficiently 'in harmony' so that they are not upsetting a stable state of their relations and needs. It is open to question whether this condition is a realistic appraisal of human nature and the quest for 'progress'. This quest is exacerbated by the need for the dominant economic system – predominantly through advertising – to generate dissatisfaction so that people are induced to purchase 'satisfying' goods and services.

In order to function, the market must satisfy people's aspirations while simultaneously perpetuating their dissatisfaction – a paradoxical condition that works against equilibrium and stability. Framed in this way, the prevailing economic set-up is inherently and necessarily 'dissatisfying' in terms of human aspirations and needs. Hence, as well as producing the environmental degradation described in *GEO-2000*, as an economic system, market capitalism is also an important social force.

Proposing a sustainable alternative economic system is a central agenda of some NGDOs, such as the New Economics Foundation, and of writers, such as David Korten.[17] This long-term macro agenda, and how to pursue it, is beyond the scope of this book, which places direct poverty alleviation as its central concern. However, this is not to deny or ignore the structural importance of reform in the economic order. What it means is that to engage seriously in sustainable development, NGDOs must be both be aware and capable of dealing with ambiguity. On the one hand, the sustainability of what they do locally is likely to be undercut by structural forces shaping the 'big picture'. On the other hand, this prospect cannot be treated as an inevitability that makes a sustainability agenda a waste of time. Efforts towards sustainable impact are still vitally necessary. Increasing insight and agility is one way of going about it.

Recognising the ambiguity described above, NGDOs should adopt as a minimum criterion a self-imposed condition that they will not knowingly engage in interventions that enhance unsustainability at their chosen human and geographic scale of activity. In addition, in terms of what they themselves control in development work – which realistically speaking is not very much – NGDOs must ensure that they adopt and apply sustainable perspectives and practices. What this means organisationally is a theme of this book.

In terms of time scale, given limited influence the best an NGDO can probably strive for in terms of sustainable impact is that the benefits of its work are retained by children in today's generation. This means the life span of children who are already living. If this test is applied to every new development initiative, impact should be sustainable into future generations.

How then can NGDOs cut through the complexity, ambiguity and relative powerlessness described above to promote change that is tangibly sustainable and helps society improve its capability to respond in sustainable ways as conditions change? An analysis of definitions is one way of approaching this question.

Choosing Definitions and Respecting Integration

Not surprisingly, there are many definitions of sustainable development. Inevitably, they tend to reflect the institutional perspective and agenda of the writer. Box 1.1 provides a sample.[18] An inclusive approach is to seek out the essential elements contained within these definitions, or to select the formulation which contains most of them. The FAO definition captures features of sustainable change to be found in the others, but without the future – next generation – emphasis.

Comparing definitions, the core elements of sustainable development, with qualifying statements, appear to be:

- Natural environment dimension: not degraded; productive with good management practices.
- Economic dimension: viable and non-exploitive.
- Social dimension: public acceptability, while enlarging choices with equitable satisfaction of needs.
- Technical dimension: appropriate (in terms of environment, economics and society).
- Time dimension: reflecting inter-generational responsibility.

It is obvious that the different components of sustainability have an interrelationship. The following quotation is one way of describing the interaction between them.

'In practice, therefore, environmental questions are inextricably interlinked with social, economic and cultural values. Economic systems determine the rate and route of flows of energy and resources from the environment into patterns of human use, and the rate and flows of waste energy and materials from human economic operations back into the environment. These economic systems are, in turn, imbued by cultural values, and underpinned by social and psychological models that influence the way that people see their options and make their choices.'[19]

BOX 1.1 DEFINITIONS OF SUSTAINABLE DEVELOPMENT

'Development that meets the needs of the present without compromising the ability of future generations to meet their own needs' (WCED, 1987)

'[Sustainability is defined as] management practices that will not degrade the exploited system or adjacent systems' (Ecological Society of America, 1993)

'Sustainable Human Development can be defined as the enlargement of people's choices and capabilities through the formation of social capital so as to meet as equitably as possible the needs of current generations without compromising the needs of future ones' (Banuri et al, 1994)

'A development which is environmentally non-degrading, technically appropriate, economically viable and socially acceptable' (FAO, 1997)

'Sustainable development is a development path that is resistant or resilient to stresses and shocks of all kinds. Sustainable development has four essential components: productivity (yield, etc), ecological sustainability, stability and equity' (Conway, 1997)

In other words, from a sustainability perspective, these five elements do not stand on their own – they interact. One immediate implication is that sustainable approaches to development must themselves be integrated. Moreover, each element is a complex system in its own right. For example, the environment operates in complicated ways that are poorly understood. For a start, the relationship between global warming and climate change is unclear and contested. The economic element contains features such as physical hardware and technology as well as the notions of market cycles, investor behaviour and interactions between them. This complexity, again, suggests the need to take an integrated perspective when working within each element.[20]

Definitions in Box 1.1 implicitly take the world as the area within which sustainability is to be gained. For many NGDOs this is not a practically useful scale. Nevertheless, what it does mean is that operational NGDOs must ensure that their interventions are sustainable at what-ever scale they work. Consequently, they need to be aware of the links between their actions and consequences for sustainability at other levels.

NGDOs of primary interest in this study usually focus on the situation of poor people. The livelihood of a poor household is therefore a reasonable and common level which they use to think about sustainable impact and orient interventions. Looking upwards and downwards from a household's livelihood system can help NGDOs be aware of the hierarchy of levels and factors which will affect the sustainability of its own work. Appendix I is an example of levels that may be relevant for rural households that gain their main livelihood from agriculture. For the urban poor, other levels would be more appropriate.

So far, we have dealt with issues of timing and levels of action which nest within each other. What, if anything, does sustainability thinking say about the content of sustainable projects and programmes? A common view is that sustainability can best be looked at in

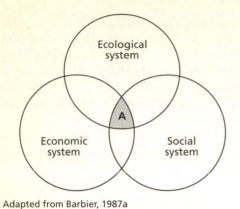

Adapted from Barbier, 1987a

Figure 1.1 *Systems in Sustainable Development*

terms of the systems that drive the world at all its different levels of human activity.[21] The challenge for NGDOs is to ensure that their interventions either contain all these system elements or fit properly with the work of others, a task explored in subsequent chapters. The question therefore, is what systems drive development and, in doing so, generate wealth, poverty and unsustainability?

Sustainable Development and Unstable Multiple Systems

Figure 1.1 captures one view of the systems that development work should take into account. A development intervention could try to optimise its effects in any one of these systems. But sustainable impact in the lives of poor people requires a combination of changes located in the area of overlap. It corresponds to Elkington's 'triple bottom line' of ecological sustainability, economic viability and social responsibility being put forward as criteria for profitability and sound growth.[22]

The ecological system comprises all elements of the natural environment. It embraces the interaction between climate and all life, including people in terms of their essential biological functions: their

physical needs, such as food and shelter, and their vulnerabilities, for example to poisonous chemicals. The resources people use exist in an evolving relationship to other natural resources and conditions which together make up the total ecosystem. For many who are poor, sustainability requires that the stocks of renewable resources to which they have access – such as air, water, vegetation, soil and animals – are not depleted, nor are they tainted or made unusable by human pollution

How all these factors interact at every level is not well known. For example, attribution of environmental instability and natural disasters – such as increasing hurricanes, floods and droughts – to global warming is contested. But as it is the poor who suffer most when disaster strikes, erring on the side of caution seems not only sensible but also a matter of social justice. Consequently, there is no chance of being absolutely certain about all the ecological effects of an NGDO's activities. This does not mean, of course, that effort is not needed to identify likely problems, for example the consequences of introducing more productive but non-indigenous species that could upset the previous ecological balance. In sum, when intervening in or altering livelihood-generating systems that depend on a primary interchange between people and nature, NGDOs must ensure that their natural resource base is not reduced or adulterated.

On the basis of supply and demand, the economic system allocates a value to resources, human efforts and tangible and intangible assets. It is 'designed' to generate economic growth built on a hierarchy of transactions. At the foundation is the extraction and technology-based processing of natural resources into tangible products, some of which are consumable. A widening variety of higher-level services has evolved from this foundation to serve people and to serve the system itself through a capitalist market place. Economic sustainability means the generation and maintenance of the value of an economic surplus, ideally, enhanced by the accumulation of capital reserves in terms of money or other economic assets.

A market-based economic system works at every scale of human endeavour. It is rapidly extending its reach throughout the globe. The market is driven by a competitive imperative to improve productivity, accumulate capital and market share and enhance the security and value of assets. Technology is a primary factor in making productivity gains. Improved communications and the opening up of economies to rule-based international trade mediated by the World Trade Organisation (WTO) are two important means for accelerating market penetration.

However, this system is itself worryingly unstable. As well as periods of wealth creation, it creates booms and busts, rocketing inflation, fluctuating exchange rates, economic depression and the 'crashes' witnessed in East Asia. It is a force that creates and feeds on systemic uncertainty which generates opportunities to make money that, in turn, lead to panics of buying and selling and over- and under-regulation.[23] With the opening up of capital markets, local distortions, herd-like investment behaviour and 'sentiments' are transmitted quickly across borders. Little progress on creating a new global financial architecture suggests that power holders cannot see or agree on a cure, or are becoming relatively powerless to implement one even if they do.

Destabilising social effects of market capitalism can be seen in escalating job insecurity, in the creation of a structural underclass of the unemployable and in the growth of 'McJobs' with little redeeming human value.[24] Despite progress in lifting people out of poverty and producing better levels of health and education, gaps in wealth – a potentially insidious force for social instability – are increasing by leaps and bounds within and between countries. Some three billion of the planet's six billion inhabitants are classed as absolutely poor while, moreover, their total incomes are matched by that of a handful of multibillionaires. The words of Michael Edwards echo those quoted at the beginning of the chapter, '"Sustainability" has little meaning in a world marked by [such] poverty and inequality.'[25]

Poor people have their own economic perspective and drives. This typically translates into:

1 increasing their financial and other assets;
2 reducing vulnerability by diversifying income sources;
3 being in greater control over factor inputs on which their livelihood depends; and
4 having better economic prospects for their children.

Here NGDO activity would be directed at ensuring that people are able to satisfy their basic needs; that (gender) equity is enhanced and that goods and services are accessible to and useful for those that the market does not reach. NGDOs can also seek to modify economic conditions in ways that reduce transaction costs for the poor as well as providing alternative, less exploitative economic terms. NGDO involvement in micro-credit is one example of the latter.

The social system derives from how people identify themselves and interact with each other. The system includes attributes such as social status and culture, sub-systems such as politics and governance and structural features such as division of power between groups and their interests. It also contains formal and informal mediating institutions and systems which society needs to remain stable and viable.

The 1990s have been a period of growing social unrest. Examples are the Kurdish revolt, ethnic cleansing in Central Africa, religious clashes in India, and political struggles to recognise the right of self-determination such as in Kosovo and the bloody separation of East Timor from Indonesia. This suggests that the search for and assertion of identity is an abiding force within social groups that must be increasingly considered. For example, it is probable that socio-economic class and economic ideology will not be primary factors in the political configurations of non-Western countries that start to embrace multi-party democracy. The introduction of a Scottish Parliament and a Welsh Assembly in Great Britain are already signs that aspects of identity other than class and wealth are equally, if not more, important. Politics which accentuates differences in identity, rather than cohesiveness, is a likely destabilising outcome.

It appears that erosion of national sovereignty as market globalisation proceeds, and the falling away of Cold War rivalry as a binding national social force, are leading to a new focal point for human self-awareness, aspirations, group behaviour and socio-political cleavages. Conditions are emerging where nationality and economic status are less defining features of people's identity and interests than they used to be. Other characteristics – ethnicity, language, religion, gender, world view – are coming to the fore as focal points for social organisation and in the definition of who belongs and who does not. In *Clash of Cultures*, Samuel Huntington posits a new world order marked by socio-political competition along religious lines.[26] Whether true or not, the point is that the way people sort out who else they belong with and where

their interests lie will be increasingly socio-cultural rather than socio-economic. In sum, increasing assertiveness of social groups, aggravated by destabilising economic forces, and opening up of political space, introduces its own type of instability to social systems and political relations.

NGDOs usually describe themselves as agents of social change – changing who wins and who loses in society's evolution is a common mission. To do this, NGDOs are active in almost all sub-systems and levels of society. Improving the status of people who are poor and marginalised; enhancing organisational capacity; changing the state–society interaction; increasing social justice and making politics and public decision-making more transparent, accountable and inclusive are typical NGDO concerns and goals. However, in the past few years, development thinking has introduced the idea of building 'positive' social capital as an important element in NGDO activity.[27] This poses a new challenge. By recognising social capital as a constituent part of the social system, NGDOs must now focus their attention on a particular set of values. They are being called upon to strengthen and expand relationships based on trust and reciprocity, between increasingly assertive people, groups, organisations and institutions.[28] Paradoxically, they are having to do so in the context of an economic system which stresses competition, (market) segmentation and mistrust.

Achieving sustainable poverty-reducing change in the lives of people is intimately tied to the way in which these three unstable and dynamic systems move. It entails finding '… better ways of blending market processes with social and environmental objectives'.[29] However, the extent to which NGDOs can push these systems in a mutually reinforcing direction is conditioned and constrained in a number of ways.

Constraints to NGDOs Adopting a Multi-system Approach

To be sustainable, changes benefiting people who are poor and marginalised must be supported by coherent, mutually supporting movement in all three systems: ecological, economic and social. In other words, the ideal is to ensure that all their interventions are located in area 'A' in Figure 1.1. This is tough. Why? Because, as noted previously, NGDOs have little influence over factors that cause change on the different levels at which these three systems operate. For example, NGDOs do not control inflation, the price of goods or internal terms of trade. They do not determine the nature of politics and power, such as how politicians use or misuse an appeal to people's sub-national identity as a source of support. In spite of this real limitation, NGDOs still need to be aware of, and as far as possible take into account, what they cannot control or influence. They cannot resign themselves to the inevitability of systems and structures remaining as they are. What they need is enough knowledge and insight to make a well considered choice about the right point of entry into these systems, often in collaboration with others.

An additional and growing problem of working in a multi-system way is that the resources that NGDOs increasingly rely on come from official sources structured around 'sectors'.[30] Typically, official aid allocates its funding through areas of professionalism, reflected in how governments organise themselves into technical and other ministries: health, education, water and sanitation, infrastructure, finance, trade and industry, the environment and so on. Too often, these vertical structures operate in mutually exclusive ways. For example, it is difficult for a ministry of health to see and employ micro-credit as an entry point for improving people's health status. In other words, governments find it difficult to link together expertise and processes associated with ecological, social and economic sub-systems.

Accessing funds along these institutional lines brings with it the hazard of steering NGDOs towards a mono- rather than a multi-system approach. Consequently their potential for generating sustainable impact is a function of the quality of the funds they access and the 'systems coherence' of the policy framework they inhabit. Studies of NGDO performance suggest that aid quality and public policy are major limitations on gaining sustained impact noted earlier.[31]

The pervasive shortcomings in aid performance are reasons for recent initiatives to make the system more coherent and sectorally integrated. The Comprehensive Development Framework (CDF) being promoted by the President of the World Bank, and the United Nations Development Assistance Framework (UNDAF) are two ongoing attempts to adopt a more multi-system approach. The danger, however, is that the rate of adoption of sectoralism by NGDOs will exceed the rate of institutional reform required for the aid system to be more integrated, consistent and coherent. If this occurs, the prospects of NGDOs being able to improve on their sustainability objectives is open to question. The next two chapters, therefore, look at what NGDOs are doing to deal with these and other constraints in terms of their direct development interventions and wider relationships.

Chapter Summary

This chapter adopts a systems approach to locate NGDOs within a global perspective of sustainability. Within this framework they must operate in the context of forces that are unstable and unpredictable. This creates both opportunities and threats to achieving sustainable impact.

To have enduring impact, NGDOs need to consider the following:

- Sustainable development is about bringing particular types of change in a dynamic system linking ecology, economy and society.
- The factors making up sustainable impact operate and interact at many levels at once, from local to global and back to local.
- NGDOs have little control of or influence over most factors that affect sustainable development. Therefore,
- A basic requirement is that, in what they do control and influence, NGDOs do not knowingly contribute to unsustainable change.
- Sustainable behaviour starts at home. NGDOs' work should not induce or reinforce unsustainable processes.
- For people who are poor and marginalised, promoting sustainable change means employing an inter-linked multi-systems approach to development where:
  - *in the economic system*, NGDOs adopt strategies which:
    - reduce economic vulnerability of households and their livelihoods;
    - increase assets and equity;
    - increase access to appropriate economic goods and services;
  - *in the ecological system*, NGDOs adopt strategies which:
    - ensure that natural stocks of plants and animals etc are increased/not degraded;
    - reduce or counter environmental hazards, such as chemical pollution;
    - increase biological productivity;
    - retain genetic diversity;
  - *in the social system*, NGDOs adopt strategies which:
    - advance social justice;
    - promote participation and inclusiveness in social and political institutions;
    - enhance mediating institutions that bridge between groups, based on trust and reciprocity;
    - respect cultural and human diversity.

Poor people and NGDOs are dependent actors in constantly changing environments. Consequently, the core of system strategies is an approach that enhances insightful agility. That is the ability to recognise, understand and adapt – in sustainably-oriented ways – to changes which determine the specific context.

NGDO impact is conditioned by the policy framework and quality of their funding. In today's aid conditions, they require approaches that not only do not over-sectoralise what they do, but also show how integrated development can be effectively pursued.

Chapter 2

Interventions for Sustainable Local Impact

'Whatever the source of the initiative, it is important that rural development programs be undertaken in a learning process mode and with assisted self-reliance as both means and ends.' (Uphoff, Esman and Krishna)[1]

The previous chapter drew attention to the relative lack of control that NGDOs have over the unstable systems that determine the sustainability of the changes they try to bring about. Nevertheless, the way an NGDO does development work – its practice – can still determine the probability of sustained change. It is all the more important, therefore, that the things NGDOs can control or influence are founded on an insightful approach to sustainability.

This chapter explores two aspects of such an approach to sustainable local development interventions: content and process. Content hinges on bringing about the right mix of three components of human change – material and physical improvement, enhanced local capacity and personal and group empowerment. These are the three legs of a platform on which responsive capacity must stand. Process hinges on the quality of local participation; on competence in linking and embedding interventions; and on an NGDO's psychological and practical ability to respect empowerment towards itself and skilfully withdraw. Shifting from dependency to independence is the key to communities sustaining the ability to cope with change.

The Content of Sustainably-oriented Interventions

A wealth of experience indicates that effective micro-development has three essential components in terms of human change.[2] NGDOs need to build these into their way of working with households, groups and communities. The three components are:

1 Tangible improvements in physical well-being, particularly: secure food supply, improved income levels, better health and education status and reduced vulnerability to seasonal and unexpected stresses.

2 Greater capacity for people to act individually, as households and collectively in organisations that they own, control and that represent them.

3 Empowerment in the sense of improved sense of self-worth and ability and willingness to act politically and negotiate in defence or promotion of own values, interests and rights.

Sustained micro-development must combine these three elements in an NGDO's approach, practice and results. How this

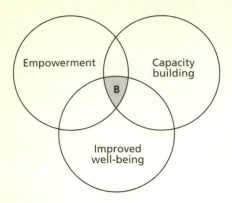

Figure 2.1 *Components of Human Change in Sustainable Interventions*

can be done is described in a wide range of manuals, studies and books listed for further reading. In a proper combination, these three elements of grassroots development create the preconditions required for people themselves, not NGDOs, to translate a 'rights-based' approach to development into practice.[3]

Chapter 1 points to one reason why, of these three components, the quality of the organisational capacity is so vitally important for sustainability. The task is not simply to build the capability of a community or group to manage or maintain the benefits of a particular input or investment, such as a school, clinic, credit fund, afforestation of a water catchment, or rural access road. Making change endure means going beyond the capacity required for this type of immediate necessity and action. The challenge is to foster organisational resilience founded on a link between sustainable insight and resulting action. For sustainability, awareness without action is sterile. Action without awareness is futile.

The necessary quality of local capacity is fed by the two other components and by the approach to capacity building itself. Improvement in physical well-being is typically associated with a stronger asset base and improved human condition.

People are less ill or physically weak and better able to cope with stress. They are more equipped to mobilise the resources needed to tackle a new problem or unexpected event which, in turn, makes their organisations more resilient and, if successful, more valued – an example of positive feedback. Another way of phrasing this is that, through material change, the resource base for local organisation and (re)action has been made more secure and success has made the organisation more capable.

In parallel, empowerment based on greater awareness allows people to interpret more accurately what is going on around them, providing a better foundation for an appropriate organisational response. Improving awareness requires an ability to accurately 'read' the environment. Often this calls for a Frierian-type of critical social analysis as a necessary component of capacity building. Without a critical awareness-raising element, enhanced capacity of community organisations will not be 'systems insightful', a necessary precondition for appropriate adaptation.[4]

A systems view of sustainability indicates that awareness raising should broaden people's horizons and perspectives from the intimacy of their physical location into an understanding of successively wider circles of power, influence and interdependency. Whether or not the concept of globalisation and its local affects are a useful point of reference is open to question. Nevertheless, a challenge for NGDOs is to identify the point of entry that makes most sense in terms of people exploring the horizontal and vertical linkages that matter to their lives. These could be the 'fish and rice' issues of improving local productivity of basic commodities. It could mean issues of land tenure or political representation. The task is to find out 'what lives' in terms of things people want to put their energy into, which is often reflected in a shopping list of demands and expectations.

Typically, NGDO points of entry are problems and the things poor people say they want. Identifying such focal points is therefore often accomplished in terms of satisfying people's problems or basic needs. This approach typifies a welfare, rather than an empowerment, perspective. An empowerment view would start with what people aspire to and are prepared to work for, drawing on their past accomplishments instead of stressing what they lack. The subsequent processes of action may not be too dissimilar. What necessarily differs is the psychological foundation established from the outset. Foundations which build on past successes respect the fact that people do already have capabilities and skilled ways of coping and surviving. The tone and style of intervention alters from one of patronage with NGDOs 'bringing something', to making people, rather than outsiders, the key force for change in their own future.[5] The task is to help people discover and appreciate the systems that play a role in their relative disempowerment that usually has a gender dimension.

The NGDO's own approach to local capacity building is obviously the key to forming an adaptive ability. It also determines the extent to which the potential contribution of the other two components sketched above is realised or lost. Much has been written about building local organisational capacity.[6] Some texts are mechanical, treating CBOs as a particular sort of machine that requires technical enhancement through soft and hard technology and training. However, this approach is less suitable if insightful agility is the answer to the vital question 'capacity building for what?' Of more use are organic views of CBOs as social units with variable environmental response capabilities.

Local capacity building requires processes that are really human-centred and 'ecological' in their view of organisational change.[7] This means perspectives and methods that place group dynamics, not project outputs, outcomes and impact at their centre.[8] While project achievement is a sign of capacity, it does not necessarily show the degree of CBO resilience to external stress and change in surrounding conditions. In other words, we need to pass beyond a project and look for unaided CBO behaviour to know if responsive capacity is present and is being applied.

This post-project condition is not easy for NGDOs to see. Consequently, part of the art of capacity building for sustainability is to employ staged processes and predictive indicators. What this means in practice is explained in more detail in the next chapter. However, adopting this type of practice makes particular demands on NGDOs. These demands stem from what community capacity is and how it can be developed.

Community Capacity

Typically, organisational capacity is regarded as an ability for a group to be who they want to be and to set and effectively achieve their goals or purposes. There are any number of features of capacity, or abilities, that CBOs need to accomplish what they set their minds to.[9] The following list is but one perspective.[10] A 'capacitated', independent CBO should:

- Mobilise, regulate, manage and account for local resources on an ongoing basis.
- Be critically conscious of the world in which they are living.
- Ensure that leadership can be censured and held accountable.
- Ensure and enable the ongoing partici-

pation of relevant stakeholders.

- Cost-effectively translate external support into sustained impacts.
- Critically assess public policies and translate them in locally appropriate ways.
- Mediate, resolve and manage internal conflicts.
- Effectively control an equitable distribution of benefits.
- Resist appropriation of benefits by those who should be excluded.
- Make legitimate claims on resources and defend local interests towards the government.
- Understand civic rights and exert them towards politicians and government officials.
- Hold NGDOs and other intervening agencies accountable for their behaviour.
- Monitor, evaluate and learn from experience.

These are, essentially, observable features of CBO behaviour and capabilities. As described previously in Figure 2.1, the three dimensions to human change should help create this complex range of features. There are, however, less tangible aspects of CBO capacity that determine how well the above are done, if at all. Two of the most fundamental are the level of trust between CBO members, allied to the degree to which their values and aspirations are shared and strongly held.[11] Where one or both aspects are weak, the CBO is likely to be fragile, despite abilities to set and achieve goals.

Enhancing trust and shared values is not a question of training. These organisational qualities stem from affinity in terms of identity, from personal experience and from observation of how others behave in relation to reaching mutually determined goals – in deeds not words. For NGDOs, this presents a challenge of understanding the sociology and ethnology of group construction. It also requires ways of dealing with elite and other power holders, where cooperation is usually a better strategy than alienation. The task for NGDOs, therefore, is to have deep local social insight and from this create learning opportunities for the CBO which test and reinforce invisible elements of its capacity. Ways in which NGDOs are doing this are explained in the next chapter

In sum, the issue with sustainability of member-based groups and of their achievements is to create a particular quality of capacity. This is the capacity to cope with change based on insight. This quality is not the same as the capacity to manage an external input to achieve a pre-planned output: a common focus of NGDO capacity-building efforts. Capacity for sustainability is concerned with the less tangible organisational characteristics such as trust, resilience, self-confidence and sound leadership. This does not mean that more tangible abilities are not relevant but rather that they are a necessary but not sufficient condition.

NGDO Competencies

An overarching competency for NGDOs is to assist the change in CBO capacity towards the area of overlap 'B' in Figure 2.1. Reaching this location in terms of human change brings a number of organisational demands.

The first requirement is information. In order to judge when and how to adjust the intervention, NGDOs face a continual struggle to know where communities or groups are in relation to their capabilities and growing autonomy. In other words, how do they know where groups stand in relation to the interplay between these three aspects of change: well-being, organisational capacity and empowerment? To gain this insight, NGDOs must have the skills to help CBOs generate their own measures of organisational strength and value and determine signs of change within themselves. This is a major topic for Chapter 3.

The second competence is adaptability – a fluid ability to change the nature of the NGDO's interaction with CBOs. For example, as economic returns and incomes or the asset base of households improve, the degree of NGDO subsidy and input should diminish; or, as groups become more self-assured and capable, the intensity of interaction with the NGDO should decrease. For example, for the Philippines Business for Social Progress (PBSP), an important role shift is from providing finance to providing technical assistance. From here, the role might again change to one of providing a bridge to other organisations. In other words, there is an NGDO role progression from financier to technical adviser to relational facilitator. This type of change in the relationship is sometimes called 'graduation' or withdrawal. The pivotal task, as Allan Kaplan puts it, is for groups to move from a dependent to an independent relationship with respect to the NGDO.[12] From this position, they can choose to become interdependent with the NGDO or any other organisation.

The third competence required is content integration. This topic, which is explored in more detail in the next chapter, can be achieved in different ways. For the present it is enough to point out that for some NGDOs, the answer lies in multispecialist teams where the group process, not the technology or type of input or level of output, stands central. For others, it lies in adopting a geographic development-area focus and seeking working relationships with other NGDOs and local government to complement the mix.

Overall, getting right the mix of these three dimensions of content over time is difficult. Moreover, the project mode of financing interventions does not make it any easier. Why? Because, amongst others, tightly predetermined projects work against continuous adjustment if, for example, new circumstances make pre-established goals less relevant, or if important actors change. Sustainability thinking brings an additional problem of relating these measures to the three systems of ecology, economics and society. Achieving this linkage is another major organisational task. A framework for doing so is the starting point for Chapter 3.

Content is one side of the intervention coin. The other is the process by which content is introduced and applied, this being the topic of the following section.

Sustainable Interventions as a Process

In terms of process, three elements stand out if sustainable local impact is to occur. The first is the quality of local participation in externally supported initiatives, even if locally defined. Second is the necessity of linking and embedding external support or innovations into surrounding, ongoing systems and processes. Third is the ability of an NGDO to withdraw in the right way at the right time. We will look at each.

The Quality of Participation

Experience also shows that interventions using good participatory methods gain more effective and sustainable results than those that do not. This does not mean that change cannot occur in non-participatory 'top down' ways. But there is compelling evidence that sustainability of benefits is positively correlated with people's authentic participation because, by co-defining change, they are more committed and motivated to take ownership of processes needed to bring it about. If this condition is not satisfied, be it in interaction with governments or communities, effects of external investments are often short-lived.[13] Critical to participation is targeting – reaching the appropriate gender, cultural, or socio-economic group. Here, the NGDO record of accomplishment is very uneven – it is difficult to reach the poorest of the poor, and NGDOs are not as gender-sensitive as commonly assumed.[14] What, then are the essential features of participation that need to be right if local ownership, commitment and embedding of change are to take place?

Participation can be looked at from three important perspectives: depth, breadth and timing. Depth is a measure of stakeholders' influence on decision making. Breadth is a measure of the range of stakeholders involved. Timing relates to the stage of the process at which different stakeholders are engaged. The way that the three are approached and made to interact determines the intensity of local and wider ownership and commitment. Inadequate depth can create frustration, better mobilised opposition, complacency or passive or opportunistic cooperation. Inadequate breadth leads to fragility in local institutional foundations. Change becomes too dependent on a few individuals or power holders and their interests. Inappropriate timing, usually late inclusion of key stakeholders, leads to perceptions of tokenism, co-optation, disrespect and disempowerment. None of these feelings bodes well for local commitment.

Good practice in participation matches depth, breadth and timing according to the possibilities of the local situation, but not in a passive way. Counteracting social and economic exclusion often calls for extending the bound-

aries of existing participatory conventions and exclusion of the poorest from existing groupings. However, when opening up participatory space, the challenge is to balance all aspects of participation so that they do not become lopsided. When depth outstrips breadth, the motivations of individuals who have helped define strategies or interventions are made vulnerable by too narrow support. When breadth outstrips depth, wide understanding may not be complemented by commitment to implement interventions because they are not perceived as sufficiently locally influenced and owned. When timing is incorrect, people feel railroaded, oppressed or disrespected. A general rule of thumb is that it is never too late to start participation, but the earlier it begins the better. The skill required is to design participation processes that are time-sensitive and do not create a significant imbalance between depth and breadth while changing the status quo in pro-poor ways. But sustainability sets even more demanding criteria in terms of this skill, outlined below, starting with depth.

Depth can be understood as a continuum of stakeholder involvement, shown in Figure 2.2. Depth of participation is shown from zero to substantial joint control. These extremes correspond to the degree to which power over decisions about an intervention is totally concentrated in the NGDO or fairly shared with primary and other stakeholders. Different types or 'contents' of participation can be plotted along the depth continuum.

For sustainability, gaining depth means reaching a point of joint control over interventions from which the NGDO can begin a stage of withdrawal. Sharing influence is not enough. If the ultimate power continues to rest with an outsider, the local organisations will not experience and learn to deal with the weight of responsibility required for independence.

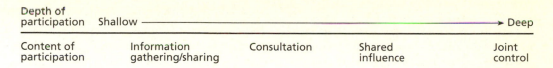

Figure 2.2 *Depth of Participation as a Continuum*

They will also be shielded from dealing with the effects of change, in other words from increasing their adaptive capabilities. We will return to this feature many times.

Breadth means the range of interested parties that are involved or whose views and actions must be taken into account. Each of these stakeholders has an interest in the NGDO's behaviour, can affect or will be affected by what the NGDO intends or does, and will behave accordingly. Commonly, primary stakeholders are those who should benefit from the intervention, but often they are not the only party that matters. For example, sustainability may require linkages to local government and to other institutions.

Who counts and in what way is situation- and purpose-specific. This typically means that NGDOs must carry out some form of institutional mapping and assessment, usually as part of an initial baseline creation and planning process. A sustainability perspective calls for mapping to have both horizontal and vertical dimensions – the NGDO and the local organisation need to decide what scale of sustainability-influencing actors they want to engage with. How far up and out should they go to see who needs to be brought into the process and in what way? Should local, regional or national government priorities and practices be taken into account? Should the electoral timetable be considered? Are there major negotiations going on between government and funders that are likely to change relevant, existing conditions? In other words, how far can they extend their influence, if not control,

towards stakeholders that will co-determine continuity of change?

Timing has both practical and symbolic importance. In practical terms, the timing of who is involved influences the quality and soundness of negotiation. NGDOs are getting much better at engaging primary stakeholders from the outset. What often seems to go wrong, however, now occurs downstream in decision-making processes with official donors and with late disbursement once the intervention is approved. Tendering and contracting procedures typically introduce a significant gap between an early encounter with communities and activity beginning. This gap feeds a symbolic dimension of delay not just as a sign of disrespect but as an expression of ultimate donor power. Rhetorical claims about partnership cut no ice – actions speak louder than words.

Consequently, as intermediaries, NGDO trustworthiness starts to suffer. Poor people stay poor and get on with their lives as best they can and trust the NGDO less. Donors do not experience the implications of the delay they may cause as life-threatening or as a significant set-back in relations with primary stakeholders. In other words, the effects of delay are unfairly spread. It is NGDOs that are most negatively affected when the timing of the system breaks down. Within the NGDO community, some donors, such as the European Union, are more notorious for delay than others. Neverthless, the problem is sufficiently widespread to be undermining the credibility of the aid system as a whole.

Finally, despite its merits and necessity, a word of caution is needed about participation in NGDO practice. There is a growing danger of participation becoming a standardised 'tyranny' or simply a marketing tool.[15] Local participation is a common part of donor requirements. This laudable criterion is, however, often accompanied by a specification of what sort of participation methods or techniques are to be employed. This requirement may arise because the donor is familiar with or trusts one approach over another. Dangers arise from this trend. First, imposing a method disempowers the NGDO in terms of its own choices, learning and competencies.[16] Second, it works against flexibility and matching methods to each situation. Standardisation does not necessarily lead to economies of scale. In fact, in participatory practice, standardisation of approach to participation generates diseconomies that lead to less efficiency overall.[17] Third, when added to other demands to become more business-like in their operations, participation becomes a marketable commodity subject to competitive rules and cost-cutting pressures, creating problems of ritualism and poor quality practice. In sum, NGDOs must be able to adapt their participatory practice to the specific situation – an important aspect of organisational agility.

Linking, Embedding and the Sustainability–Accountability Paradox

Development interventions are essentially investments to accelerate and redirect change in an ongoing situation. By definition, an intervention is an outsider's purposeful, time-bound engagement with existing forces, systems and processes. Explicitly, therefore, an externally induced or supported change will only become sustainable if and when it becomes linked

with and embedded into the ongoing situation. In other words, change becomes part and parcel of a new reality. NGDOs must therefore adopt processes that ensure linkage and embedding. Unfortunately, the aid system has inbuilt barriers to this happening, One barrier is the sustainability–accountability paradox.[18]

In applying best practice, NGDOs are frequently trapped in a paradox of an expectation that they will achieve sustainable impact and be directly accountable for such a change. On the one hand, sustainability requires progressive integration of the products and effects of interventions into the ongoing processes of economic, social, political and cultural life that surround them. Only by creating the necessary linkages – horizontally and vertically – will the effects of temporary external resources be locally supported and carried forward – in more assets, in new behaviours, in better resource use, in knowledge and in altered patterns of relationships. On the other hand, to demonstrate and be accountable for performance and resources, the effects of NGDO interventions must be kept distinctive and attributable to their efforts alone. Consequently, to satisfy funders, projects are deliberately or unconsciously 'ring-fenced' to show differences resulting from specific inputs. Where this phenomenon occurs – irrespective of what integrated project documents call for – it acts as a constraint to necessary linking, embedding and sustainability.

One way of overcoming this barrier is to clearly designate what linkages need to be made to which ongoing processes. CETEC in Colombia, for example, does this very consciously in terms of agricultural production, processing and marketing. It uses a farming systems approach and numerous technical packages to ensure an ecologically sound improvement in agricultural productivity. Backward linkages into the physical requirements of sustainable production are complemented by forward linkages into farmer-owned, cooperative processing and marketing ventures and to credit supply and management. Further, joint ventures in building construction provide a link to improved smallholder habitation, as well as to commercial building contracts in urban areas that generate cost-reduction through bulk purchasing and a cross-subsidy. The creation of farmer-owned organisations is another critical element of the intervention. The overall approach is to recognise and develop mutually reinforcing linkages across an array of agro-technical, economic and social systems.

Another way of embedding is to link into and alter existing systems. For example, in Nepal the Association of Craft Producers (ACP) sought to change market conditions for domestic weavers. This craft group are usually exploited by middlemen who provide poor quality looms at a high charge and then pay low prices for the products which they sell in India. By introducing better looms and an alternative outlet in Nepal, prices paid by middlemen have risen significantly. Change brought about in market conditions, such as prices, is one useful indicator of system impact and embedding.

Another vital element of embedding is selection of the right institutional set-up. The choice an NGDO makes between inducing a new local organisation or working with an existing one is crucial. For reasons of time pressure and lack of pre-intervention investment funds, the too-common tendency is to start a new group. The next step is to hope that it becomes respected and valued enough to continue and sustain itself once the NGDO leaves or the money runs out. Yet, comparative studies by Mick Howes indicate '... that successful outcomes nearly always seem to depend on the NGO beginning with a careful reconnaissance of the context in which it intervenes.'[19] This process can take many months, as it did for the founder of Saptagram in Sri Lanka. It can take many forms, ethnographic studies being one employed by the Agency for Co-operation and Research in Develop-ment (ACORD). However, '... the precise way in which knowledge is acquired is not, in itself, important. What is critical is that, by some means or other, the NGO should arrive at a clear understanding of the institutions that are already in place before embarking on any particular course of action.' The choice still remains of who to work with: the advantages and disadvantages of induced versus indigenous CBOs are detailed in *Striking a Balance*.[20] My own view is that, from an embedding perspective, problematic as it may be, wherever the opportunity presents itself NGDOs should err on the side of indigenous CBOs.

Too often, in planning development interventions as logically-framed projects, systems not central to the intervention are placed in the assumptions column: they are treated as boundary conditions, not as hooks to which a project must be coupled. For embedding, interventions need to clearly specify – from the participatory creation of a baseline or similar initial mapping exercises – what couplings must be made in order for change and benefits to be sustained. As we will see, an increasingly common sustainability linkage is to local government decision-making and public subsidy.

In sustainability-oriented practice, an NGDO must see and be able to explain what process of linking and embedding is built into its intervention strategy. The three systems described in Chapter 1 are an obvious frame of reference and starting point. Without this clarity, projects are too likely to remain as externally supported islands of change that crumble when the external prop is withdrawn.

Respecting Community Sovereignty – Empowerment and the Psychology and Practice of Withdrawal

A third essential element of sustainable process and practice is the mode of separation of an NGDO from the community or group it is working with. In the words of Indian observers:

'Withdrawal with sustainability is possible if from day one the donors (internal and external) and the NGOs have a clear perspective based on a long term withdrawal strategy.' [21]

The starting point for such a strategy is an honest acceptance that dependency is an inevitable initial outcome of external inputs and support. The aid system in general, and NGDOs in particular, seem to be in a state of denial about this, hopefully temporary, effect. Ideological predispositions and political correctness steer them away from the honest acceptance that new inputs to a context have the tendency to be dependency creating. There is no problem with accepting this initial relationship if they have a sound strategy for changing this condition into one of independence. Unfortunately, too few have. Consequently, this develops into a structural, self-perpetuating pathological condition.[22]

There are a few thoughtful pieces to be found on the process of 'exit', for example by Barry Smith and Richard Holloway.[23] Smith couples withdrawal to a discussion about sustainability as part of the 'contracting process'. He identifies twelve factors or signs that help assess the prospects for an NGDO's sustainability after a funder's withdrawal (see Chapter 12).

But, overall it is clear that NGDOs (and their funders) lack a theory of organisational growth to draw on and guide their practice of engagement and disengagement. Taking an organic view of CBOs is one way out. It suggests an evolutionary perspective of antecedents, context-linked origination, identity formation, growth, self-awareness, differentiation, enhanced self-confidence, autonomy and carrying responsibility. However, rather than dying in a natural cycle, organisations can regenerate themselves by learning and adapting to new conditions, a central topic in Chapter 10. In addition, in keeping with an ecological and evolutionary perspective, there is no inevitability about what independence will look like or when it will be achieved. Many factors and variables condition the process and outcomes. Nevertheless, there are general features of a mature, autonomous and healthy CBO, described above, that NGDOs can use. The issue of concern is that an NGDO has a perspective on organisational maturation and on how its own role must change as part of this process.

A common impediment to changing the relationship between NGDOs and CBOs is that dependency can be comfortable for both parties. For the CBO, it allows avoidance of responsibility. For NGDOs, it permits a perpetual claim on subsidies for its work and the satisfaction of 'being needed'. At a deeper psychological level, it maintains a parent–child relationship built on innately familiar roles that make both parties feel secure. Taking on responsibility and forgoing 'parental' authority are painful, discomforting transitions.

Yet, if empowerment is to mean anything, it must mean CBO freedom from and assertion towards the NGDO, not just towards surrounding power holders such as the local elite, government officials or politicians. A number of interviews suggested that 'letting go' by, for example, an NGDO allocating funds directly to a CBO to manage itself, is a common problem.[24] With a threat to its role and own sustainability, an NGDO is often motivated towards finding fault and weaknesses with the CBO, rather than encouraging self-responsibility and learning by mistakes.[25] Of course, knowing when to pass over funds is a difficult judgement to make – it is a measure of NGDO professionalism. However, there are intangible disincentives to doing so, or to delaying such a step well beyond what is necessary. CBO autonomy is felt as a threat, not an achievement. An NGDO that cannot cope with CBO empowerment cannot engender a sound sustainability-oriented process. In short, NGDOs must be able to deal with their own transformation to a non-funding role in their intervention process.

A complicating factor in withdrawal is that capacity building of local groups is not a linear process. A detailed study of local organisational sustainability in Bangladesh likens the process to the game of snakes and ladders.[26] Gains towards autonomy and independence can quickly be reversed by internal and external group dynamics. This is all the more reason why NGDOs must both properly read what is going on and have the adaptability to temporarily re-enter and re-build.

Some NGDOs are adopting strategies that, from the outset, are designed to counter a dependency syndrome. One strategy is setting a time limit to engagement. CETEC, for example, only works with a group of farmers for six years, before moving on to a new area and farmers. ActionAid is introducing a seven- to ten-year time limit in a development area. However, a drawback of holding too firmly to a time-bound strategy is that conditions for sustainability may not have been achieved in the time limit set. Nevertheless, by starting with a time horizon the rules of the game are made clear and transparent – a mutually agreed end

point of CBO responsibility, independence and responsive capacity is known to both parties.

Another strategy is to negotiate benchmarks as part of a phased or staged approach. This is explained later. Groups that lag behind in terms of benchmark timings are identified, reasons are sought and remedial steps negotiated with them. In a phased approach used by the Philippines Rural Reconstruction Movement (PRRM), for example, the stress is on community 'sovereignty', that is, a respect for the right of communities or peoples' organisations, in the quest for their own development, to make mistakes and to deal with the consequences. But, whatever the perspective, the crux is that saying 'goodbye' accompanies saying 'hello'. A strategy of incremental disengagement is an integral part of the initiating negotiation.[27]

Obviously, the idea that an NGDO will withdraw can be introduced at any stage. However, if it is not there from the outset, the discussion becomes much more fraught and possibly acrimonious. This is especially difficult when an NGDO has pushed hard on the idea of partnership. Introducing withdrawal at a later stage is seen as hypocritically and unilaterally changing the rules of the game.

Typically, by default, NGDO withdrawal is not a planned or staged affair but is determined by the ebb and flow of the availability of funds. To avoid this happening, NGDOs actively redesign or relabel existing interventions to satisfy new community needs and development fashions. For example, today much project reframing is going on in terms of governance, civil society and building social capital.

Finally, the notion of withdrawal must be looked at in a subtle way. It does not mean, necessarily, that the NGDO disappears from the area. It can equally mean that it is present but fulfils a different role towards the CBO, for example as an adviser, network facilitator or information source, but not as co-manager and financier of the CBO's plans, affairs and decisions.

The question now is, how can NGDOs relate these sustainability-oriented practices and competencies to the systems described in Chapter 1?

Chapter Summary

This chapter examines important aspects of content and process for sustainably-oriented interventions by NGDOs.

Content requires an evolving interplay between three aspects of human change:

1   Physical and material well-being.
2   Organisational capacity.
3   Empowerment.

The first and third components have important elements contributing to the needed insightful and responsive quality of local capacity. Improved well-being reduces vulnerability and strengthens the economic base from which to act. Empowerment creates the wider systems awareness required to respond with insight. In terms of capacity building, NGDOs must factor in and work with invisible elements of enhancing group trust and shared identity, values and aspirations.

In terms of process, to introduce and apply content properly, NGDOs need three types of competencies. They are:

1   An approach to participation which marries and balances depth, breadth and timing with skill at targeting.
2   Linking and embedding interventions with existing forces, systems and processes.
3   An appropriate shift from dependency to independence of the CBO premised on foreseen change in the role of the NGDO and withdrawal, for example from funding, to advising and to facilitating other relationships.

Chapter 3

Framework and Indicators for Sustainable Local Development

'If you can't measure it, you can't manage it.' (Anon)

'Not everything in development can or should be measured, but it still has to be managed.' (Anon)

'An over-reliance on target setting in the context of social development can distort reality in the process project.' (Philip Harding)[1]

Achieving enduring local impact means combining the systems, content and process perspectives explained in previous chapters. The combination creates a composite framework that NGDOs can use to assess and formulate a sustainable approach. This chapter begins with such a framework and explains its use to identify points of entry to ongoing processes. Subsequent sections look at two important aspects of carrying out the strategy, first in terms of horizontal and vertical integration and second in terms of prediction-oriented information and the proxy indicators that leaders and managers use to assess the probability of sustainability.

Strategising for Sustainability – A Composite Framework

A composite framework must bring together the three systems that determine sustainability – set out in Chapter 1 – with the three features of practice described in Chapter 2. A simple way of doing so is by creating an intervention matrix as shown in Table 3.1.

Gender and generations are included as important reminders. Differences between men and women call for dis-aggregated data and assessment of initiatives and measures in gender terms. Significant gender differences can be found in almost all boxes. For example, women are subject to socio-economic systems that make it less likely that they own or control productive resources or are equally rewarded for their work; they face socio-cultural conditions that restrict their access to formal education; they live within political systems that reduce their participation in governance, and they are more likely to be dependent on fragile domestic agricultural production systems for their food security.

Generations prompts thinking about the time scale over which sustainability is being considered. For example, a primary education programme would probably not show its effects on households until many

Table 3.1 *An Integration Framework for Sustainable Micro-development*

Systems for NGDO intervention	Dimensions of sustainable human change		
	Well-being (Individual, groups, households)	Capacity (local organisations)	Empowerment (groups, households, individuals)
Economic			
Social		X	
Ecological			
Gender and generations			

years after the boy or girl has left school. Tree planting with good husbandry may be designed, as is done by Green Cross in Côte d'Ivoire, to have both motivational short-term economic returns and long-term environmental effects.

The dotted lines in the table signal that there are many interactions between the cells. This corresponds to overlapping areas in Figures 1.1 and 2.1.

Interaction between cells can be seen, for example, in how the economic system – be it profit-making corporations or poor people making a livelihood – exploits natural resources in ways that can be environmentally degrading. An overlap between economic and social cells is often seen in potentially corrupting ties between businessmen and politicians.

In terms of interventions, economic empowerment for women can lead to gains in other areas, such as their representation in local leadership. Women's political assertiveness can have positive economic effects in terms of claim-making, and beneficial social effects through better access to more appropriate services. Improved health status is a physical change in terms of well-being, but can be economic as well by reducing household expenditure on medical costs and productive days lost due to ill health. Empowerment can also have economic effects when people press for and gain greater access to public resources and

services. Where to place the effects of interventions in a cell is a question of judgement. In its turn, this judgement is tied to selecting points of entry for NGDO interventions.

Each cell of the matrix can be used to identify strategic goals or specific objectives with indicators to assess achievement, as discussed below. The content of each will inevitably vary between different types of NGDO activity. Any one development programme or project would not necessarily fill all the cells. For example, the Bangladesh Rural Advancement Committee (BRAC) has three major types of programme: the rural development programme, which is essentially credit funding tied to economic activities and technical asistance; a non-formal primary education programme; and a health programme. In areas where all three programmes are active together, they would be expected to effect change in many, if not all, of the cells.

For most NGDOs, however, their range of activities is quite small. Many specialise in a particular type of development initiative: credit, health, education, agriculture, technology innovation and so on. Consequently, they would not be able to directly influence every cell in the table in terms of their own intervention. They can, however, gather information about other areas of change to assess the extent to which their work is properly complementing initiatives of others agencies and of primary stakeholders. Baseline studies are a common mechanism for establishing a composite picture. Whatever the method chosen, it should enable an NGDO to work out its best point of entry into complex, ongoing systems.

Filling in the Boxes – Choosing Points of Entry

A matrix is not the same as a system description. The boxes are not divisions in the real life of poor people. But together, the nine cells provide a memory-jogging tool and a framework to ensure that important dimensions of change are not overlooked.

Many things guide selecting entry points to ongoing processes, for example the NGDO's own mission, the dynamics of the 'big picture', the specific group and context, that is the 'little picture', and the activities of others. This would suggest that an NGDO could select any one of these boxes and its linkages as its primary point of entry or focus. However, from the sustainability perspective described in Chapter 1 – coping with instability and change – the conceptual point of entry should be the central box marked 'X'. In other words, building the responsive abilities of local groups is the key. Doing so will involve any of the other boxes as means. Nevertheless, in all cases the ultimate ends are increasing people's capacities to deal with a changing context in sustainability-oriented ways without the NGDO being in control.

The only certainty in development work is that contextual change will occur. Safeguarding gains made because of NGDO interventions must mean a local ability to understand what is happening and adapt accordingly. Consequently, the core competence of NGDOs must lie in bringing about capacity change of the groups they work with, both for and beyond the specific type of 'technical' intervention chosen. With this requirement in mind, how do NGDOs go about selecting entry?

First, selection should reflect the mission and 'theories' about poverty that NGDOs use to define their work: those without a clear mission, cause analysis and 'theory' of how 'underdevelopment' can change lack the internal foundations for making coherent judgements and interpretations. Importantly, this understanding helps to identify a hierarchy in the structure of causes and effects, akin to a problem tree analysis associated with logical framework planning. This will help NGDOs ascertain how many levels they need to work on directly or indirectly. The official aid system provides many sources of information about the 'big picture'. However, the contents are typically apolitical. This means that NGDOs will often have to factor politics into the context and seek out non-governmental sources.[2]

Strategic planning or 'future search' types of exercise are a usual way for NGDOs to reach a sound 'big picture' judgement. The value of relying on rigorous strategies for operations is open to question. For, no matter how thorough and well thought through, a strategic plan can never be like a railway line leading unerringly to a future goal. However, what good strategic planning should do is enhance the NGDO's own knowledge base and insights about the poverty-inducing effects and dynamics of the three systems described in Chapter 1. Moreover, if done in an iterative and participatory way, as described in *Striking a Balance*, the process spreads this knowledge and insight throughout the NGDO. Without a good appreciation of what is going on in the wider world, NGDOs are less able to lift the horizons of local communities to help them form their own judgements and responses. If NGDO staff meeting with communities have little understanding of the bigger forces that shape poverty locally – for example, international trading rules and government policies – they cannot heighten local awareness and horizons. Typically, this type of awareness-raising is founded on some form of participatory social analysis or action-research with communities.[3]

Second, judgement must be informed by the 'reading' of the levels of context and the specific conditions and aspirations of the community concerned. Typically, this requires deep insight into how local society works and how the historical forces that keep poor people poor are expressed. As noted in the previous chapters, building a coping capacity requires that an important feature of 'small picture' analysis should be about institutions. How is local society organised? Who is in and out of the various local groups? For what purposes and for whose benefit are local groups established? Mick Howes describes many different techniques for this type of enquiry.[4] Sound local institutional analysis – allied to an identification of institutional roles in relation to different systems – is vital for choosing the social foundations for intervention and capacity enhancement. Such insights are a precondition for working out the most appropriate approach to capacity building. They are also needed to establish the basis for negotiation and time scale for withdrawal.

An NGDO's interpretation of causes of poverty and the functions of local institutions needs to be validated by the people themselves. This is a common element in participatory planning techniques. What sustainability requires, however, is that in this process people's local experiences and insights are expanded to locate them in the wider systems that shape their reality. CETEC's approach to farming systems analysis with small-scale producers

embraces these three components. It includes farmers' examination of seasonality, gender divisions of agricultural labour, operation of global markets and credit programmes and sustainable land use. The underlying goal is to build the collective capacity of farmers to understand the forces affecting the sustainability of their livelihoods while simultaneously selecting activities to expand the economic base from which to act in other areas – in other words to increase their insight and resilience.

Sound judgement leads to selection of the points of entry that seek to change systems as well as local capacities and circumstances. Good entry strategies are those which are likely to have wider effects that contribute to change in other cells and systems. Today, microcredit plays such a role. The idea is that a strengthened economic base, especially for women, will have positive and enduring impacts on other systems. The issue less addressed, however, is whether or not economic activities undertaken with credit actually improve the productivity of local resources in sustainable ways and create greater local value-added. Are local economic foundations being enhanced to provide an enduring increase in a local economic surplus, for example by promoting innovation among local producers?[5] If most credit is applied, for example, to petty trading, the market will quickly be saturated and unsustained if there is not a corresponding increase in disposable incomes.

Finally, from a systems perspective, selecting points of entry must be informed by the policies, activities and initiatives of others. From the outset in choosing entry, an NGDO needs to think about linkages, embedding and complementarity, that is, to be aware of what is happening around the community and who is trying to do what in the other boxes. If, because of this assessment, it appears that some boxes remain empty, the NGDO will need to think seriously about what the consequences will be and, wherever possible, take initiatives to fill the space. More importantly, trends or actions of others in the other boxes are often working against what the organisation is intending to do. For example, governments are reducing their social responsibilities and budgets for social services. Consequently, it may be necessary to revise plans or consider the probability that the impact of an NGDO's efforts will not endure or, as a recent NGDO impact study shows, for high aid dependency scenarios to simply accept that sustainable impact is an illusion.[6]

For example, in Ethiopia as in many other countries, government policy on education has not looked kindly on non-formal approaches to improve access for poorer primary level students. As a result, the prospects of government finance being available to meet recurrent costs of non-formal teachers are not high. However, opting for community-based approaches and recurrent financing can suffer from the problem of equity – poorer localities are less able to finance teachers than others and hence sustainability will be less

probable. A high-risk mode of entry would therefore be to experiment with alternative, low-cost methods of primary education. Bringing about a systemic change would require government approval for students from the informal schools to move into the formal schools with their previous years of schooling being recognised. If this strategy does not work, broadening poor people's access to primary schooling is unlikely to endure (but at least a few cohorts of students will have benefited while the NGDO was active).

Similarly, if governments are intent on opening up their markets to imports of basic foodstuffs or clothing, resulting price trends may work for or against the economics of interventions in those areas targeted at local producers. Income diversification may therefore be a more appropriate choice.

In sum, filling in the boxes in terms of an NGDO intervention must take into account linkages across cells, as well as levels within them. It also requires knowledge about what others are doing and about forces and policies. Inevitably, this requires NGDOs to think and act in integrative ways.

Integration – The Crux of a Sustainable Approach

Integrated rural development has had a chequered history. While fashionable in the 1970s and early 1980s, disappointing results led away from integration to today's emphasis on sectoral policies and investment strategies. The toll is now being paid in fragmentation of effort and frequent lack of complementarity, fed by funders' preferences in terms of their own domestic expertise, markets and self-perceived comparative advantages. One recent response to incoherence is to use a

macro-matrix approach to establish a national level comprehensive development framework. The objective is to bring compatibility to the efforts and investments of important governmental and other stakeholders but with the government taking the lead.[7] Another official reaction is to focus integration geographically by concentrating on a single sector in an area, by assisting grassroots initiatives, by multi-donor budget support or by assisting integrated regional planning.[8]

Integration for NGDOs has two primary directions: horizontal and vertical. As cases below illustrate, they are often achieved though some form of collaboration with others. One aspect of horizontal integration is a local development process that allies three types of human change described in the previous chapter. This type of integration is required within an intervention in any of the three systems set out in Chapter 1. It is a basic best practice within any type of community-oriented initiative, no matter how small. It corresponds to the competence required to work horizontally across the rows of the composite matrix (Table 3.1). Another aspect of horizontal integration is how NGDOs span the three systems, or pursue an intervention mix that deals simultaneously with local aspects of ecology, society and economy – the columns in the matrix – dealt with below.

Previous chapters argued that NGDOs have no control and only selective, modest influence over the 'big picture' factors that determine sustainable impact. Nevertheless, sustainability calls on NGDOs to exert whatever pressure they can on 'big picture' issues. The task is to alter 'big picture' forces and structures so that they reinforce rather than undermine their local efforts. Consequently, in addition to horizontal linking, NGDOs also need to integrate vertically to address different levels within and across each system.

The practical NGDO approach to integrating horizontally and vertically can be found in two trends. One is to concentrate a broad array of interventions with CBOs in a given physical area. Another is to collaborate in national and international advocacy and lobbying.

Horizontal Integration – Adopting an Area-based Approach

An increasingly common NGDO approach to horizontal integration is to focus on a geographic area that may be whole or part of a government administrative unit. One reason for this trend is that decentralisation of state functions is creating local government units with more responsibilities, albeit not necessarily complemented by adequate resources. The Panchayat Raj reform in India is one example, as is the Philippines' decentralisation through a local government code. Ethiopia's federal model and Uganda's multi-tiered committees are others. Similar downward shifts in governance are evident throughout Latin America. This reform creates an opportunity for strengthening the interface to the state, as well as a greater risk of co-optation into governmental delivery and a substitution role for decreasing local availability of government services.

In Brazil, POLIS has been working for over ten years with local government and communities in urban areas. Its approach is founded in the concept of building municipal democracy from below.[9] The goal is to foster new linkages between civil society and systems of urban governance, to embed the relationship into local government processes and change the attitude and behaviour of both sides. Its main work focuses on teaching local government how to work with communities and vice versa, in particular by making communities less passive. POLIS has published and disseminated some 120 case experiences of constructive, and problematic, collaboration. POLIS facilitates the initial interaction with the intention that this relationship remains when it withdraws. Case studies show that councils which ignore community participation and try to do everything on their own are more fragile and politically vulnerable than councils that have active community involvement and negotiated sharing of tasks. Strong civic links are also seen to improve a local council's standing with and leverage on central government.

Behind a trend of greater NGDO interest in negotiating and working with local government lies a sustainability strategy. One aspect is that negotiating ongoing support and demonstrating innovations that could be adopted by local government is much easier if the existing administrative structure and its responsibilities are taken into account. In addition, it provides access that could be used to scale up innovations through the government system and its sectoral policies.

Leaders of Latin American NGDOs interviewed by Mariano Valderrama are aware that they must be realistic and concentrate on experimentation that can be integrated into bigger scales and arenas beyond the local.[10]

'In several of the interviews, colleagues from large, traditional NGDOs that have now re-routed to different activities, stated with almost surprising coincidence "…either we are very naïve or we believed we were omnipotent…" Therefore, in terms of their efforts, NGDOs must, above all, experiment with new ways of making policies, programme and projects that can be replicated and assumed by the state or more powerful institutions (i.e, acceptance of the value of innovation on a micro scale as a springboard to the macro scale)'.[11]

For NGDOs that have evolved in settings of political struggle against military or civilian dictatorships – common in Latin America and parts of East Asia – a shift to working with the state requires overcoming a collaborationist stigma. It also requires a shift in perspective for NGDOs and CBOs to actually realise that they 'own' the state and have rights. It is not the other way round.

Demonstrating local innovations in order to alter the policies and practices of government requires some form of linkage to low-level state agencies and the governance system, such as local and municipal councils. This is a fast-growing type of NGDO collaboration with multiple intentions. One objective is to open up interaction for CBO claim-making on government. Another is to negotiate ongoing public support to NGDO initiatives where this is necessary. In addition, local level horizontal interactions are meant to feed into vertical linkages to alter 'bigger pictures', typically within a technical sector, specific project or loan or an area of public policy.[12]

Within a local geographic area, it is only possible for an individual NGDO to establish an integrated set of interventions – economic, social and ecological – if it is large enough to have many skills. Moreover, the skill mix must be accompanied by a sufficiently flexible or broad resource base. NGDOs financed through child sponsorship, such as ActionAid, PLAN International and World Vision, are able to adopt an area-based multi-intervention approach and commonly do so. However, the vast majority of NGDOs are small and specialised. Their option is to collaborate with other small NGDOs in a variety of ways. In doing so, they can link across cells and systems. If they can find ways of working together, they can behave as a big, multi-skilled NGDO.

With this concept in mind, a coalition of Philippine NGDOs has developed an integrated approach to working in a given area. Their approach is known as Sustainable Integrated Area Development (SIAD).[13] SIAD relies on collaboration between NGDOs that agree to adopt a common multi-systems framework in which each contributes its own particular expertise. The framework is complemented by shared standards and measures of working with communities.[14] The framework adopted for this combined approach uses the acronym COCO-BREAD.

Creative, collective, critical
   consciousness raising
Organisational development
Coalition efforts in advocacy
Overcoming gender and other biases

Basic services and infrastructure
Resource tenure (eg, land reform)
Economic self-reliance and
   strengthening
Agricultural development with
   ecological concern
Democratic participation and
   governance

As can be seen, this type of integration embraces all boxes in the matrix. It is applied to interventions with communities in selected administrative areas. The specifics of interventions are negotiated with People's Organisations. Resulting tasks are divided between the organisations and among participating NGDOs. For example, the Institute for Popular Governance (IPG) brings expertise in the political dimensions of community empowerment. The Congress for People's Agrarian Reform (CPAR) contributes to change in terms of land tenure, while Community Organising for People's Enterprise (COPE) works on local economic development. An agreement on theory, practice and division of labour brings about integration of the efforts of small individual NGDOs in a coherent way. However, it calls for substantial investment to build trusted working relationships and operational agreements.

The COCO-BREAD strategy recognises and works towards three stages of strengthening the capabilities of People's Organisations. Indicators are defined for each of the seven constituent elements for each stage. Progress in each element can be assessed by each local group. The tough part, however, is in the final stage of NGDO handover of funds and withdrawal.[15]

The stress within COCO-BREAD is on a coherent horizontal linkage of mutually reinforcing interventions. However, the element, 'coalition efforts in advocacy', calls for dedicated efforts to create vertical linkages to higher system levels through better placed NGDOs and through meeting with governments directly. This type of integration moves beyond coalitions of NGDOs and CBOs to include other types of development actors. This also brings a less commonly appreciated perspective to local capacity building, that of NGDO 'downward accountability'.

Vertical Integration through Multi-institutional Collaboration and Alliances

An alternative form of integration is to bridge different types of development institutions. In Costa Rica for example, CR-USA negotiates a 'triangulo de solidaridad' (triangle of solidarity) between communities, local and state governments, for the building and maintenance of rural access roads. In Colombia, the Fundaçion FES (FFES) promotes the negotiation and signing of 'solidarity contracts' between communities and the government for the protection of national parks and reserves. These links are intended to establish ongoing working relationships once the NGDO removes itself. The NGDO acts primarily as a catalyst, using its resources as seed funds for relational development, which may have projects as a focal point for building up trust and mutual understanding. Linkages are also intended to shape government behaviour through its policies and practices, while reinforcing people's impact on governance.

Inter-institutional collaboration is also being actively explored in what are known as multi-sectoral partnerships beyond governments to included socially responsible businesses. It is argued that this type of integrated effort is better able to solve complex social problems and will be needed more and more in the next century.[16] The Synergos Institute in the USA has examined these types of integration. Its studies in Africa sound a cautionary note in relation to their ability to enhance capacity for local sustainability. Findings suggest that, in relationships that are essentially unequal in terms of power and resources:

> '...governments and official aid agencies must be careful to avoid undermining community initiative and the sustainability of community and civil society actors while ostensibly supporting such partnerships'.[17]

In order to gain impact on higher levels within systems, NGDO linkages to different types of institutions often have an advocacy or lobbying intention. Here the basic idea is to bring local testimony to the table in international decision-making forums. Some observers point out that circumventing the domestic political process in this way may undermine the governance system within a country.[18] In addition, NGDOs are also being challenged about their credentials with respect to the people on whose behalf advocacy or lobbying is being undertaken. Much has been written about this challenge in terms of government 'backlash' questioning the legitimacy of the positions taken on issues by NGDOs. There have also been problems of the mandate of Northern NGDOs who speak on behalf of their Southern counterparts, particularly towards Bretton Woods institutions like the World Bank.[19]

From the perspective of this book, the aspect of concern is the place of CBO capacity-building in NGDO vertical integration as part of their lobbying efforts. In other words, is CBO capacity enhancement part of NGDO advocacy?

A recent study has shown that NGDO success in policy advocacy towards an institution like the World Bank requires the vertical integration of local to global efforts and involves multiple types of institutions.[20] Its main conclusion is that achievement depends on finding allies and building coalitions both within and outside the institution. Importantly, allies must provide and combine a number of elements. These are:

1 Credibility for the civic messengers or advocates towards the Bank, founded on 'technical' professionalism and a legitimate case to be made, derived from local concerns and activism, such as protests, in the country concerned.
2 Non-patronage relations with those most likely to be affected – the grassroots – including mandates that give sufficient assurance of civic accountability.
3 Political support from actors strategically located at critical decision-making sites: within the borrowing country's civil society and governments; within World Bank staff; and within donor governments and their executive directors in the Bank.

Without an ability to demonstrate a mandate, NGDOs are less credible as well as vulnerable to charges of pushing their own agendas and interests, which are not necessarily those of the poor.

A common way for NGDOs to deal with the issue of mandate is to form alliances and operate in coalitions with those whom they support. Examples of such coalitions seeking to change World

Bank policy, projects, loans or practices are the Kedung Dam in Indonesia, the Mount Apo thermal plant in the Philippines and the Planafloro Natural Resource Management loan to Brazil. Coalitions were formed between CBOs, with domestic and international NGDOs acting as knowledge and bridging organisations. However, this and other studies argue that it is not simply enough to have CBOs on board, but only in a token way. It is necessary to have a 'downward accountability' towards them. What does this mean?

Using three components, Catherine Bain examines what civic, downward accountability should entail in transnational advocacy.[21] The three components are representation, capacity building and social capital. These are defined as follows:

'Representation: *The manner in which an organization, or group of organizations, speaks for its members or constituents and is held to account for this representation.*[22]

Capacity building: *The ability of a network to coordinate actors and bridge differences to achieve impact and leverage in a way that pools skills and builds the capacity of its members – primarily its Southern members – to represent their own views in national and global arenas.*

Social Capital: *The ability of a network to promote trust, solidarity, respect and unity among its diverse members and reinforce democratic practices by conducting itself in a transparent and accountable manner.*' [23]

She goes on to examine these components in relation to three cases of transnational coalitions involved in policy advocacy towards the World Bank. These are the Structural Adjustment Participatory Review Initiative (SAPRI); the Women's Eyes on the World Bank Network; and the NGO World Bank Committee. An overall conclusion from this study is framed in the following way.

'*While some progress has been made in addressing low upward accountability …, it seems that downward accountability – at least within transnational NGO networks – continues to be the Achilles heel of the NGO movement. In an era when NGOs aim to become "vehicles of international co-operation in the mainstream of politics and economics" and have successfully won a place at many global negotiating tables, they now seem to be having difficulties in adjusting to their new role. While it would be unreasonable to expect all NGOs to adopt strategies of partnership and collaboration, it is not unreasonable to expect NGOs to begin to practise the downward accountability that they preach.*' [24]

From a sustainable systems perspective, an NGDO lobbying effort related to an on-the-ground reality must contain ways of developing CBO capacity to lobby and advocate for itself.

Case studies show that an empowering multi-level awareness as part of capacity building is easier to bring about when the issue directly affects people's lives, as in resettlement schemes and the loans supporting them. The task is more difficult when the system issue is one of general policy support, such as structural adjustment loans and the conditions that go with them. Here timely NGDO access to and provision of information, in locally adapted ways, is vital.

Another challenge for NGDOs is to identify and then seek agreement to work with whatever membership-based movements already exist. In Ecuador, for example, NGDOs formed alliances with indigenous people's movements, such as the Confederation of Indigenous Nationalities of Ecuador (CONAIE) that were engaged with land rights, greater access to productive resources and protection of ethnic identity.[25] The link between Northern and Ecuadorian NGDOs to gain access to information about the World Bank and the Inter-American Development Bank (IDB) proved an important part of reshaping local people's views of how their own government worked. It enabled them to reframe their previous understanding into a 'bigger picture' of power and decision-making. Public demonstrations about government policy were one sign of both greater awareness and civic assertiveness.[26]

If capacity building is successful, the role of NGDOs shifts from representation to mediation. The perspective informing this shift is one of 'growing policy from the grassroots' – how the realm of practice can inform the world of policy and the place of NGDOs in the process. It involves not just 'scaling up' but also 'scaling out' with a greater diversity in forms and greater depth in quality of participation and engagement between different actors.[27] Appropriate capacity at the grassroots is a vital element in a vertically mediating strategy and practice.

No matter how NGDOs tackle the issue of horizontal or vertical integration, the question arises of how NGDOs know the extent to which the right quality of local capacity is developing. This raises the issue of indicators and staged approaches to CBO capacity-building.

Process Indicators of Local Capacity Development for Sustained Impact

To manage an integrated intervention effectively, NGDOs need to be constantly aware of the capacity change they are bringing about. They need to answer the question: how much closer to independence and insightful agility are CBOs getting? To answer this question they need signs and measures. Sustainability places particular demands on indicators and measures for effective management for enduring impact. They need to be predictive. What this means is explored in the following section.

Signs and Symbols – Direction and Prediction

There is an exhaustive search for development indicators across all the systems described in Chapters 1 and 2.[28] For example, the Organisation for Economic Cooperation and Development (OECD) has a set of 21 indicators to measure large-scale progress. They are grouped under four categories: economic well-being, social development, environmental sustainability, and regeneration and general.[29] Specific goals for each have been derived from commitments made at a number of UN conferences. In parallel, an ongoing search for small-scale indicators, for example in food security,[30] has gained a new impetus and direction emanating from the concern to understand and measure social capital.[31]

By and large, and partly as a result of logical framework approaches, the hunt for indicators tends to concentrate on measures to assess achievement in reaching the predetermined goals of a development project. The Harding quotation at the start of this chapter corresponds to this way of thinking. This method is usually not easy because of poor baselines, problems of attribution of cause and disputes about qualitative measures.[32] However, a sustainability perspective introduces an additional complication of finding signs and indicators that have a predictive value – will change endure once the intervention ends?

One answer is that in any cell of the composite matrix, indicators must always signal a status in relation to the previous condition. Something of relevance could be more or less available, better or worse, increasing or decreasing, or more or less frequent, for example. Simply giving a figure for infant mortality at a given moment, or attendance at a meeting, or membership of a CBO is not enough. Managers need to know whether this is higher or lower than before – in other words how things are developing. In short, any sustainability indicator must be dynamic and show the trend or direction in the condition being tracked.

Table 3.2 illustrates possible indicators initially identified by BRAC.[33] This does not mean that all these indicators are being applied in practice, nor that all BRAC-related village organisations are capable of achieving them. For example, the ability of village organisations to enforce control over the use of common property is probably a long way off. The point is that this could be an indicator of the type of change empowerment should bring.

The task for an NGDO is to check and see if the trends are mutually reinforcing. If they are, then the probability of sustained impact is higher than if they are not. A common contradictory trend is economic improvement coupled to ecological stock depletion and pollution, globally and locally. For example, projects to introduce prawn farms to improve the livelihoods of fishermen in Bangladesh appear

to be at the cost of environmental degradation of rivers and estuaries.[34]

Obviously, gathering this type of information is technically difficult, time consuming and often too costly. Consequently, as the last section explains, NGDO leaders and managers use proxies to inform themselves of the probability of sustainable impact.

One new way for NGDOs to build up an integrated picture of what change is occurring with CBOs is by using a social audit. This method is being applied by the Philippine Partnership for the Development of Human Resources in Rural Areas (PHILDHRRA) and the Triple Trust Organisation (TTO) in South Africa. Social audit requires an NGDO to identify its key stakeholders and their criteria for change. Progress against agreed criteria is assessed each year. Applying social audit principles in an integrated way is slowly being applied to businesses in relation to a 'triple bottom line' of their economic, social and environmental impacts. For CBOs, it would mean using these three dimensions to determine what change they will work for with the range of institutions they relate to, not just the NGDO. This exercise would generate a set of composite criteria that could be checked, say, annually.

Stages and Milestones in CBO Capacity Building

In the critical area of local capacity building, a practical approach to prediction is being introduced. The method is to identify and negotiate 'milestone' indicators that are applied at different stages of a change process. In other words, NGDOs are 'predicting' the stages that CBOs should go through to be independent and 'capacitated'. Indicators in any one stage can be 'static' in that they do not themselves indicate a change but a condition or ability. The trend comes from comparison

Table 3.2 *Sample Indicators of Sustainable Development Impact*[35]

| System for intervention | Indicators of sustainable human development | | |
	Well-being (individual, groups, households)	Organisational capacity (local organisations)	Empowerment (groups, households, individuals)
Economic	Increased savings and ability to repay higher levels of credit. Greater disposable income. Income sources diversify. Capital assets increase. Decreased health costs. Productivity is enhanced.	Equitable distribution of economic benefits is maintained. More joint economic initiatives undertaken without external assistance. Greater local financial resource mobilisation.	Greater freedom in choice of services through enhanced demand. Growth of more appropriate economic services.
Social	Improved nutrition, eg, no hunger for longer periods. Increasing literacy levels. Reducing mortality rates. Increase in preventable morbidity and disability.	New members attracted. More links established to similar groups for mutual support. More social services defined and overseen by users. Greater adoption of new ideas and self-spread of practices.	Government recognition of group legitimacy and voice. Women's freedom and autonomy increased. Greater assertiveness in formal political systems. Greater self-esteem, eg, inclusion in communal affairs.
Ecological	Maintenance or increase in quantity of natural stocks. No degradation in quality of stock due to man-made pollution and contamination. Biodiversity is maintained/enhanced.	More effective local protection of common natural property. Improved local management of access, eg, reduced resource conflicts.	Natural resource rights better secured. Improved exclusion of illegal users of natural resources. Increased action taken against polluters.

Gender and Generations

with previous stages. For example, an inability to resolve conflicts may be a sign in an early stage: ability to resolve them a sign in a subsequent stage. The SIAD coalition has established three stages of capacity growth in People's Organisations. PRRM has identified seven 'levels of capacity' that such organisations should progress through and have constructed a Composite Village Empowerment Index (CVEI) as a self-assessment and management guide.[36] BRAC has six stages for the groups involved in its rural development programme. The BRAC stages are shown in Table 3.3.

The stages reflect progress in altering two characteristics of BRAC's village organisations. First is a shift from BRAC-dependent management to self-management. Here, the village organisation moves from credit to other self-selected activities with BRAC support. Allied to this is a change from a BRAC-related credit channel, though a development actor to a fully autonomous and new type of local civic body – a *Palli Samaj*. The village organisation ceases to be a BRAC organisation, becoming an independent civic entity in its own right with the ability to select whom it wishes to work with.

The intention is that each stage builds on and incorporates the criteria of the previous stages. One sign of shifts from dependency to independence to self-chosen interdependence with BRAC, is the ability of the organisation to choose the supplier of the services it needs: if BRAC can provide what is required at a quality and price it can afford, the relationship will remain. This is a marked shift from the present tied situation. It calls for significant revision to BRAC's way of working with communities that is now underway.

Engagement with and membership of a *Palli Samaj* would also follow stages as they gain experience from linkages to other groups. Ultimately, a *Palli Samaj* could form a distinct, civic entity, representative not necessarily of a complete village but of its poorer groups, and would interact with *Polipolislot*, a recently introduced institution for local governance.

As a management tool, based on past experience BRAC assigns target timings for the move from one stage to the next. Information about group progress is collected regularly, at least twice a year. Given the thousands of village organisations they relate to, this enables local and higher-level managers to identify overall progress and problem areas. The 'snakes and ladders' nature of organisational evolution noted earlier makes this type of management information necessary if a pattern of delay or CBO regression is to be noticed.

Wherever possible, specific signs and measures are negotiated with the CBO, often as a process of participatory self-assessment.[37] In the terms used by FFES in Colombia and the Integrated Social Development Centre (ISODEC) in Ghana, CBOs are co-researchers and co-creators of capacity signs and measures. The list of characteristics of a capacitated NGDO to be found in the previous chapter is one possible starting point for selecting research areas and questions. Once identified and agreed, indicators are tracked by CBO members as well as by NGDO staff.

Insightful NGDOs are using the process of negotiation and participatory identification of measures as a capacity building method. For example, raising the issue of indicators of good leadership opens a dialogue on what people value and expect – it allows a debate about personal characteristics and standards of group, local and other leaders that can alter people's tolerance level and make them averse to poor behaviour. They are also used to 'expand horizons' to other levels of system behaviour to debate how CBOs could better position themselves, for example, by talking about criteria for selecting and electing political representatives and the value of their vote.

To help with this type of dialogue, some NGDOs (for an example see Box 3.1) are specialising in political awareness and capacity development . This type of organisation provides information that other NGDOs can use to help communities reflect on what they believe to be good representation: for example, the track record of candidates for elective office. Enabling communities to better vet candidates constitutes empowerment in the form of 'preventive quality control'.

In addition to the use of indicators by CBOs to track and evaluate their own progress in building capacity, managers need information too. For many small

Table 3.3 *Stages of Capacity Change in a Village Organisation*

Village organisation sustainability stage	Criteria (time)	Indicators/Measures
Stage 0 (Credit organised)	Unable to meet all BRAC credit requirements. (0–12 months)	Members correspond to BRAC targets.
Stage 1 (Credit organised)	Able to meet all BRAC credit requirements. (13–36 months)	80% members receive credit. Village organisation discipline is consistent ie, members meet attendance, credit repayment and savings requirements.
Stage 2 (BRAC) Stage 0 (*Palli Samaj*)	Able to engage effectively with all BRAC programmes. (37–48 months)	*Performance* % change children at school. % change legal marriage /divorce. % change in latrines, safe water. % change in immunisation, contraception. 80% members receive all BRAC programmes. *Capacity* Equitable access to benefits. Ability to resolve conflicts. Stable membership (low attrition rate). Maintain mobilisation of local resources.
Stage 3 (BRAC) Stage 1 (*Palli Samaj*)	Engages effectively with non-BRAC development initiatives and institutions, inter-village activities and coordination. (49–72 months)	Mutual funds established and managed for village organisation needs. *Evidence that organisation:* •agitates for social action; •asserts rights and claims; •takes corrective action against injustices; •exercises control over para-professionals. Effective member of inter-village *Palli Samaj.*
Stage 4 (Civic organisation) Stage 2 (*Palli Samaj*)	Self-managed and self-sustained groups able to negotiate and purchase BRAC and other services and to effectively engage politically. (73–96 months)	Members contest local elections. Effective demand (payment for full service costs). Stable relations with other institutions for services. Form other sub-groups/specialist groups.
Stage 3 (*Palli Samaj*)	Self-managed local federation of village organisations able to negotiate with and provide oversight on local government.	Stable, democratic local institution is sought to endorse local government initiatives. Can enforce sanctions when needed.

Box 3.1 Fundacion Poder Ciudadano (Foundation for Citizen Power)[38]

In the last few years, the Fundación Poder Ciudadano has carried out different activities aimed at increasing citizens' abilities to know and exercise their rights, as a way of strengthening democracy and generating greater equity. One of the institution's activities since 1992 has been the formation and dissemination of a data bank of candidates for elected positions, so the citizenry can exercise what they call preventive quality control of candidates. Another project with a similar aim is the Citizen's Monitoring of Public Interest Actions. This programme 'attempts to activate instruments and mechanisms that permit citizens to claim, through the courts, effective compliance with the law, exercising actions of public interest...'. Projects of this type are also being initiated in Chile and other countries of Latin America.

NGDOs, the costs and sophistication of 'scientific' methods are prohibitive. Instead, experienced NGDO leaders, managers and staff use proxy signs and indicators. This study tried to identify what they are in general and in relation to sustainable impact in particular. The following final section describes what was found.

Sustainability Indicators in Practice – Management and Prediction by Proxy

Over time, people running NGDOs adopt indirect or proxy indicators to assess the likelihood of a sustained impact of their intervention and of an enduring increase in CBO capacity. The signs and measures they employ are based on both experience and intuition. When observing and 'reading' what is going on, proxies form a handy, proven aid to check on the probability of change remaining.

Intervention Proxies

What do NGDOs look for when gauging sustainable progress? The following items bring together answers to this question from many people interviewed.

Spontaneous Adoption and Replication

When, without NGDO effort, an idea or a new practice it has introduced spreads by itself, it is likely to have resonated with something that people value and will continue without external support. For example the Centre for Conflict Resolution (CCR) in South Africa saw that two teachers who had gone through CCR training had, on their own initiative, introduced the techniques with nurses and the police in their local area. The initiative has now become a formal programme. The Centre de Recuperação Nutricional (CREN) in Brazil observed a 'wave effect' as families in surrounding slums took up improved nutritional practices that were being shown at CREN's nutritional recuperation and education centres. The ACP in Nepal saw a wide adoption of a block printing technique for fabrics it had introduced as a commercial undertaking – from a domestic craft, there are now 25 commercial producers. For the TTO in South Africa, a sign of spontaneous spread was their business expenses and saving training (BEST) board game – designed to teach the basics of business – being taken by schools to other schools. In the words of one respondent, 'intervention impacts are not sustainable until they have been adopted by people themselves'. Self-perpetuating spread is one sign of this.

Excess Contribution

Another proxy indicator is the greater contribution by the CBOs, in terms of money, time or other resources, than had initially been agreed with them. In Costa Rica, for example, in one year community contributions were 240 per cent more than had been agreed with CR-USA for an access-road programme. This excess allowed for the construction of an extra 150 kilometres of rural access roads that are maintained by the communities themselves.

Increase in Linkages

One sign of future sustainability is embedding where CBOs develop new sets of linkages and relationships that have not necessarily been part of the intervention. For POLIS in Brazil and for PBBS in the Philippines, a CBO's active engagement with local government units and municipalities signals a relational connection beyond the NGDO. The Centro Internacional de Education y Desarrollo (CINDE) in Colombia looks for the emergence of reciprocal support systems between CBOs that have been established and negotiated without outside help. A further sign of a CBO gaining access to local government resources is used by DESCO in Peru.

Adoption by Local Government

Another sign of likely sustainability is when government adopts and applies the principles and practices demonstrated by NGDOs. In the Philippines, the Department of Agricultural Reform has adopted the basic SIAD approach to elements under its remit. In addition, NGDOs look for reallocations in government budgets in response to their work with CBOs and to policy changes that create a more supportive environment for and beyond their work. A good test of government reform is not new rhetoric, but the ways budget allocations and rules of access are amended.

Breadth of Participation

Some NGDOs, such as those operating within a SIAD frame, look for a minimum level of voluntary participation that includes the better off as well as the poorest. For the SIAD coalition the target is 30 per cent of the population in an area. They also look for composition in terms of inclusion of some of the better off, not solely the poor. This profile suggests that potential resistance and sabotage by the local elite may have been attenuated, if not overcome, increasing the likelihood of continuation.

Alteration in Individual and Group Behaviour

Some NGDOs work with individual clients. For the Child Workers in Nepal Concerned Centre (CWIN), attention is paid to changes in the behaviour of destitute children who have passed through the organisation's support systems. One example is a street child reunited with his family, who subsequently took to the streets again, ending up in a carpet-weaving factory which was exploiting other children. Many children were sexually abused and chained to their looms, but this child managed to escape and brought the police to the factory, leading to the release of 23 children, something that was highly unlikely before. CINDE looks for the way in which families change their style of upbringing of their children by adapting what they do to different stages of a child's growth. In other words, they were no longer simply applying traditional practices that were not always child-centred.

Inevitably, some of these indicators overlap with others and with those used to gauge CBO capacity. In addition, to be meaningful, signs have to be seen in the context of the nature and history of the setting. It is local insight and experience that make proxies more valid and hence of real use. In the last analysis interpretation of proxies is a matter of informed judgement.

Capacity Proxies

In addition to whatever formalised assessment methods are employed, NGDO staff look for other signs of CBO capacity.

Energy and Attitude

Some NGDOs look for the 'light in people's eyes' – they try to sense the energy and excitement with which people undertake shared efforts. Energy and fire stem from a combination of anger and hope. Having only the former often leads to burn out and frustration. Laughter shared by all, rather than sullenness, is a useful reflection of satisfaction. Forward-looking energy and drive is fed by incremental successes that motivate and keep a group alive. NGDOs therefore keep an eye out for a continuation of gains and selection of new initiatives.

Quality of Leadership

Groups tend to stand tall or fall fast depending on the quality of their leader. High quality leaders succeed because of their integrity, vision and commitment. In the words of the director of CETEC, 'they know how to manage the "privilege" of being selected'.[39] However, this must be complemented with an ability to reach sound judgements by correctly reading the condition of the group and the environ-

ment in which they live. Technical competence is seldom a sufficient basis on which to inspire and motivate members as followers. Followers trust and respect the leader enough to accompany him or her into uncharted territory and experiences that may be stressful and, at times, confrontational. Expectations of leadership are deeply culturally embedded. Consequently, local knowledge is a key to understanding the quality of leadership a CBO has chosen and why. Moreover, the nature of leadership usually needs to change over time to reflect different stages of group maturity. NGDOs therefore look to see how CBO members are selecting leaders and for what characteristics. A too static, unquestioned leadership may not be an encouraging sign.

Role and Relational Shifts

Accompanying increased CBO capacity should be well-reasoned calls for the NGDO to shift its role. If this does not occur, there is a likelihood of CBOs being in a comfort zone, complacent and insecure. For example, the Village Development Resource Centre (VDRC) in Nepal looks for the extent to which a CBO is tapping new resources and developing linkages under its own steam and negotiating on its own terms. In particular, NGDOs look to see if their role is being replaced by CBO links into unaided local systems, such as gaining access to inputs or services or for marketing products. NGDOs also look at the way CBOs respond to changes in the external environment, for example in local politics. Do such changes cause a CBO response in terms of a shift to recognise new patronage dynamics that are a common element of politics and power relationship in much of the developing world?[40]

Management

Of the numerous formal measures employed to assess CBO capacity, two stand out. They are the CBO ability to effectively manage conflict and financial resources. Failure in these two capabilities cannot be compensated by abilities elsewhere. Poor management in these areas breeds distrust, eroding a necessary foundation for effective collaboration.

Continuity and Stability

High turnover of members and uneven, spasmodic application of group efforts are typically a sign of lack of consolidation in group relationships. For example, irregularity in individual contributions is regarded as a warning signal of lack of strong commitment. A typical sign used by NGDOs such as PRRM is continuity in financial or in-kind support for the work of local cadres that the NGDO may have trained or otherwise relied on for its outreach.

Inquisitiveness and Critical Enquiry

A further proxy is the type of questions groups ask about the NGDO, such as its resource base, internal ways of working, transparency and power distribution. Instead of adopting a recipient stance, do they push forward issues that may discomfort the NGDO and challenge often subtle, paternal behaviour? NGDOs also look for group questioning about things 'over the horizon' – such as the behaviour of markets – that people may not understand but sense are conspiring to block their progress. Inquisitiveness acts as one proxy for active engagement with the environment.

Internal Readjustment

An additional sign NGDOs look for is the internal adaptation of the CBO to its own growth and to changes in external circumstances. For example, success and growing strength typically lead to better application of norms and roles, and may also lead to growing differentiation of tasks, with more

and more sub-groups being formed to look after different activities. There may be active recruitment of members with beneficial external relations, such as to newly chosen representatives on local authorities.

The Stance of the Elite

NGDOs try to take measure of the position adopted by the local elite towards a CBO and what it is trying to do for whom. This is an ambiguous measure. Upsetting the status quo could be a necessary path to CBO empowerment. One cannot expect local power-holders to be happy with this. On the other hand, interventions that set out to antagonise existing power-holders are most likely to be undermined. The reading NGDOs make is therefore one of the extent to which the CBO can manage relationships with the more powerful in an ebb and flow of assertion and accommodation. This may involve using the NGDO's presence, protection and external relationships. A negative sign used by the Institute of Politics and Governance (IPG) in the Philippines is when this remains a perpetual claim of the CBO on the NGDO.

In summary, proxy indicators are on-the-surface approximations. They are most useful when they capture important underlying issues and processes, such as incentives and changes in attitudes, behaviour and power relations. But more significantly, NGDOs use them because they exist in 'real time'. They are not the product of scheduled monitoring, evaluation and review. These types of formalised and ritualised procedures are just not sufficient for reading a situation as it happens and making adjustments while 'on the move'. That is one essence of responsive management and development agility.

Proxy signs must be read together before an interpretation can be made of the strength and quality of NGDO capacity. CBOs that are unquestioning, docile, sombre, not innovative, do not manage conflict or money well, do not continually generate something of value for members, or retain the same leadership for too long, are unlikely to sustain themselves or the benefits of external interventions. CBOs that pose critical questions, readjust them-selves as they grow, innovate and take initiative on their own, manage money and contention between members, and change their relationships and leadership as inter-nal and external circumstances demand, are more likely to have both insight and agility.

Chapter Summary

This chapter has explored three facets that enable NGDOs to assess progress in sustained impact beyond their intervention.

Process entails adopting a composite view in order to select points of entry and relate them to other areas of change beyond the NGDO's own contribution. Clear theories about underdevelopment, poverty and change are a prerequisite for the analysis needed, typically through a strategic planning process that is widely spread and understood. This type of process has to be complemented by situa-tional analysis and local validation. Once points of entry are chosen, NGDOs need to integrate their efforts

- in terms of their own internal processes;
- horizontally to others working at the same systems level; and
- vertically to other levels that influence the NGDO's own work.

Integrated area development is one approach to doing so, coupled to upward linkages to policy and advocacy. In its turn, downward accountability of NGDOs in advocacy calls for local capacity building to enhance the CBO's own claim-making and advocacy abilities. They cannot simply be treated as a source of testimony to substantiate or mandate an NGDO's own advocacy efforts.

NGDOs need to find ways of predict-ing the likelihood of sustained impact and increasing such probability through the way they work. One way is through measurements, periodically performed, that indicate the dynamics and direction of change. For capacity building, using a staged or phased approach and indicators is one way of identifying trends. However, complexity and cost often stand in the way of extensive or intensive studies of change. Two practical solutions are used to deal with this difficulty. One is to negotiate indicators of change with CBOs them-selves, which they monitor as part of their own capacity building. Another is to use experience and local knowledge to identify proxy signs. Examples are given for proxy indicators in terms of sustained benefits of an intervention and the capacity of CBOs. A living assessment of insightful agility as a quality of CBO capacity comes from reading and interpreting what the combi-nation of proxy indicators tells NGDO managers and staff as they go about their day-to-day work.

Part II

Maintaining Activities – Strategies for Sustaining Resources

Part II concentrates on one dimension of sustainability that is currently preoccupying NGDOs – mobilising resources for their work and for their own existence. The approach adopted complements the growing number of publications on this topic by paying attention to the trade-offs NGDO leaders and managers make in selecting between an array of possible strategies. An underlying question throughout is: what do strategic options mean for an NGDO's insightful agility and its position in society?

The first chapter in Part II starts with a brief review of a fixation that equates finance with sustainability. While understandable at this moment in history, the equation is dangerous if an organisation wishes to be viable, autonomous and civic. From this cautionary opening, the concepts of resource dependency theory are used to analyse NGDO reactions to changes in resource supply and demand in the external environment, including domestic trends and shifts in aid policy and practice. The third section looks at components that influence resource mobilisation trade-offs. The concluding section sets out the major strategic resource options faced by most NGDOs, together with a simple framework for subsequent analysis of the practical choices they are making.

Chapter 5 begins with a critical reflection on the push of NGDOs towards the fashionable concept of civic and social entrepreneurship. These concepts complement the discussion on resource dependency in Chapter 4. Together they serve as the backdrop to a focus on one strategic option – human and material resource mobilisation. The treatment links back to the previous chapters on capacity building of member-based CBOs. The discussion centres on involvement of volunteers and approaches to community resource generation.

Chapter 6 looks within a strategic choice of an NGDO to become a 'hybrid' organisation, that is, becoming a non-profit organisation engaged in commercial activities. Again, possible sub-strategies and their trade-offs are examined along with the dilemmas they bring, for example in relation to government stance. Chapter 7 looks at a third strategic option where NGDOs gain access to finance generated by others: from governments through taxes, from businesses from their profits and from civil society through a variety of methods.

Chapter 8 acts as a summary for Part II in two ways. First, it illustrates how different decisions about NGDO identity and role in society lead to different strategic priorities in fundraising. This is illustrated by a case of an NGDO that wishes to locate itself as a reform-oriented, autonomous organisation, that also deals with today's development problems. Second, the chapter shows the link between NGDO resource mobilisation strategies and four stages of organisational growth. BRAC 's approach to resource mobilisation over the past 25 years is used as an example.

Throughout, the focus is on resources that are not directly obtained by NGDOs from the aid system, which is analysed in many other publications.[1] Strategies that alter the profile of resource dependency from foreign to local are examined.

Chapter 4

Options, Strategies and Trade-offs in Resource Mobilisation

'... many CSOs can benefit by stepping back from their day-to-day demands ... to take a strategic view of resource enhancement possibilities.' (Schearer, de Oliveira and Tandon, 1997)

Resources steer organisations. How you raise the resources you need, and from which source, has a strong influence on what an organisation is and what it can be. This chapter examines how resources impact on NGDOs. It provides a framework of 14 resource options and characteristics against which different options can be assessed for their likely effects.

The chapter starts with a cautionary note about equating money with sustainability. Finance is a necessary, but not sufficient, condition. The subsequent section takes a broad view of what is going on in terms of resource supply and demand that is likely to affect NGDO strategies. Then, using insights from theories of resource dependency, the chapter identifies the strategic choices available, together with the major trade-offs they imply. The options are then used for the analysis and discussion to be found in the rest of the chapters that make up Part II.

Fixing the Financial Fixation

There is an old American school of thought arguing that the final measure of non-profit performance is continuity in raising money.[2] If the organisation is not doing something right for someone, it will eventually wither away and die.[3] As the saying goes, you can fool some people all of the time and all of the people some of the time, but you can't fool all of the people all of the time. This holds particularly true for NGDOs that, in many countries, are the object of government mistrust and public suspicion. They face a tough test in ensuring resource continuity.

The underlying point is that success at resource mobilisation is the standard by which NGDOs should be judged. This is the ultimate 'bottom line'. No resources means no organisation. Consequently, a perceived threat to resource supply leads to a natural tendency to concentrate on finding new sources as if this is what solely matters. As described below, such a threatening perception exists, leading to a concerted effort to look for alternatives.

A concern to secure an NGDO's resource base – away from international aid – started in the late 1980s. The book *Towards Greater Financial Autonomy*, was probably a seminal start to what has followed.[4] The approach adopted by the writers was for NGDOs to become completely self-financing. This goal is no longer seen to be realistic or necessarily desirable. It has been displaced by a number of trends. For a start, this book was written before the 'discovery' of civil society in relation to development. This new concept provided both a framework for and impetus to investment in studies, training courses and specialist organisations, such as the International Fund Raising Group and the World Alliance for Citizen Participation (CIVICUS).[5] Another change has been the adoption of partnership by all and sundry in the official aid industry. Collaboration and cross-financing between sectors of government, business and civil society is now a common part of a financing agenda. Further, there is a growing assertiveness and increase in claim-making by NGDOs on government for subsidies to help provide public goods and services. If governments are prepared

to provide tax and other concessions to attract businesses – a forgone income – why shouldn't NGDOs have a right to support for the added value of social provisions?

But the last point leads to one reason why resource mobilisation is not the sole answer to organisational sustainability. As Part I argues, the case to be made rests on demonstrated NGDO performance. In its turn, maintaining performance requires an organisation that can learn and adapt to environmental changes and to stay its civic self in the process – the topic of this chapter and of Part III. In short, organisational sustainability is more than just a question of dollars and cents.[6] Sustainability pivots in the interplay between resources, impact and organisational regeneration. With this fact in mind, we turn to the issue of resource mobilisation.

NGDOs and Resource Supply and Demand

All organisations are both shaped by and shape their environments. The degree to which both occur varies enormously. For example, transnational corporations resulting from recent mergers in the banking, oil, transport and communications industries can and do wield enormous economic clout, as well as producing far-reaching social effects in terms, for example, of employment.[7] Nevertheless, they have to continue to raise and retain capital by generating value for shareholders. And, as the Monsanto case illustrates, they also have to maintain a positive reputation with present and future consumers. Apparent arrogance about the merits of genetic engineering and the benefits of 'terminator genes' tarnished the Monsanto brand name, causing loss of consumer trust, market valuation and share price.

The damage to public image was so severe that the name Monsanto was dropped in a merger with another corporation.

Despite a perception that Northern governments are all-powerful, their behaviour is increasingly bounded by the demands of globalisation, particularly the free movement of capital and elimination of trade barriers. Unless they make conditions for domestic and inward investment attractive, capital will go elsewhere. In addition, in an increasingly democratic world, the regimes elected to control the bureaucratic machines and public resources must satisfy enough citizens if they wish to remain in power. Hence, governments must behave in ways that recognise international competition for resource and produce policies and outputs that ensure public acceptance of domestic taxation.

The contribution of non-profit organisations to a country's economy may be more than people realise.[8] Nevertheless, they remain modest economic actors overall. However, through public pressure and interest groups, size is not necessarily the determinant of impact. Non-profits can have significant effects in terms of politics and policy if their agendas resonate with, and are sufficiently sustained by, civil society. The impact of civic institutions depends on public trust and support, even if this is expressed through public finance.

These generalisations indicate that no matter the type – or how big or how small – organisations are continually challenged to adjust and optimise their exchanges with the world outside their boundaries. The current flurry of studies, proposals and initiatives aimed at improving the sustainability of NGDO resources, especially money, can be seen as an accelerated adjustment to both perceived and real changes to their environment. The major contextual changes influencing NGDOs can be looked at in terms of alterations in supply and demand.

Supply-side Dynamics

On the supply side, the rapid growth of Southern and Eastern NGDOs has been fed by and resulted in a heavy dependence on foreign aid.[9] Aid resources reach them both directly from official donors and Northern NGDOs and indirectly via loans and grants to their governments.[10] There is an overall trend of official aid to finance Southern NGDOs directly in-country and to bring them into projects and programmes to be implemented by governments. Southern NGDO experience of these modalities is mixed, summed up in the question: are we partners or contractors?[11] This question reflects a strategic issue for NGDOs that reappears in subsequent chapters. The fact that it matters so much relates to the substantial degree that NGDOs rely on official aid.

The past decade has seen a decline by 21 per cent in the real levels of finance allocated to overseas development assistance. After steady reduction in real terms, a recent increase in official aid, the first since 1994, added US$3.2 billion to the 1997 level of $48.3 billion. This amounts to a growth of 8.9 per cent. At 0.23 per cent of donor GNP, this level still falls far short of the agreed target of 0.7 per cent.[12] However, even these improving figures should be read with caution. Detailed study suggests that official figures suffer from conscious, elevating distortions.

'Recently, aid flows have tended increasingly to benefit activities that do not fit the Organisation for Economic Cooperation's (OECD) strict definition of aid. Changes in OECD conditionality and in donor ideology after the Cold War also appear to weight the scale against recipient countries.

Official data from the OECD support the view that there was no resource shift to the East and that official aid was additional. Closer examination, however, suggests that changes in reporting and recording have artificially boosted ODA figures, thus hiding both indications of a geographical shift and a decline in ODA in the strict sense of a proportion of Gross National Domestic Product. Further findings of the study suggest that:

- *Changes in the OECD's interpretation of ODA have increased officially declared aid in the 1990s.*
- *The inclusion of expenditures directed at "solving global*

common problems" – not development aid according to OECD definitions – has boosted.

- *A new ideology of donors and new forms of conditionality could be used to justify giving less aid.*
- *New conditionalities have shifted the balance against recipient countries. State-led development appears at times to have been substituted by state-subsidised private sector activity, often favouring investors from donor countries.*[13]

In sum, aid as originally understood is probably still decreasing, while policy conditions are changing the parameters by which it can be accessed and by whom.

For NGDOs, the effect of this supply-side trend has been very mixed. On the one hand, donor policies that develop civil society and concentrate on poverty are opening NGDO access to official funds, some previously assigned to government.[14] Consequently, the total finance available to NGDOs has increased from about US$6 billion at the beginning of the decade to about $13 billion today. Private funding has remained more or less static while other, previously very limited sources – such as for-profit activity or business support – are increasing minimally. Consequently, the proportion of official, tax-derived, funds in the NGDO total has increased from about 20 to about 50 per cent.[15] In other words, NGDOs have become more tied to official aid and hence more exposed to changes in its policies and priorities.

However, a growth in official aid to and through NGDOs is very unevenly distributed geographically and between NGDO types.[16] Latin American NGDOs

continue to experience a rapid drop in the foreign aid available to them. A similar reduction is being felt in the East Asian 'tiger economies'.[17] At the same time, poverty focus and political considerations are starting to concentrate official assistance. A poverty focus is moving foreign aid towards countries in South Asia and sub-Saharan Africa with a high number or high proportion of people who are poor. Politics directs aid to countries, either emerging from civil war, as for example in Cambodia, or a communist history, such as Vietnam and Laos, that would benefit from private enterprise, voluntary association, civic growth and finance for social compensation programmes during a period of transition.[18]

The bureaucratic threshold for gaining access to official aid is high. It requires 'spare' resources for pre-investments in participatory investigation and writing proposals. It also requires a high degree of 'development literacy' and professional competence. For many Southern NGDOs both of these commodities are in short supply, and this therefore benefits their Northern counterparts. In addition, there is still a tendency for foreign donors to prefer, or in the case of Canada require, a domestic NGDO in funding to Southern NGDOs. Therefore, again, the South is relatively disadvantaged in terms of access.[19]

An additional feature feeding the supply of resources to NGDOs is the global instability caused by climatic and man-made disasters. What this means for the demand side is explained below. On the supply side it means a growing proportion of aid allocated to humanitarian action – currently amounting to some 7 per cent of the total in 1997, up from 2.6 per cent in 1990.[20] Again, Northern NGDOs tend to have more capacity to respond and deliver than their Southern counterparts, which is one reason why the

United Nations High Commission for Refugees (UNHCR) is intent on local capacity building in the South.[21]

NGDO access to domestic funds is dependent on the political economy of a country, its historical and cultural circumstances and legal conditions. Together, they create an environment that determines the extent to which NGDO resources can be mobilised locally and with what types of strategies and degrees of difficulty. Where there is a tradition of NGDO-type intermediary organisations, government support, civic awareness and propensity to give are likely to be already established. However, at risk of gross generalisation, the purpose of such support is likely to be the provision of institutional welfare rather than development as currently understood.[22]

Conversely, there are countries where informal relations and reciprocal networks – the 'economy of affection' common to sub-Saharan Africa[23] – are the foundation for social support. The notion of funding an intermediary runs counter to the needs of sustaining social capital and a system of mutual obligation. An emerging and enlightened middle class may be prepared to finance NGDOs, but mass support is less probable. And even middle class support is more likely to be premised on social welfare rather than activism.

Where NGDOs have been active in establishing a new, democratic political order, as in much of Latin America and in South Africa, relations with the new regimes could be expected to result in policies that open government funding to NGDOs. The question arising is: on what terms does this occur? Can and will such support be accessible in ways that respect the autonomy that was an essential feature of the NGDO contribution to political reform? Alternatively, will the new regime expect NGDOs to continue as 'brothers and sisters in arms', by playing an uncritical supportive role?[24]

For countries now adopting a market economy while retaining single party, communist-inspired political systems, as in China, the whole notion of autonomy is questioned. In China, despite an unclear legal status and ambiguous regulations, that are not uncommon elsewhere,[25] both domestic and foreign NGDOs are required to have a 'partnering' governmental or party institution.[26] Government resources – salary maintenance and subsidies, for example – are consequently a common foundation of domestic NGDO operations and sustainability, albeit with some modest progress in fund-raising from Chinese citizens.[27]

Finally, recent developments in China reflect a common problem faced by many NGDOs when trying to gain access to domestic resources; this is the problem of political and social legitimacy.[28] Where NGDOs are perceived to be a product of external interventions, colonial history, or extensions and instruments of foreign aid and its masters, the foundation for domestic support is inevitably weak. In countries newly independent from the Soviet Union and in Russia itself, a new breed of non-profit organisation is already perceived as a cover for organised crime, or simply to provide employment generation for those establishing them.[29] The basic ethics of voluntarism and trust in philanthropic intentions are insufficiently present or, if present, are more likely to be expressed through long standing, informal and intimate relationships – not through support to intermediary NGDOs.

From these broad generalisations, it is apparent that the present supply-side picture is both positive and negative for NGDOs. Crudely put, an NGDO's ability to capitalise on supply-side shifts depends on where it is on the globe and if it is Northern or Southern with already good capacity for development and/or emergency work.

The Demand Side

The demand side for NGDO development work is dominated by policy shifts associated with aid conditions and particular aspects of globalisation. On the policy front there is consistent pressure for governments to do less, and do better at what they should do well. Typical tasks are sound economic management; creation and maintenance of an enabling environment for business and citizen initiatives; a fair and just application of the law; protection of human rights; provision of social safety nets as a last resort; and ensuring physical security for the population. Correspondingly, people should carry a bigger responsibility for their own welfare and costs of social service. They must learn to expect less from government services and hopefully, in much of sub-Saharan Africa, less state predation as well. In parallel, public ownership of productive enterprises should be reduced, if not eliminated, as should barriers to trade and capital flows under rules and agreements of the WTO.

Within this global policy framework, it is assumed that the social costs of adapting to the economic demands of globalisation – such as unemployment or impoverishment – will only be short-term. The eventual acceleration in national economic growth because of more efficient market operation and investment, together with lowering prices – as international comparative advantages of factor inputs 'kick in' – will produce benefits for everyone in the end. In sum, there are transition costs of globalising adjustment that temporarily overlay and add to the social impact of structural reform in state–society relations

Aside from the realism of the assumptions underlying the growth model being employed,[30] the demand-side question for NGDOs is: who wins and who loses from the additive effects of adjusting and structural changes? A crude answer is those – the poor and marginalised – already least able to cope before and while these two transitions were underway. The nature and breadth of this category are situationally dependent. But the general scenario is one of growing disparities between an emerging group of a few super-rich, a growing but insecure middle class and a perpetual category of the poor, relying for survival on subsistence, mutual support and public subsidy.

Identifying who is most likely to lose has been discussed in previous chapters. But whoever they may be, the structural nature of the anticipated shift in state functions will inevitably create a public service demand on Southern NGDOs. The demand is akin to that already manifested in the majority of their domestic counterparts in the North. Domestic non-profit organisations, predominantly in the North, fulfil a 'Third Way' welfare substitution and social service role based on a social compact or contract financed by a mix of government subsidy, contracts and user fees for service[31] – the developmental dimension of NGDOs will be under pressure unless their response offers an adequate counterweight. This is an important dimension of the strategic choices that NGDOs face in selecting how they want to mobilise domestic resources.

Combined, the forces sketched above are poverty inducing, and not just in the short term, for the capitalist free-market economic model has no intrinsic redistribution method or intention. Equity remains in the realm of politics and public choice. Consequently, the demand for policy advocacy should remain high on an NGDO agenda. However, as previously alluded to, will this be possible if there is greater dependency on public funds? Compromise in policy assertiveness is therefore another strategic issue and choice to be made in selecting a resource mobilisation path.[32]

Southern governments have mixed views about the real agenda of aid conditions and its lessening of their role – not to mention a reduction in the potential for patronage on which much of their politics is based.[33] Nothing as clear-cut as a state–NGDO compact yet exists in most Southern countries where overt or covert mistrust on both sides is attended by increasing exploratory engagement.[34] Nevertheless, for heavily aid-dependent countries it is reasonable to anticipate that aid conditions reflecting donor domestic policies will push their way down the aid chain into the state-society arena, creating expectations of, and funds for, an NGDO service role. Spill-over of funders' domestic policies have usually had this effect in the past. For example, the Thatcher-Reagan era of supposed state retrenchment corresponded with the introduction of the cruder forms of structural adjustment conditions on recipients of aid. Subsequent refinements to adjustment and the drive for partnership with everyone for development corresponds to the Clinton-Major era, now reinforced by 'Third Way' harmony of the Clinton-Blair-Schröder and guarded Jospin quartet in their ode to 'social-liberalism'.[35]

However, governments are also under pressure to be more efficient so that taxes can be kept low, competitive and attractive for international business and knowledgeable manpower. This requirement can increase an interest in learning from NGDOs about how more can be done with less. Hence innovation and experimentation may be an NGDO niche role that is better appreciated and called upon, but probably in domains selected by government and not by NGDOs themselves, unless they make it happen. Southern NGDOs and their governments can also be allies, for example in setting out positions in terms of the rules and practices of WTO. Through their international contacts, NGDOs are sometimes better placed to gather information and help develop government capacity for negotiation, as happened prior to and during the WTO Seattle debacle. However, to expand this type of demand would require a change of the typical government perception that NGDOs are 'the opposition' and insufficiently professional or internationally connected enough to have anything valuable to offer.[36]

Another potential source of demand on NGDOs will not come from government, but will be directed against it. Greater and less inhibited flows of information across borders and a more educated public are forces for greater assertiveness towards state policies and actions. In other words, NGDOs can be at the forefront of increased popular activism for pro-poor structural reforms and trading conditions. One example is the month-long tour, in June 1999, of a caravan of Southern peoples' organisations through G8 industrialised countries as a symbolic protest highlighting the negative impact of the global trading system on their lives and livelihoods.

Alongside structural and transition demands on NGDOs are the natural and man-made disasters that help them gain public profile and substantial resources that, on occasion, can cross-subsidise development work or at least secure a better cash flow. Hurricane Mitch devastated parts of Central America in 1999; a cyclone hit and killed 8000 people in Orissa in India in November, 1999; Turkey and Taiwan sustained major damage and loss of life through earthquakes in 1999. Conflicts in Kosovo, Africa's Great Lakes region, Sierra Leone, southern Sudan and atrocities in other locations, like East Timor, all conspire to maintain local and global instability and human tragedy. These instabilities and the humanitarian demands they cause – in 1997 some 14 million refugees and asylum seekers and 19 million internally displaced people – create opportunities for NGDO humanitarian action. Much of this support is provided by official sources and channelled through Northern NGDOs.[37] The question currently being asked is whether or not this work can move beyond UN–NGDO sub-contracting to a more equitable arrangement of pre-agreed 'task-sharing'.[38]

Overall, there is every reason to expect a continuation in the escalation of demand for certain types of NGDO activity. The biggest source is state unburdening through substitution for government welfare and social services – health, education, water and sanitation, for example. It would be burying one's head in the sand to suggest that – faced with government cutbacks –

this role is not what poor people would want NGDOs to play. Non-service roles, such as advocacy for reform, innovation and government reinforcement, are also possibilities, but are unlikely to be of a comparable size or as prevalent. For the foreseeable future, humanitarian demands will continue to arise.

Setting supply possibilities against the profile of demand in a given context – and making the right choices – is an important part of creating a resource mobilisation strategy. Another element is examining and dealing with trade-offs in terms of the implications for the organisation itself associated with different courses of action. The concept of resource dependency can, and without them knowing it, does, help NGDOs in making trade-offs.

Moving from Dependency – Criteria for Resource Mobilisation

Within changes in supply and demand, NGDOs have to make decisions about where to invest their energies in terms of mobilising local resources. From a sustainability perspective, one task is to reduce resource vulnerability. But an NGDO is vulnerable in another way as well. Strategic choices in terms of resources have a ramification beyond their reliability. Why? Because the choices made can also affect what the organisation stands for, which equates to a second task of protecting its mission and identity. In more technical terms, the profile of resources employed co-determines organisational identity. Using ideas generated by theories of contingency and resource dependency, this section explores various aspects of this dual vulnerability as a foundation for understanding the trade-offs NGDOs employ when choosing which resources to mobilise and how.[39]

Resource Dependency

A contingent view pays central attention to the transactions and exchanges between an organisation and its environment. On the input side, an organisation is dependent on what the environment has to offer in terms of resources. On the output side, organisations can act to alter the environment in ways that increase, secure or stabilise the resources it requires. Typically, this is through providing goods and services that society wants and values, as well as pursuing interests in the political arena. NGDOs do both. For example, they draft proposals for funding and submit them to donors, while simultaneously seeking to change the conditions donors use to allocate their resources in order to make them more accessible. Their ability to do the latter depends on being seen to produce something of social value. In terms of organisational types, 'pure' non-profit organisations are particularly susceptible to change in the characteristics of their resources. This is because they do not control their generation as profits, like business; nor do they control their extraction as taxes from citizens, the resource base of government. Consequently, those providing resources to NGDOs can, and do, exert a significant element of control or power. Even if not their intention, it is a common, almost inevitable effect, paralleling the problem of CBO dependency described in Chapter 2. The consequences of resource instability, therefore, fall more heavily on NGDOs than on those funding them. The relations between NGDOs and typical resource providers, donors and governments, are heavily unbalanced: funders typically exercise more control over NGDOs than NGDOs do over their funders.

As a result, NGDOs are particularly sensitive to the stability of resources they rely on. In unstable periods, as sketched above, they have to adjust their external relationship to try to restore continuity and stability. A vital issue is how to do this in ways that are not at the cost of mission and identity. The phenomenon of an NGDO's client group or activities altering because of changes in resource conditions has been called 'mission creep' or 'goal displacement'. One result is an inconsistency between mission and action on the ground. Another result is internal confusion as the gap between rhetoric and reality increases – not an uncommon feature of NGDO behaviour.

Sensitivity also depends on how critical the resource is for organisational functioning and outputs. Typically, because the project-mode of development funding is averse to paying general overheads, resources that cover an NGDO's core costs are usually the most critical. As we will see, this translates into a compelling desire to set up endowments that generate untied funds.

In appraising alternative resources, NGDOs face the issue of maintaining autonomy in their own decision-making. Being able to negotiate fair terms without compromising on freedom of internal decision-making is important, as is the ability to say 'no' when it is necessary. Such ability can be eroded to different degrees by different sources of resources. This raises the issue of proportionality. Excessive reliance on a single source of funding not controlled by the organisation is a normal sign of high vulnerability, high sensitivity, high criticality and low autonomy. It is not necessarily indicative of low consistency if the mission of both parties is sufficiently similar, but this problem comes readily into play if the provider shifts policy or perspective.

Finally, an NGDO must assess the organisational implications of taking on a new type of financial resource. How much internal adjustment will need to be made? What management and human resource demands will arise? How compatible will new resources be with existing processes, values and culture? Low compatibility brings significant organisational demands; high compatibility few if any.

The concepts used above help in understanding the factors involved in NGDOs' strategic choices for resource mobilisation.

- *Vulnerability:* an NGDO's ability to suffer costs imposed by external events. Highly vulnerable NGOs are unable to cope, invulnerable NGDOs are unaffected.
- *Sensitivity:* the degree and speed at which changes in a resource impact on the NGDO. Low sensitivity means that external changes do not cause immediate severe disruption, high sensitivity means that they do.
- *Criticality:* the probability that an existing resource can be replaced by

another for the same function. Highly critical resources – such as core support – cannot be easily replaced; resources with low criticality can.

- *Consistency:* an ability to alter a resource profile without compromising mission and identity. High consistency resources mean that an NGDO is less forced to compromise than it must do if it is to gain access to low consistency resources. Typically, swapping donors creates a consistency challenge as each has its own conditions and preferences.[40]

- *Autonomy:* the degree to which the resource affects the ability to say 'no' when it is needed. Turning away or not pursuing available resources – when the demand side is essentially infinite – is not easy but it should always be possible. If it is not possible, NGDO decision making is effectively enslaved to the dictates of others. It is not autonomous. Hence autonomy is reflected in an NGDO's freedom in decision making about resources it wishes to access and the outputs and social value it will provide.

- *Compatibility:* the degree of similarity between new and existing resources that call for minor to major modification to the organisation's processes, structure and functioning; for example, creating a new department or recruiting staff with different professional cultures, values and aspirations.

An NGDO with a resource profile characterised by low vulnerability, low sensitivity, low criticality, high consistency, substantial autonomy and high compatibility is likely to be more agile and adaptive than an NGDO with the opposite profile. Commonsense would suggest that an NGDO that achieves the preferred profile is not only more insightful but also has its strategic house in order – it is capacitated. As we will see in Part III, achieving this condition has a lot to do with reputation, learning, leadership, a secure identity and self-awareness.

All the foregoing feeds into two features that dominate thinking behind the many efforts currently being put into NGDO resource mobilisation. They can be summed up in two words: 'dependency' and 'diversification'. Given the high degree of NGDO reliance on foreign funds and the perceived unreliability of this source, the basic goal of resource mobilisation is to reduce dependency on foreign aid by diversifying the resource base.[41] For example, studies in the US confirm that '... diversified revenue sources are more likely to be associated with a strong financial position than concentrated revenue sources.'[42] The question arising is how do NGDOs go about this task in relation to the six aspects of resource dependency summarised above? This is the topic of the next section that sets the guiding structure for the rest of Part II.

Strategic Options, Trade-offs and Dilemmas

What strategic options do NGDOs have as they seek to reduce vulnerability and dependency? What trade-offs and dilemmas do they face in making the best choices? This concluding section sets out the way in which the next four chapters answer these questions.

Strategic Options

The major options available to NGDOs in terms of diversifying and localising their resource base are summarised in Figure 4.1. The first major strategic choice is between human and material resources

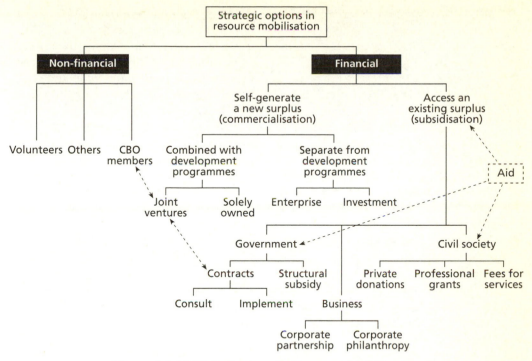

Figure 4.1 *NGDO Options in Resource Mobilisation*

and finance. Given that NGDO dependency is essentially monetary, the latter tends to dominate over the former. But the former option is most likely to avoid the dilemma of mission creep and introducing inconsistency. Mobilising volunteer and community resources is also a strategy that keeps an NGDO closest to the real commitment of CBOs and, hence, to sustained impact. This strategic option is the focus of the next chapter.

Within the financial option, NGDOs face two immediate decision paths. One is to generate financial resources itself, the topic of Chapter 6. This keeps the NGDO in greater control. The threat to autonomy is likely to be minimal. Own control also means that vulnerability to outsiders is not necessarily increased, that sensitivity can be decreased and that critical resources can be replaced because the NGDO decides where to put the surplus it produces.

An alternative option is to access a surplus created by others, the focus of Chapter 7. This choice brings with it issues of reduced autonomy, heightened sensitivity and vulnerability, a threat to consistency, but the possibility of reducing high dependency on foreign aid. The probability of such negative aspects actually occurring depends, in turn, on the source generating the financial surplus: government, business or civil society.

For NGDOs, potential drawbacks of opting to gain access to a surplus produced by others must be set against the benefits of diversification. This is where proportionality comes into play. Simply shifting from a heavy dependency on foreign aid to a heavy dependency on domestic government revenues may make things worse, rather than better. The effect will depend on state–society relations and the willingness of government to negotiate rather

---

BOX 4.1 THE SOCIAL CAPITAL FIDUCIARY FUND OF ARGENTINA (FONCAP)

In July 1997, the executive branch of the Argentine government signed the decree creating FONCAP. The initiative was generated in the Argentine Secretariat of Social Development and its main purpose is to get community organisations to become the leading players in the creation of a structure to provide financial services to the huge quantity of small economic units. It is hoped that this would make it possible to build a consolidated and independent social sector. From this perspective, it is the intent of FONCAP that access to credit should improve the economic conditions of the most needy families and help to generate bonds of trust and links between social and public sector organisations and the national private sector and international cooperation sector. The fund is designed to last 30 years and has been started with US$40 million in capital from the national budget.

Source: Mariano Valderrama

---

than impose conditions. There is no straightforward answer. It is a question of judgement.

Figure 4.1 is a simplified version of a much more complex reality. All sorts of linkages and combinations are not shown. For example, it is quite possible that joint ventures with CBOs are made possible by the CBOs' own access to government funds as well as from their own resources. In turn, government finance to CBOs may be from its own resources, such as from the Social Capital Fiduciary Fund of Argentina (FONCAP) described in Box 4.1 or from aid grants or loans. World Bank social funds are a typical example of the latter.[43] In fact, in the period 1993–1997 some 40 per cent of World Bank funded projects made some provision for NGDO/CBO involvement. Within these projects, about 80 per cent of funds were designated for supporting CBOs.[44] In addition, NGDOs may raise capital to start up self-generating enterprises from voluntary and in-kind contributions (Chapters 5 and 6). Nevertheless, the framework corresponds reasonably well with the division of options that NGDOs face in practice.

Moreover, these options are not a question of either/or. Sensible NGDOs look to all three major strategic possibilities as they seek to diversify and reduce aid dependency. For example, in its 25-year history, BRAC has used all of them (Chapter 8), the latest additions being the establishment of a bank (transforming the credit-based rural development programme) and a fee-paying university. Few NGDOs become as complex as BRAC in terms of its strategic mix. But NGDOs should be able to explore all possibilities, while bearing in mind that the organisational and management difficulties they pose multiply as the mix expands.

In terms of overall strategic choice, Table 4.1 summarises likely effects on the six factors described in the previous section for each of the three major resource options discussed so far. It can be seen that the non-financial and self-financing options are more likely to beneficially alter an NGDO's resource profile as it moves away from aid dependency than the third alternative – gaining access to a financial surplus generated by someone else. Shifting from aid dependency to dependency on local sources other than

Table 4.1 *Probable Effects of Different Resource Options*

Resource factor/ likely impact	Non-financial option	Finance option: Self-generating a surplus	Finance option: Gaining access to an existing surplus
Vulnerability	Reduced	Reduced	Increased
Sensitivity	Reduced	Reduced	Increased
Criticality	Unchanged	Reduced	Unchanged
Consistency	Reinforced	Retained	Reduced
Autonomy	Unchanged	Reinforced	Reduced
Compatibility	High	Moderate	Source dependent

your own generated internally is the less advantageous choice. The rest of the chapters in Part II explain why in more detail.

Entries in the third column are the least certain: the outcome of tapping a surplus generated by others is so highly dependent on the specific source. However, like donor agencies, whoever it is will have an agenda and interests that will need to be satisfied if agreement is to be reached. Some compromise will be inevitable. Hence, dependency on the stability and reliability of resources generated by others will at least remain, but is more likely to increase, particularly where the source is not 'developmental' in its nature, for example businesses.[45]

Resource Trade-offs and NGDO Positioning

Finally, we need to pay attention to two major organisational concerns. This is the effect that resource diversification can have on:

1 an NGDO's contribution to society; and
2 its ability to act in its own terms.

In short, what role does an NGDO play and produce that is of social value? In addition, how autonomous is the organisation from governments that also have social responsibilities and agendas or corporations that want to be more citizen-like in their behaviour? These two factors critically affect an NGDO's position and identity in society and are shown as the axes of strategic choice in Figure 4.2.

The nature of the resource base constructed by NGDOs determines both what they do and their distance from the state. In terms of contribution to society, their impact lies along a vertical axis with, at its base, welfare provision that responds to state and market failure without attempting to change the structure of each: their work essentially maintains the *status quo*. The other extreme is where NGDOs are solely concerned about reforming how state, market and society work in favour of the poor and marginalised. Their agenda is activism and structural change.

The horizontal axis signals NGDO distance from state or corporate influence or control over their internal affairs, particularly decision making about what role to play in society.[46] In the case of China, domestic NGDOs are closely allied with state and party. At the other extreme are NGDOs not affiliated to the state in any way at all. Within whatever the law allows, they enjoy complete freedom of decision making that may or may not correspond to government agendas and priorities. Foundations deriving income from market investments may enjoy this degree of autonomy. This horizontal axis

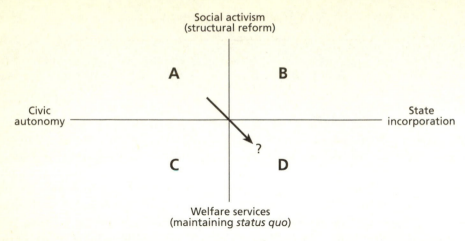

Figure 4.2 *Important Trade-offs in NGDO Strategic Positioning*

is therefore a very rough guide to an NGDO's 'civicness'.

The combination of role and autonomy locates NGDOs somewhere in this graphic framework. If recent data on non-profit organisations in industrialised countries are anything to go by, most organisations appear to inhabit quadrants 'C' and 'D'. In terms of services, the ratio between welfare and recreation and advocacy is about 70:30. While in terms of revenues, the split between government finance, fees for service and private giving is in the order of 40:50:10.[47]

Not surprisingly, quadrant 'B' is relatively uninhabited. Public finance for 'autonomous' non-profits to pursue reform agendas 'against' those providing the finance is almost a contradiction in terms. The bulk of resources in this quadrant come from private giving, especially from philanthropic foundations.

Many NGDOs would consider themselves – or would like to be – somewhere

in quadrant 'A'.[48] However, the summary of forces shaping supply and demand, suggests a pressure from NGDOs to move towards quadrant 'C'. In political terms, such a move would imply that NGDO legitimacy is altering from civic to public with direct accountability to citizens being replaced by accountability to and through public bodies.[49] The trade-offs NGDOs make in terms of changing their resource base will influence whether or not this happens.

The issue of staying true to 'civic' position and role underlies much of NGDO self-questioning and soul-searching as they consider what to do in a 'future beyond aid'. The next three chapters therefore examine what occurs when NGDOs address these and other dilemmas. The starting point is a critical look at the current fashion to recast NGDOs as 'social entrepreneurs'. This concept should, it is believed, help NGDOs retain their position in quadrant 'A'. The question is, 'will it?'

Chapter Summary

Using a resource dependency perspective, this chapter covers strategic options, choices and trade-offs associated with resource mobilisation towards sustainability. Generally speaking, the goal in changing the resource profile is to reduce dependency on foreign aid by diversifying towards domestic sources.

There are major shifts in resource supply and demand that shape the NGDO operating environment. The overall picture is of an uneven change in availability of aid resources for NGDOs that is often not being made good by domestic sources, especially from government. Hence, there is the fear that some NGDOs will not survive.

Environmental changes are to the disadvantage of some types of NGDOs and to the gain of others that are already better resourced and more capable. There is a squeeze on weaker, middle-sized NGDOs, and those that do not have a clear 'niche', to the benefit of larger, often Northern, organisations. Increasing humanitarian demands are reinforcing this differential impact of changes in resource levels and conditions for NGDO access.

Six concepts assist in understanding the factors NGDOs take into account when assessing options. They are:

- Vulnerability: an NGDO's ability to suffer costs imposed by external events affecting the resource.
- Sensitivity: the degree and speed at which changes in a resource will impact on the NGDO.

- Criticality: the probability that an existing resource can be replaced by another for the same function.
- Consistency: an ability to alter a resource profile without compromising mission and identity.
- Autonomy: the degree to which the resource affects free decision making and ability to negotiate terms and say 'no' when necessary.
- Compatibility: the degree of similarity in organisational demands between new and existing resources.

NGDOs face a primary division in the types of resources they can mobilise. They can choose between non-financial and financial sources and, within the latter, between generating funds themselves or tapping into finance generated by others. A comparative table suggests that the first two options are most likely to bring positive change in the above six factors. The latter option is more prone to creating contrary effects and to introduce organisational stress. However, the extent to which this occurs depends on which sub-source is accessed.

An important trade-off for NGDOs is one which links the profile of resources to its position in society in terms of its role and 'civicness', or distance from government. The external environment is tending to push NGDOs to more welfare roles and closer proximity to government and business. Countering or accommodating this trend is an important feature of strategic decision making.

Chapter 5

Mobilising Non-financial Resources

'If the cause is right the means will come.' (Rita Thapa, TEWA)

One relatively unexplored area of resource mobilisation is for NGDOs to actively pursue non-financial resources. This option should be obvious for two reasons. First, because of the altruistic spirit of voluntarism, social energy and the 'caring enough about something to act' from which NGDOs are supposed to emerge. Second, when dealing with poor people, they are least likely to have money to contribute. It is the non-monetary aspects of CBO contributions that therefore need to be explored. Consequently, primary paths within this strategy lead towards volunteers, communities themselves and to material 'gifts' or concessions from others, such as government businesses.[1]

One reason these options receive modest attention in publications about resource mobilisation is that they do not increase, diversify or stabilise insecure income.[2] Instead, they reduce an NGDO's costs. Given that securing money is perceived to be the major problem of organisational sustainability, this preoccupation tends to displace attention from non-financial options. Consequently, there are less case studies available in this area.[3]

In addition to reducing cost, non-financial resources have other positive attributes. They also bring a number of intangible but vital benefits, such as a relational network, that improve an NGDO's resilience and viability.

This chapter examines the non-financial options shown in Figure 4.1. The following two sections look at volunteering and community resource contributions in the light of the six features of resource dependency defined in the previous chapter. We also review what they may mean for an NGDO's insightful agility. To frame the task, a link is made between non-financial resources and the concept of social capital.

NGDOs and the Volunteer Option – With a Brief Look at Social Capital

As a category of human behaviour, voluntarism is yet to benefit from agreed standards or constant definitions that allow for analysis of trends over time or sound comparisons between locations or countries. For some, the concept is captured in formal systems like student community service. For others, it is a less formal activity such as bearing witness and the 'buddy system' used by People with Aids,[4] or in the exchange of child-care between households. For yet others, it is a form of pooling of human assets, mutual aid and communitarianism, exemplified in, for example, the Kibbutz movement in Israel and the Eitowan community in Japan.[5]

This section does not attempt a definition of what voluntarism means in terms of NGDOs save for a distinction between paid staff and unpaid individuals who give their time for free. In other words, the NGDO may fulfil many aspects of a volunteer's life, apart from one – it is not the source of their livelihoods.[6] This section uses examples of NGDO volunteers to help illustrate what they can mean for the nature of a change in NGDO resource dependency.

Social Capital and NGDOs

People contribute their time to non-profit organisations and civic associations for a variety of reasons. For example, motivation can stem from boredom, through curiosity, to a deep-rooted commitment to the organisation's cause and calling.[7] A renewed interest in understanding why people volunteer their time and energy is emerging from the concept of social capital. It is allied to concerns about community breakdown and social issues, such as divorce, pregnancy outside of marriage, drug abuse, street violence, escalating imprisonment, suicides and the like – what Fukuyama has called *The Great Disruption*.[8] Disputes about whether or not voluntary association, and hence social capital, is in decline are ongoing and likely to continue.

One important 'big-picture' argument is whether or not market capitalism – through its values of individualism, competition, contract-based mistrust and so on – is a structural force eroding positive social capital. The implication of a positive answer is a future of social break-

down – the fundamental weakening of the foundations and fabric of society.

Similarly, investigations into the relationship between social capital, poverty and development are generating disagreement.[9] Such contention will continue to colour the degree of interest and investment that the aid system will allocate to operationalise the concept. Perhaps it will also affect politicians who are expected to find solutions for the social dysfunctions of market capitalism and limits to competition.[10] They may be induced to pay more attention to values and to the relational rather than the material aspects of progress.

Social capital theory, its findings and debates, are relevant to NGDOs' non-financial resource mobilisation to the extent that:

1   They help understand, assess and select volunteers and voluntary contributions. Why is an individual wanting to assist? What are their motivations and expectations?
2   They can help sharpen insights about risks associated in mobilising different types of local resources.
3   A social capital perspective helps to chart and assist in the dynamics of local group cohesion, wider association and the enhancement of insightful and agile institutional capacity on which sustained mobilisation depends.

It is beyond the intentions of this book to work through these issues. Many studies are in progress. At this point, it is enough to signal the potential relevance of social capital thinking for the way NGDOs identify and negotiate both financial and non-financial contributions.

The Volunteer Option

For NGDOs, the volunteer option is soulful, functional and tangible. As well as embodying the original spirit of the NGDO movement, if selected and treated with care, volunteers can provide substantial technical, material, informational and relational advantages.[11] In addition, recent studies indicate that when volunteer input is included in measures of, say, employment, it can significantly increase the Third Sector's contribution to the economy. For example in Western Europe the figure alters from 6.9 to 10.3 per cent of national employment. In terms of their field of employment, volunteers make a greater proportional difference in recreation and advocacy as compared with provision of welfare services.[12] However, figures for Latin America show far more modest changes once volunteers are included. Nevertheless, despite potential problems, the volunteer dimension cannot and should not be neglected in NGDO resource strategies.

NGDO volunteers are of two basic types, the professional and the non-professional. They both bring two direct benefits – cost-reduction and a channel for civic rooting and enhanced legitimacy

In the case of Foundation Omar Dengo in Costa Rica, for example, professional volunteers in education, the media and computer technology are an important resource. The foundation was instigated in 1987 by professionals and financial entrepreneurs who wished to bring modern technology into the school classroom. However, the perspective was not technology literacy *per se*, but the ability of technology to capacitate individuals. The originating vision was nationwide. Technological human capacity was seen as a critical element in the development of the country, a view endorsed and therefore supported by the business community and the government.

The foundation was intentionally organised to bring together, as founding members, citizens from different political parties and disciplines. This helps to deal with political transitions inherent to a democracy. Founders not only act as an intellectual pool, but as activators of political support when necessary. Some of them continue to provide free technical advice that reduces costs.

'We have been able to involve professionals to do work for us for free. I do not consider this to be "voluntary work". It is, rather, a different form of activity that demands involving people in the ideas and the projects being developed and requesting their participation because we need their expertise for greater results. Professionals find this fun and become committed because these activities have a beginning and an end and they can plan the use of their time.'[13]

In addition, volunteers' institutional positions can bring useful access and linkages into both the business community and government ministries and agencies. For example, as part of a fund-raising strategy, some are able to organise lunches for business leaders as peers. Others are positioned to lobby with ministries of education for in-kind support or for the release of teachers for technical training provided by the foundation.

An alternative example of non-professional volunteers can be found in Nepal. As part of a programme to provide start-up finance for women's income generation, the Women's Support Organisation (TEWA) organises a training programme for women, typically urban housewives with time to spare. Their role is to assist staff appraise requests for assistance. They can also serve as co-field workers, talking to applicants about their ideas and possibilities. In addition, depending on their own backgrounds, they can provide technical advice. Further, they become part of a system of local committees that decide about grants.

After three days of training, volunteers are mentored for three months. Two groups are trained each year. As a *quid pro quo*, they are asked to act as fundraisers within their own extended families. TEWA members are also expected to be annual donors. To this end, they are encouraged and helped to form a 'trusted circle' of neighbours and friends committed to providing regular support.

Volunteer selection is undertaken with care. First, there is an intense appraisal in terms of individual motivation. Second, the unstable nature of Nepali politics means attention must be paid to not being seen to endorse one political party or faction or being allied to a particular political camp. In addition, TEWA wishes to reflect the country's heterogeneity in terms of culture, caste, class and age. Correspondingly, after selection, significant effort is placed on team building and active involvement of office bearers in internal meetings and planning.

After a year of service, volunteers can become TEWA members with a place in the governing general assembly. In a period where religious and cultural giving is declining, the governing body and staff have a shared vision of TEWA as an organisation dedicated to the promotion of modern philanthropy in Nepal. However, the model is one that must be sustainable in terms of Nepali capabilities. A stress on local rather than foreign resource mobilisation is aimed at building self-confidence in the ability of Nepalese people to solve their own problems. More immediately, and complementing the vision, TEWA's work is intended to help reduce the social costs of the economic transition the country is going through. Through its local efforts, TEWA has created an endowment and the annual funds raised are used for the grants given, amounting so far to some five million rupees. An average grant is Rs 30,000. Members are also encouraged to take on an advocacy role, using their own networks and linkages in society to promote TEWA's ideals, vision and agenda.

Another example of volunteer input is to be found in the origins of Child Relief and You (CRY) in India. CRY relies on volunteers for a range of activities: from putting cards and promotional materials in envelopes, to providing technical advice on graphics and for international marketing. In addition, at its inception, CRY mobilised donations of materials, advertising space, marketing advice, the skills of local artists and free use of printing presses. This illustrates that volunteers can provide other types of assistance beyond their time and labour. And even when an NGDO is able to afford such facilities on its own, there is always a buffer reserve to be used at times of overload, stress or unexpected set-backs. NGDOs solely financed by external aid are at a severe disadvantage in terms of resilience because they do not have such voluntarism at their roots, or have not invested in building such support in 'the good times'.[14]

Volunteering and other non-financial support is also vitally important for NGDOs that do not undertake development projects and programmes with CBOs. Typical are NGDOs that specialise in advocacy and lobbying, like the Third World Network (TWN) or the African Network on Debt and Development (AFRODAD) A similar case exists for NGDO coordination bodies that operate nationally, regionally and globally, such as the Forum for African Voluntary Development Organisations (FAVDO), the Association of Latin American NGOs (ALOP) and the Asian NGO Consortium (ANGOC). The difficulties they face in demonstrating 'products' of interest to businesses or governments make access to these sources quite difficult. Volunteers and other forms of non-financial support are hence more valuable than for NGDOs that can rely on tangibles and projects as a focus of volunteer attraction.

The examples suggest that volunteers contribute to both civic innovation in creating new forms of citizen giving and in the development of local philanthropy. They also reflect different expressions of social entrepreneurship, as exemplified by CRY raising much of its income from sales of products, such as greetings cards.

How can Volunteers Influence Resource Dependency?

As a strategy for diversification, volunteers can reduce vulnerability, sensitivity and criticality, reinforce consistency, strengthen autonomy and challenge compatibility.

Spreading technical and other skills over volunteers with other sources of livelihood can reduce an NGDO's vulnerability to the costs of unexpected events. When called on, committed volunteers will put in extra time, use their contacts and whatever else is needed to help the NGDO cope. Conversely, they cannot be relied on in the same way as paid staff. (Although the truth of this depends on the local market. Due to under-investment in formation of NGDO cadres, poaching is common. The general rate of staff turnover can be quite significant in some countries where needed experience is in short supply and where there is active recruitment by official aid agencies to strengthen their 'civic interface'.)[15]

Sensitivity to the speed at which external change affects an NGDO can be reduced if volunteers can act as a human resource buffer or reserve. CRY is one example, where its voluntary origins have established a reserve of social capital that can be called on in times of need. Moreover, the social links and political contacts volunteers have can be useful in negotiating with whatever the source of disruption might be.

Criticality can be reduced if volunteers have parallel skills to those of staff. This is common if volunteers are acting as technical advisers in core areas, such as financial management. For the Omar Dengo Foundation, for example, staff turnover is small, but volunteer professional backup is more often than not available as a well-informed transitional resource. If well-chosen and nurtured, volunteers are more likely to lessen criticality than increase it.

Consistency can be one challenge if volunteer skills and experience are not what is needed. Volunteers can bring perspectives, ideas and opinions that may lead to positive innovation or to awkward compromise if they are not to be alienated. One disgruntled volunteer spreading negative messages can undo what has taken years to build in terms of public confidence. This is one reason why TEWA pays so much attention to selection. The leadership is convinced that it is not appropriate to accept whoever happens to turn up and then face the potential stress and inefficiency of having dysfunctional volunteers. It is a question of conviction about getting the right people and actively selecting or pursuing them.

Autonomy can be both enhanced and compromised if care is not taken to ensure that volunteers do not bring with them expectations of preferential treatment and allegiance to external patrons. An NGDO's political insight and reading is vital. It is of doubtful benefit if a charge of 'serving foreign masters', common to high dependence on external funding, is replaced with a charge of 'serving local masters' instead. The introduction of multi-party politics in many countries is presenting NGDOs with such a political dilemma.

Probably, the most demanding part of opting for volunteers is in the area of organisational *compatibility*. Volunteers do not come under a leader or manager's span of control in the same way as staff. They need to be motivated and nurtured differently. For example, their contribution needs to be structured into the way the NGDO works. They should not be left hanging on the periphery waiting for something to do. Moreover, what they do, no matter how menial, must not be seen as tokenism. Volunteers need to see how their contribution is being used and how it is making a difference. In sum, volunteer management can be very time-consuming and must be sensitive to personality differences and the motivations that make people contribute their time.

Tensions can arise when the views and ideas of staff and volunteers differ, or when the authority or competence of staff is challenged. This is almost inevitable with the involvement of professional volunteers who have skills, position and status that confer 'authority'. Demands on relational and conflict management may increase. Correspondingly, the need for team approaches increases as well.

Other organisations, such as governments and businesses, can volunteer to provide non-material support. They can offer items such as land, buildings, new or used equipment, furniture or vehicles. They can also second personnel, forgo rent, give items for resale, allocate free advertising space or carry an NGDO's message on their own products.[16] Assuming the conditions for acceptance will not lead to government dependency or commercial misuse of the NGDO's name and reputation, such contributions can be a significant way of reducing investment costs.

Overall, volunteered inputs are likely to bring more benefits than problems in resource diversification. However, it is hard work to find and maintain volunteers. The relative lack of use of this option would suggest that it is too daunting for many NGDOs, or that money is a more flexible substitute, if it can be found. This is unfortunate from a perspective of civic embedding. It is doubly unfortunate when the intangible benefits of a volunteer's relational network are not taken into account. When volunteers commit themselves to what the NGDO is doing and stands for, it is akin to casting out a relational net. Appropriate selection means that the right 'fish' are likely to be caught.

Volunteers are an important way for NGDOs to root themselves socially, especially if they have been dangling above society, suspended on the umbilical cord of international aid. Attracting the right volunteers is an important way of bringing credibility and trust. In today's jargon, they are an essential source of social capital that it will take ages to build in other ways.

In terms of insightful agility, volunteers can make important contributions in terms of knowledge and information. Volunteers may be strategically placed in institutions or in families that broaden the information base that NGDOs can draw on. Their multiple perspectives are inputs to a more thorough and potentially accurate interpretation of what is going on in the environment and why. In short, they increase insight. In terms of agility, aside from being a flexible resource that can be tapped in different ways, volunteers can help create political and social space for NGDOs to move into. They can reduce external barriers to change, explain the NGDO case to a wider audience, open doors, give confidence about an NGDO's intentions and so on. To this extent, their potential informal 'gifts' to NGDOs may outweigh the technical resources they have to offer.[17]

Non-financial Resources from Communities

Another option for gaining access to non-financial resources is through community-based organisations themselves. This is a common pathway for NGDOs with or without a strategy for resource diversification. It is inherent to the content and process of micro-development explained in Chapter 2. Typically, NGDOs use participatory mapping exercises to ascertain what resources a community has access to individually and collectively. From these the organisation must make essential decisions. First, what complementary inputs are needed to make better use of existing assets and potentials? Second, how to deal with inclusion, exclusion and free riding; that is, people getting benefits without contributing to their creation? Third, is to ensure that NGDO inputs can be phased out over time.

This section begins by briefly reviewing the major type of non-financial resources that CBOs may be able to commit. It goes on to apply features of resource dependency to examine trade-offs that NGDOs face.

Community-based Non-financial Resources

There are many ways of identifying and grouping CBO non-financial resources. For example, the Mysore Relief and Development Agency (MYRADA) in India identified 20 such elements, while the SIAD handbook points towards seven areas.[18] The categories chosen arise from the local development perspective adopted by the NGDO in question. In our case, the consolidated framework detailed in Chapter 3 (Table 3.1) guides the resource grouping and content.

Reflecting the problem of overlap discussed in Chapter 3, the allocation of a particular item to one category in Table 5.1 is somewhat arbitrary. For example, communication systems are both an economic and social resource.[19] Similarly, physical assets are a source of empowerment and of reduced vulnerability, which is one dimension of well-being. In addition, physical assets, such as land or trees, have productive economic value.

Each resource brings with it issues of risk, (gender) ownership and access and, frequently, the effects of vertical linkages. The task for NGDOs is to identify local non-financial resources that do not affect its resource security. In fact, the search is for a local resource mix that positively contributes to an overall resource profile. What local non-financial resource mobilisation should ideally do is:

- Decrease vulnerability by reducing risk.
- Reduce sensitivity by ensuring a buffer is available.
- Reduce criticality by not relying on a very special type of resource.
- Enhance consistency by including only people who are directly related to the mission.
- Increase autonomy, by not creating a structural dependency on its inputs that call for continued subsidy that the NGDO has to find – from government, donors or own sources.
- Maintain compatibility by not taking on resources that call for new skills, procedures and incentives.

Fulfilling all these conditions is highly unlikely for any local resource or resource combination. But it does provide a guide to choices and trade-offs.

All resources carry some degree of risk. The origin and type of risk can be

Table 5.1 *Local Resources Matrix*

System/ non-financial CBO resources	Dimensions of sustainable human change		
	Well-being	*Local organisations*	*Empowerment*
Economic	Physical infrastructure: roads, electricity supply, and irrigation. Equipment for land use, product processing. Transport system. Input supply system. Energy supply system.	Cooperatives. Credit schemes and groups. Income-generating groups. Government extension workers and their knowledge.	Market sites, demand and outlets. Savings and other assets. Productive know-how. Local skills in demand (with gender divisions). In-kind remittances.
Social	Service availability: education, health, potable water. Quality of housing. Communication systems.	Trusted leadership. Indigenous institutions for community management. Relational conventions, norms and practices. Associational ties to other communities. Rural–urban linkages and access.	Political representation. Participation in local governance (with gender equity). Patronage relations. Legalised property rights.
Ecological	Food sources (per socio-economic group). Natural assets: land, water, vegetation, livestock and minerals. Energy sources. Local knowledge for sound management of natural resources.	Common property management rules and organisation.	Enforcement mechanisms for resource access and use and protection of rights.

Gender and generations

man-made – for example, legal, policy or price changes – or natural, such as floods, droughts or earthquakes. In addition, all resources have some claim against them in terms of ownership, be it traditional or legal. Moreover, claims may be in contention, introducing another type of risk. Contention is frequent with common property resources such as forests, where access by traditional users comes into conflict with public ownership and issues related to logging.

Moreover, resource ownership is more than likely to be gender biased. Land is typically owned by men, but worked by women. There may also be gender division in control of agricultural products. For example, men control processing and sale of cash crops, women of food crops.

And what is local is not necessarily locally controlled. For example, in much of Africa, clan-based urban-rural linkages may be called upon to decide about common property, to provide economic security or remittances, to gain political access and leverage, or to adjudicate in disputes.

Finally, as Chapter 2 argues, NGDOs must pay attention to intangible resources. Examples are the quality of relationships, such as trust, as well as associational linkages, informal institutions – which may be very formal for those within them – intergroup relationships and the norms, rules and conventions by which people live. They determine who is included or excluded. They inform and shape the core elements of local organisational capacity – the 'home' for insightful agility. What, then, must NGDOs look for when seeking to bring community non-financial resources into its mix?

CBOs and an NGDO Resource Profile

The general overview in Table 5.1 can be used to guide NGDOs in terms of how to select and mobilise CBO resources from the perspective of improving and diversifying its resource profile.

In terms of vulnerability, it is dangerous to use CBO resources that are not legally secure or in dispute. This is one reason why the issue of land tenure is often so important when deciding on local investment. Reliance on any type of insecure local resource introduces risk-sharing with CBOs themselves. One way to reduce this type of risk is active advocacy for land tenure, part of the agenda, for example, of Harnessing Self-Reliant Initiatives and Knowledge (HASIK) in the Philippines in its work with urban squatters and their resettlement. This type of action achieves most when it is allied to direct action of the squatters themselves. The Conoal Cooperative in Brazil is one outcome of the government's allocation of 10,000 hectares of land to 1000 poor families. Supported by the Landless Rural Workers

Movement (MST) families invaded and squatted on the land for three years, prior to establishing their co-operative.[20]

Risk also applies to relying on local resources provided by government. For example, in many African countries rural health services suffer from acute shortages of drugs and low pay for staff. A search for sufficient income takes staff away from their stations and into parallel private practice. Consequently, this public service can seldom be relied on. More generally, local services provided by government are under both stress from under-funding and under threat from privatisation. Including such resources in an NGDO intervention requires circumspection.

Control of the local market can also be a source of vulnerability. Where NGDOs are assisting in the production or processing of local commodities, the way markets behave can determine economic success or failure and hence ability to withdraw. Consequently, opening up new avenues and institutions for trading is a common remedy, as is setting up CBO trading outlets, for example by Jiros Jiri, an association of disabled people in Zimbabwe.[21]

Vulnerability can be reduced or enhanced by the effects of patronage. For example, it is not uncommon for a politician to claim that he or she has 'brought the NGDO' to a community. This type of assertion can give an NGDO a reverse hold on the patron, but at the risk of a new political incumbent trying to undo or undermine the predecessor's initiatives. Local patronage is always a high-risk game and a double-edged sword.

Assisting CBOs with activities that generate an economic return and increase disposable incomes commonly reduces vulnerability for NGDOs. This is one reason why credit is so fashionable. Together NGDOs and CBOs must construct interventions that allow for a gradual replacement of external inputs with those locally generated or purchased. Too often, external levels of aid investment cannot be met by an increase in productivity and growth of the recurrent income required for their operation and maintenance. These have been termed the COMIC costs – the local costs of sustaining a common good.[22]

- Capital and Construction
- Operation
- Maintenance
- Information
- Coordination

The issue for NGDO resource profile and vulnerability is the extent to which COMIC costs (including reserves for capital replacement) are progressively shared with communities. If there is no prospect of the CBO meeting the recurrent burden from an improved resource base, then the NGDO faces an ongoing drain on its resources.[23] This situation has knock-on effects in terms of a perpetual demand for NGDO subsidy with the risk of structural dependency and weakened autonomy (see below). In other words, NGDO autonomy is not just a question of state control, but also freedom to decide and act on what social goods it will produce. A commitment to perpetual inputs for an intervention is akin to a mortgage restricting future choice, and hence autonomy.

Local resource impact on NGDO sensitivity and criticality is a question of proportion and type. Where local inputs are substantial relative to the NGDO contribution, but are near the limits of what a community can afford, substitution is improbable and criticality is increased. Hence, care is needed in not expecting too much while trying to keep a buffer. For example, if the labour commitment required is near the limit of that available, sickness or seasonal stress can severely affect this input, which cannot simply be replaced by, for example, hiring labour from outside.

Mobilising resources with and from CBOs is likely to reinforce and strengthen consistency. However, the requirement is that NGDOs have done their homework and are indeed working with people that correspond to those envisaged from their mission and strategic goals – the issue of targeting. An additional requirement, however, is that the benefits of an NGDO's intervention and community input are not simply captured by non-target populations or by those who have not contributed. Local resource mobilisation, therefore, always has an element of inclusion and exclusion. This must be negotiated with, but ultimately enforced by, communities themselves. Some NGDOs, like BRAC, do this by restricting inclusion to households with less than a certain size of land holding. Other NGDOs might focus on, for example, female-headed households, the aged or types of land use.

Demonstration of sincere, self-motivated and sustained community inputs to an external intervention should enhance NGDO credibility and hence ability to assert itself towards government officials and others. This reflects back to the quotation in the introduction and the thrust of Part I. Autonomy is enhanced if the NGDO is seen to be performing well. Ongoing resource commitment by CBOs is a proxy for this. In addition, by reducing NGDO costs, local resources also reduce the pressure to find resources from elsewhere.

The effect of CBO resources on compatibility depends on whether or not communities are mobilising for something that is not within an NGDO's existing repertoire of knowledge, experience or skills. For example, a community may be willing to donate land for better watershed management, but the NGDO's skills lie in credit. This incompatibility takes us back to the discussion on integration in Chapter

3. The question posed by such requests is whether to incorporate required capacity within the organisation or to make agreements or form alliances with those better placed to do so, as occurs with SIAD. The answer is a judgement by the NGDO about the long-term implications of taking on new skills. Generally speaking, from a compatibility viewpoint, NGDOs should only internalise new skills if their strategies already point in this direction. If not, alliances are probably a better approach.

NGDOs face a common dilemma about local resource mobilisation in terms of community volunteers. Should interaction with communities be led by an NGDO staff member or someone selected and supported by the community itself? The former has advantages of bringing in the required professionalism but disadvantages in terms of cost, local knowledge and acceptability. The latter has potential disadvantages in terms of 'neutrality' within the community and an expectation of getting a salary from the NGDO.

This question was dealt with in some detail is *Striking a Balance*. My conclusion was that embedding, local commitment, ownership and capacity building all benefit from investing in local people as focal points for an intervention, but without financing them. A proxy test of future community dedication is its mobilisation of local resources to cover the opportunity costs of the time allocated by a local person. No matter how the NGDO leaves, some new level of knowledge, skill and useful experience will remain as important aspects of enduring impact.

Overall, in non-financial resource mobilisation NGDOs should subject local possibilities to the six tests outlined above. From perspectives of sustainable impact and NGDO resource mobilisation, there are overwhelming reasons to emphasise CBO social investment and other non-financial inputs to interventions.

Finally, how can local non-financial resource mobilisation from CBOs contribute to NGDO insight and agility? Local contribution to insight is primarily through the provision of local knowledge and the generation of learning by experience. All development interventions can be classed as action-learning events and opportunities. Careful attention to what is (not) going on, why and how, is an important source for NGDO self-development and insightfulness. But generating and distributing insight requires dedicated action beyond monitoring and evaluation (a topic of Part III).

It is quite possible that mobilisation of local resources will hamper rather than improve agility. In theory, risk spreading should make organisations more resilient and better able to respond to change and stress. But it all depends on the way in which NGDOs structure their joint risk. They must also ensure that their interventions do not create a permanent level of resource commitment that is unattainable by communities or supplementary sources such as local government. For agility, interventions must not act as a tether, but as a springboard to learning and new innovation.

Chapter Summary

The concept of social capital can help inform NGDO identification and assessment of the intangible resources that may be available in a particular community setting.

Mobilisation of non-financial resources – from volunteers and communities, but also from businesses and governments – should be a primary strategic option for NGDOs because of its potential for:

- cost reduction,
- social support and civic embedding,
- network effects and information enhancement,
- 'space creation' through informal linkages to power holders and brokers, and
- enhancing public awareness and organisational credibility.

Volunteer recruitment and acceptance, be it professional or non-professional, should be rigorous in terms of the NGDO's mission and values.

Volunteers can bring useful and dangerous patronage linkages. They must therefore be assessed with care. Caution is the watchword.

Community resource mobilisation brings some degree of risk sharing and therefore a need for risk analysis. Resource demands on communities should always allow for contingencies through a risk buffer. Community inputs to an intervention should never be at the limit of what is available.

Local resource mobilisation is a source of insight, but may or may not restrict agility. To ensure agility is increased means both a careful match between external resource inputs and growth of local compensatory assets, coupled to a withdrawal strategy.

Table 5.2 *Overview of Non-financial Options and Probable Implications for Resource Profile*

Resource feature	Volunteers	CBO members
Vulnerability	Reduced	Reduced
Sensitivity	Reduced	Reduced
Criticality	Reduced	Reduced
Consistency	Challenged	Improved
Autonomy	Challenged	Enhanced
Compatibility	Challenged	Depends on type of demand

Chapter 6

Commercialisation – A Profit-making Non-profit

'There is no escape from the market in a world with declining aid.'
(Fernando Aldaba)[1]

'In general, development organisations are not adequately trained in implementing self-financing projects that will gradually lead to their activities being financed by local resources.' [2]

Opting for non-financial resources can do much to reduce costs and enhance social embedding. As an option, it is probably more accessible for operational NGDOs because it provides an identifiable human factor that motivates.[3] It is a more difficult path for NGDOs that make less tangible contributions to social change and reduction in poverty. However, in either case the non-financial option is unlikely to sustain an organisation, apart perhaps from in the early formative, pioneer stages (see Chapter 8). Nor will it fully compensate costs for services provided directly or indirectly.[4] In addition, some NGDOs have moral discomfort and problems of principle in expecting the poor to pay for the full costs of an intervention when there are indecent concentrations of wealth in the hands of a few. Consequently, any strategy for resource mobilisation must look at ways of raising real money.

There are basically two ways of doing so – either generating a new financial surplus oneself or gaining access to funds created by someone else. In Figure 4.1 these choices are shown as opting for a commercialisation or a subsidisation path. However, before getting into the substance, there is a need for an additional reflection on the broad framework in which both financing options are being exercised.

The structure and content of this book reflect a concern that many NGDOs are concentrating on resource sustainability at the cost of attention to the other two dimensions: enduring impact and organisational viability. There is no doubt that financial continuity and security are crucial NGDO issues: they are the topic of this chapter and the one that follows. Nevertheless, a question to be asked is why is there this bias, rather than balance, in the way NGDOs understand and are pursuing sustainability?

Chapter 4 offers one reason for NGDO concentration on financial diversification and stabilisation in terms of the dynamics of supply. However, there is also the issue of the 'ambience' or sense of the times, where the initial solution to almost all problems is sought in the market. For example, global warming will be solved by trading in emission permits, not through statutory enforcement or civic compliance.[5] The problem of unemployment will solve itself once the world has adjusted to trading without barriers and the invisible hand of comparative advantage rules supreme. Income disparities will attenuate as more people have more opportunities in a non-protectionist, rule-based economic order. Social problems will, apparently, be resolved through a new breed of social entrepreneurs dedicated to the public good but not reliant on state funding.[6] Moreover, it is in this latter category that new style NGDOs will be found: organisations not living on public subsidy but on commercial skill applied for public benefit.

Examining the idea of social entrepreneurship is important for this and the next chapter because the term is introducing confusion about NGDOs' future identity and function in society. More worryingly, it is being presented as if there is no alternative or that alternatives are a retrograde step towards a discredited era of left-right polarities.[7] Therefore, as a necessary prelude to dealing with the trade-offs and substance of options within self-generated finance, this chapter starts with a brief review of social entrepreneurship and possible alternatives: civic innovation and development enterprise.

With this backdrop, the following section looks at what it means for an NGO to become a for-profit, non-profit 'hybrid', examples of which follow. Five implications are examined. All are demanding and stress-inducing. What, then, makes this complicated and stressful option so attractive? The answer lies in the high quality of funds it can generate, that is, untied money controlled by the NGDO itself.

Section Three describes the costs and benefits of two options within a combined approach: joint and solely-owned income-generating activities. Section Four performs a similar exercise for a supplementary approach and its options of running an enterprise or making investments.

The concluding section provides a summary and a comparison of what the different options mean in relation to NGDO resource dependency.

Social Entrepreneurship, Civic Innovation or Development Enterprise?[8]

One sign of the dominance of market thinking is that, as part of modern society, the answer to future NGDO resource mobilisation lies in social entrepreneurship. In keeping with much development jargon – empowerment, participation, and partnership – the term is already a confusing blanket covering and hiding important distinctions that affect NGDO identity and practice. For example, as Bill Drayton, founder of the Ashoka Foundation, points out '...people who run businesses as part of hospitals, that is called social entrepreneurship.'[9]

An important enquiry about social entrepreneurship is whether the concept should be distinguished from civic innovation for structural reform. This is an enduring community development goal – now referred to as civil society strengthening – that NGDOs have been pursuing for many years. From an NGDO resource perspective, does the new concept imply a significant difference with consequences for role, autonomy and civicness? What does it mean for positioning within the framework provided in Figure 4.2? In order to clarify civic innovation, social entrepreneurship and how they influence strategic choices, this section explores answers to these questions. We then look at a third option, a development enterprise that focuses on commercialisation as a means of enhancing social capital and the deep relations that underlie all human transactions.

Distinctions, Definitions and Choices

The term 'social entrepreneurship' is much in vogue in the North.[10] Its contemporary use links the morality and objective of generating a public benefit to characteristics commonly attributed to entrepreneurs in the for-profit sector: commercial vision, awareness of opportunities, risk-taking, self-confidence, self-motivation, competitive drive, determination and keen attention to an economic 'bottom line'.[11] An entrepreneur is an individual with a specific attitude towards change who embraces and creates change, rather than actively conforming, resisting or going with the flow.

Entrepreneurship is a question of talents, predisposition and conduct of a person that is not necessarily limited to the economic realm.[12] From this perspective, what drives a social entrepreneur is the value placed on the public good. However, this value is allied to an economic agenda of generating and reinvesting a surplus to ensure viability in tackling social problems, rather than a profit to be distributed to the organisation's owners, typically shareholders.[13]

This Northern interpretation of what it means to be a 'post-modern' non-profit organisation translates into creating and using commercial undertakings to cross-subsidise social interventions.[14] Such an interpretation is strongly informed by the current privatisation climate. It is especially the case in the US and Great Britain, where citizens and their non-profit organisations are being asked to carry a greater share of the burden of social well-being.[15]

However, the concept of non-profit organisations commercially generating their own income for social means is far from new. For example, the *Fondaçion Social* established in 1911 in Colombia, has the specific aim of both generating and applying income to create social benefits, for example, by producing goods and services which benefit mid- and low-income sectors of the Colombian population and by establishing viable, democratic business models. The Grameen Bank was similarly established to produce social benefits from surpluses generated through micro-investment in the productive activities of poor women and from the redeployment of those surpluses to create a member-owned capital base.

Where an NGDO's development programmes are specifically designed to generate positive socio-economic outcomes as well as disposable income for the NGDO, we can talk of a combined approach. Where generating surpluses does not produce social benefits, but is simply a source of cross-subsidy, for example holding shares in a technology company or running a garage or commercial franchise, we could usefully talk of a supplementing approach. This distinction corresponds to the two principal choices for self-generating a surplus shown in Figure 4.1, and discussed in this and the next chapter. Either option turns a non-profit into a more complex organisational hybrid.

However, it can be argued that neither of these variants captures the primacy of the social dimension of social entrepreneurship in the sense of introducing innovation in how society works to solve human and other problems. Such entrepreneurship frequently draws on and innovates from the values and conventions of cooperation, collaboration and mutual assistance that already exist in the civic or 'citizen base', described in Chapter 7. Guiding points of reference for civic entrepreneurs are prevailing cultural and civic norms and reforms to systems that produce dysfunctions such as poverty, intolerance and exclusion. The guiding perspective is not diversification of funding to generate an income.

In other words, a useful distinction can be made between civic innovators and social entrepreneurs.[16] The former innovates in terms of how society works for whom. The latter innovates in terms of an economic base to produce public benefit.[17]

Working definitions of each could be:

Civic innovation is the creation of new or modification of existing social conventions, structures, relations, institutions, organisations and practices for public benefit demonstrated by ongoing, self-willed citizen engagement and support.

Social entrepreneurship is the creation of viable economic structures, relations, institutions, organisations and practices that yield ongoing social benefits.

Unlike social entrepreneurship, civic innovation has a distinct political connotation and intentions. The former term effectively takes the politics out of development; the latter does not. This is one reason why social entrepreneurship is the preferred 'mainstream' term for NGDOs' 'new style'. It fits more snugly into the prevailing and all-embracing notion of a harmonious model of social change, linguistically captured and consciously ignoring or downplaying necessary redistribution of power and contention as forces and interests realign themselves.[18]

This preference is further fed by a false implication that social entrepreneurship has an economic dimension to it, while civic innovation does not. This is not the case. The approach to local institutional development described in Part I stresses the importance of a sound and sustainable economic and material base for civic strength. This holds equally true for NGDOs as civic actors. But the point

of departure differs in terms of roles and perspectives on resource mobilisation. Social entrepreneurs adopt market perspectives, language, relations and practices in their approach to resource mobilisation. Civic innovators look towards the citizen base, mutuality, self-help, systemic change and claim-making as fundamental rights. There is, however, another option that ties, rather than lies midway, between these two. The option draws on recent attention to the social capital dimensions of society, civicness and development. This is the concept of a development enterprise.

A Commercialised NGDO as a Normative Development Enterprise

Some argue that social capital is the missing ingredient in understanding economic growth as well as the relationship between development, poverty reduction and conflict resolution.[19] As noted in Chapter 4, whether or not this is true is an ongoing debate. The point is that the notion of social capital offers a way of allying society – as a dynamic interplay of human relations – with civicness as a set of normative values, as well as a political phenomenon.[20] This alliance can be applied to the notion of development.

Social capital is a quality of human relationships and exchanges. The concept can be understood in terms of two principal types, labelled 'embedded' and 'autonomous'. Embedded social capital arises from ascribed and inherited relationships, cultural practices and political contexts. Autonomous social capital arises from experience of exchanges and transactions built up by individuals and institutions over time. At the micro-level embeddedness expresses itself in intra-community ties, while at the macro-level it refers to state-society relations. Autonomy at the micro-level connotes extra-community relations and networks, at the macro-level it refers to institutional capacity and credibility.[21]

Social capital of either type has positive and negative aspects. For example, reciprocity between individuals, groups and communities can be used to disrupt society as much as to stabilise it. Ethnic cleansing relies on strong common identity and mutual support between groups to actively harass and chase away others. Cooperative ventures use mutual support to produce economic benefits. Similarly, social entrepreneurship can be used for different normative goals, as can civic innovation. Depending on one's norms, both can be applied for positive or negative purposes – for example, for or against abortion, for or against religious tolerance, for or against political pluralism, for or against economic or gender equity.

Development as pursued by NGDOs, and the aid system more generally, is also a normative exercise. Crudely, NGDOs' normative goals are to foster inclusion, rather than exclusion; to promote mutuality and sharing, rather than individualism and exploitation; to create greater social and economic equity rather than inequity and so on. From a social capital perspective, such:

> 'Development outcomes are shaped by the extent to which basic social dilemmas at the micro and the macro level are resolved. Positive outcomes are attained to the extent that both embedded and autonomous social relations prevail at both levels. This happens when people are willing and able to draw on and nurture social ties (i) within their local communities; (ii) between local communities and groups with external and more extensive social connections to civil society; (iii) between civil society and macro-level institutions; (iv) within corporate sector institutions. All four dimensions must be present for optimal developmental outcomes.
>
> If social relations are "wrong", development outcomes will be sub-optimal. Entrenched poverty, inequality, discrimination, underemployment, and lawlessness all serve to undermine the particular combinations of social relations required for sustainable, equitable and participatory development. At the macro level, external development assistance should be conditional on these objectives being seriously addressed. At the micro level, internal development projects should seek to nurture participatory organisations that are empowered to assume increasing levels of responsibility for their own well-being while also building linkages between local communities and formal institutions.'[23]

In as far as development progress does indeed mean making good deficits in social capital, a challenge for NGDOs is to use the commercial option for this end – to be a development enterprise. This option counters the implied neutrality of social entrepreneurship or civic innovation. It names commercialised NGDOs as a category in their own terms, rather than simply adopting labels conjured up in other contexts. In addition, the commercialisation agenda is clearer, using enterprise as a means to enhance certain types of social capital. It is not as an end in itself. A working definition of a development enterprise could therefore be:

> 'employing commercial means to construct the "missing" dimensions of social capital required to optimise and sustain intended change'.

NGDOs regarding themselves as social entrepreneurs, civic innovators or development enterprises does not mean jettisoning all that they have done or learned. However, because language counts in terms of self-image, internal culture and perceived role in society, a choice must be considered and made. The three options sketched above should help NGDOs answer the question 'commercialisation for what and how?' The options do not lead to mutually exclusive ways of working. But they do give different emphases and interpretations of what self-generation of income should mean for the primary function the organisation wants to fulfil, that is the type of change that it wants to bring about: socio-economic, political or deeply relational.

Irrespective of the ends, for an NGDO to decide to generate its own income brings a complicated set of implications. It turns the organisation into a sort of hybrid.[24] The challenge is to achieve an optimal combination of for-profit and non-profit thinking and practice.

On Becoming a Hybrid

For years, NGDOs have been involved with local development initiatives intended to generate incomes and disposable surpluses for individuals, households and communities. Typical approaches are described in the next sections. This type of intervention is made possible by grant funding with NGDOs acting as intermediaries. However, a decision to generate income for the NGDO itself – be it combined with or separate from development programmes – crosses a threshold in a number of ways. Five issues of importance in choosing for self-financing are political, public, legal, fiscal and managerial.

Political Suspicion

The way politicians look at NGDO commercialisation depends on many factors. Predominant among them is the level of electoral legitimacy that politicians themselves enjoy. Where elections have been truly free and fair, the regime in power has less reason to feel insecure. However, to the extent that all politicians are wary about existing or potential opposition, irrespective of what they say or do, NGDOs will always be seen in a political light.[25]

Three examples help illustrate the political factor. During military rule in much of Latin America, NGDOs were frequently a refuge for left-leaning academics and Jesuit-trained intellectuals who could not remain in universities. This lingers on in the new democratic era. The government in Peru is looking with suspicion at the economic initiatives undertaken by NGDOs as they diversify away from shrinking international aid. It recognises that financial autonomy can provide an economic foundation for new left-leaning political parties and social movements.[26] In mid-1999, the government in Colombia forcibly took over the commercial and banking activities of the Fundaçion FES (FFES) in Cali, claiming these functions were incompatible with being an NGDO. Founded in 1964, FFES had been operating commercially since 1974. It is not clear what drove the government to act at this particular moment, but Colombian politics is thought to lie behind the move. In Egypt, a more restrictive NGDO law was recently introduced because, the government argued, non-profit organisations were being used as a cover by Islamic extremists that pose a political threat.[27] The law also enables the government to restrict NGDO activity, for example profit-making. Obviously, the law applies to all non-profits, not just those suspected of having religious-political agendas.

In the East, the transition to democratic political systems is proceeding very unevenly. The whole notion of 'non-profits' is treated with suspicion, and not without cause. For it is not unknown for failed, losing or excluded politicians to use the vagueness of legislation to create non-profits as fronts for their activities and cloak their real intentions in 'NGDO-speak'.[28]

Generally speaking, governments in the South and East think that they know where they are when dealing with businesses and what they want – they exist to make money. The situation is already more confusing when dealing with a myriad of non-profit organisations with diverse agendas. This is even more the case when, as an organisational type, NGDOs are not firmly historically rooted. Prevailing government discomfort and doubt about what NGDOs are and what they want can only worsen when making money is added to the mix.

Ambiguous Public Image – Confusing Means with Ends

Not only politicians, but also commonly the general public in the South and the East, are suspicious of NGDOs.[29] For example, in Tanzania civil servants are being retrenched as part of externally aided government reform programmes. A number of ex-civil servants are starting NGDOs because that is where funding is growing and where old contacts in government can be useful for gaining finance.[30] Establishing an NGDO is observed by people at large to be a self-employment strategy, not a personal commitment to voluntarism and public benefit. This story

is repeated in many African countries undergoing adjustment and civil service reform. In sum, a growth in the number of NGDOs cannot, and must not, be equated with an increase in public trust.

With royal and religious organisations as probable exceptions, public doubt about NGDOs is to be expected where there is no tradition of private giving to 'secular' intermediaries to provide some form of public good. Although to be found in India in, for example the Tata Foundation established in the late 1800s,[31] this model of 'philanthropy' is a predominantly northern creation that is not a part of many other cultures.[32]

When NGDOs add moneymaking to their repertoire, it is only to be expected that a doubting public confuse means and ends. The NGDO may be perfectly clear that self-financing will be used to further serve and secure its mission. The reading from outside is likely to differ. For example, in Bangladesh the NGDO clamour to initiate micro-credit programmes is seen by some to be more for the self-survival of the NGDO as lender, than for the benefit of the poor as borrowers.[33] Embracing profit-making will only confirm what many suspected all along, namely that self and not public interest is ultimately the basis of NGDO behaviour.

In sum, in many countries, becoming a hybrid loads ambiguity on top of an already suspicious public base. This is but one reason why demonstrable impact is so vital for an NGDO's reputation. It enables the organisation to stand above the clouds of basic public mistrust.

Legal Conditions

The ability of an NGDO to make a profit and redeploy it for its own maintenance or to subsidise development work is conditioned by the legal framework under which it operates.[34] In the South, non-profit law seldom expressly forbids such activities and so NGDOs enter a grey area of interpretation. However, when for whatever reason the issue starts to become significant, a common response is to reformulate laws that are more restrictive. The substantial and rapid expansion in NGDO credit programmes is one source prompting legal reform. For example, in Ethiopia it is now illegal for an NGDO to run its own credit programme. This must be done by a separate micro-finance institution. The official argument is that NGDOs are not registered as financial institutions and such activities are not consistent with the operating licence they are given by the Ministry of Justice.

In the East, non-profit law is commonly in such a state of flux that NGDOs enter a high-risk zone when they commercialise what they are doing.[35] Moreover, it would be naïve to expect that political interests do not enter the legal equation.

Fiscal Policy

Another source of government concern is the fiscal effects of not gaining tax income from profits generated by NGDOs. Here governments face contradictory pressures. On the one hand, the International Monetary Fund (IMF) is pressing governments to reduce tax exemption categories and plug other loopholes, such as duty free imports and not being subject to value added tax, that can be misused. On the other hand – as part of its good governance agenda – while supporting better discipline in revenue collection, the World Bank is persuading governments that it should create tax incentives to increase private giving to non-profits. In addition, to help expand civil society, the Bank recommends that there should fiscal incentives for the establishment of non-profits.

At the same time, where NGDO self-financing operations start to have notable market effects, as in Bangladesh, businesses complain about unfair competition. In the case of BRAC, opening a milk processing plant drew criticism from Milk Vita and other commercial companies. Grameen Bank's cell-phone initiative caused a critical and restrictive response from Bangladesh Telecom. The latter saw that Grameen's agreement to lease BD Railway's fibre-optic network to expand its cellular system would undermine its monopoly over long-distance calls.[36]

Not only do NGDOs get grants or investment support on concessionary terms, their profits are not taxed and so can be reinvested to a greater degree than for-profit organisations. Many Southern and Eastern governments therefore face a dilemma in terms of fiscal and tax policy towards non-profits that choose self-financing. This creates uncertainty and risk, as well as awakening business as a potentially adversarial lobby.

Managerial and Organisational Dilemmas

Finally, becoming a hybrid can create internal dilemmas for NGDO leaders and managers that stem from a number of issues: the problem of combining for-profit and non-profit cultures; dealing with different incentives between staff engaged in for-profit and non-profit activities; bringing in and retaining required expertise; and introducing complexity into financial and accounting systems to ensure transparency so that non-viable schemes are seen to be so and are not shielded by hidden cross-subsidies.

Depending on legal possibilities, NGDOs have a number of structural choices to deal with these problems. The least complex, from a legal perspective, is simply to embed self-financing into the existing structure. Another is to establish a separate for-profit department. Alternatively, an NGDO can establish a legally separate business entity that it owns and controls in some way. For example, this could be a holding company, owned by the NGDO that, in turn, owns the enterprise and decides whether to reinvest or transfer profits to the parent institution. In all cases, commercial skill and acumen is something that NGDOs have not traditionally required.

Embedding with the organisation usually creates the most serious management complications and tensions, unless the non-profit staff develop for-profit skills and attitudes. This is possible but difficult, and requires substantial investment in human resource development. Bringing in new staff with the requisite skills and attitudes and expectations of market rewards for good market performance introduces a mixed set of incentives that can cause friction.

In addition, the financial system must be adapted to deal with profit and loss accounting. It requires determination, for example, of how community mobilisation, capacity building, training or technical advice are to be 'priced'. Without such clarity, management does not have the information on which to manage commercially. Two points of reference – the development and the commercial – must be simultaneously applied to all activities and budgets. In my experience, this seldom works well. Staff get confused and hidden subsidies turn profits into losses without them being seen or being written off as the price of development impact – a non-sustainable decision.

Placing income generation into a separate department at least brings some clarity – bookkeeping can be tailored accordingly; business plans can be generated and followed. An NGDO can go so far as to create an internal market where business services are 'sold' to development departments and shown as income, for example. Necessary economic management information can be better generated.

Staff in different departments know what is expected of them. But a critical decision is whether or not to have different conditions of service for the for-profit and non-profit departments to reflect different incentives and market conditions for different skills. FFES in Colombia has adopted this approach. However, it is at great pains to ensure that the for-profit and non-profit departments are similarly valued for what they are both contributing to the overall mission. To this end, a competition is held where staff are asked questions about the work of staff in other departments. The winners are awarded prizes at an annual event. In addition, for-profit and non-profit teams are created to help develop new financial products. For example, the environmental department was actively involved in the development and marketing of a credit card where a proportion of the transaction fee would be allocated to environment development programmes.[37]

A more far-reaching solution is to incorporate a new for-profit entity with financial targets and professional management operating along strictly commercial lines. One way of doing so is the legal possibility, available in Britain, of covenanting all profits so that they must be allocated to the non-profit owner. If this guarantee cannot be made, there is every reason for governments to apply company law and require tax payment. In itself, this may not be a bad thing, as long as the NGDO makes a profit after tax. Why should this option be considered and potential development resources be 'lost' to government taxation? A straightforward answer is to deal with the elements of political suspicion, risk and commercial adversarial lobby noted above.

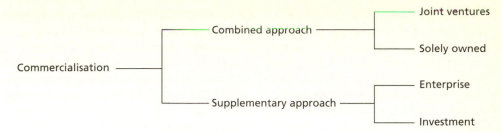

Figure 6.1 *Choices with Commercialisation*

As will be seen later, some NGDOs make a strategic choice and create a holding company that owns subsidiaries. Strategically, the developmental intention is for the holding company to initially act as a 'nursemaid'. Eventually subsidiaries will be spun-off as viable enterprises owned by stakeholders the NGDO has been working with, for example farmers and artisans.

Irrespective of the structural solution chosen, opting to be a hybrid brings complications and changed demands on leadership and management.

So, Why Become a Hybrid?

Given all the potential internal and external problems cited above, why would an NGDO choose the commercialisation option? The simple answer is that, despite all the probable difficulties, self-generating a surplus has a greater potential for positive effects in terms of reducing dependency than subsidisation – the other principal financing option, which is described in Chapter 7.

The biggest gain for NGDOs in commercialisation is to be in control of their own resource base. This has significant positive effects on two highly valued features of resource dependency: autonomy and criticality. Generating one's own resources means not being tied to the agendas, conditions and compromises with others. Criticality is reduced because it is up to the NGDO to decide how it will apply the resources it generates: to cover overheads, for staff or organisational development, as investment in an endowment, as a subsidy, as a start-up fund for a new initiative or innovation, as a participatory investment in a project design, for example. The NGDO is free to choose.

Having opted for becoming a hybrid, the six features of resource dependency identified in Chapter 4 – vulnerability, sensitivity, criticality, consistency, autonomy and compatibility – can be used to illustrate trade-offs between the options shown in Figure 6.1.

The Combined Approach

Figure 4.1 shows two principal options. One is a choice to combine NGDO income generation with development activities undertaken with and possibly co-owned by CBOs – or legally independent of, but still beneficial to them. This will be referred to as a combined approach. An alternative is for the NGDO to establish enterprises or create investments that are separate from and have no direct relationship with development programmes and their impacts – a supplementing approach.

This section deals with the former approach and two important variations within it: joint ventures and solely-owned operations.

A critical choice for NGDOs when tying resource generation to development programmes centres on ownership. The question is whether or not commercialising ventures are jointly owned and managed with communities or separately owned and run by the NGDO, albeit serving an economic and social function within its development work with CBOs. We will look at each in turn and then at the implications for resource dependency.

Joint Ventures, Yes or No?

A common way of working for NGDOs as intermediaries is to provide initial investment costs that communities should turn to productive use. At a minimum, community economic operations should recover the COMIC costs of physical investments and service delivery (see previous chapter). Examples of NGDO investments are production units added to vocational training centres; cooperative infrastructure for supply of inputs and marketing of products; and the capital for community managed water supplies with kiosks to sell water. In such an arrangement, the NGDO does not carry the burden of non-performance of the investment, beyond having to deal with a perpetual claim on its resources. In short, the NGDO does not depend on a return from local investment for its own functioning. It is economically immune from CBO performance (though its reputation may well suffer).

Some NGDOs want to alter the imbalance and patron-client relationship implicit to this arrangement by sharing the consequences of economic interventions with CBOs. CETEC in Colombia has already been cited as an NGDO that has consciously chosen to form collaborative economic ventures with the farmers it works with. One example is joint ownership of a factory processing manioc, a typical smallholder crop. CETEC also acts as a holding company for other ventures with joint control, such as low-cost housing construction that will eventually be turned over to employees. As part of its organisational transformation, Centro de Estudios y Promoción del Desarrollo (DESCO) in Peru (see Chapter 10), has embarked on a number of commercial ventures. Some are jointly owned and controlled by CBO members, as in a small building company in the south of Lima and at Ariquipa, for rearing of vicuna sheep and processing of their wool. In Ethiopia NGDO microcredit institutions, such as PROPRIDE, are moving towards joint ownership with borrowers as shareholders. In this case, because of Ethiopian law, PROPRIDE is one shareholder of a legally separate micro-finance entity.

The developmental choice for joint ventures is threefold. First, it maintains close association with the intended beneficiaries in a way that ties the risks of both. Financial risk-sharing works against patronage relations. Second, it provides a nurturing and learning opportunity for communities and NGDOs in terms of businesses linked to both their livelihoods. NGDOs can act as an economic guide but must do it well or suffer the results in terms of its own income stream. Its development practice and performance are fed back into its own financial sustainability. In the process the organisation becomes locally economically rooted and co-dependent. In sum, the terms of engagement between NGDO and CBO are altered and made more equitable. This change should have a positive effect on CBO institutional development and eventual self-management when the NGDO withdraws.

Another element of this option is that an NGDO's ability to raise development finance can be enhanced. The fact that it is prepared to share risk can attract development investors who can see the NGDO's own interest in ensuring financial returns, increasing the probability of sustainability for the organisation and the CBO. The developmental intention and degree of NGDO commitment with CBOs and the latter's formal role are likely to be attractive to professional development financiers. For example, DESCO has reached agreement with the Netherlands Development Bank (FMO), the Inter-American Development Bank (IADB), an Andean development cooperative and a small American NGDO to provide the risk capital for investment in a number of small- and medium-scale enterprises.

The shared ownership or combined approach has differential impacts on features of NGDO resource dependency. Vulnerability is likely to be increased as the NGDO shares performance with CBOs that are subject to internal and external pressures that the NGDO does not control but cannot easily escape. Sensitivity can increase because the NGDO is coupled more firmly with contexts that it depends on financially. To the extent that the NGDO is able to real-locate income as its chooses, that is not having to reinvest in the joint venture, crit-icality may be reduced. And, if successful, alternative financial institutions may be interested in financing what has been economically proven, also reducing criti-cality. However, this achievement requires a sound NGDO economic assessment in the first place.

Consistency with mission is likely to be enhanced if the NGDO is changing the rules with CBOs in areas of intervention that it is already involved and skilled in. A positive aspect is that NGDOs become embedded, with a demonstrable civic link. Autonomy may become restricted because of joint decision making. However, this also has a positive civic dimension. Finally, a threat to compatibility is unlikely, but the NGDO will have to adapt to a reverse income stream generated together with CBOs, rather than simply giving grants to them. This will affect financial and accounting systems and probably internal decision making. To the extent that existing technical expertise is not comple-mented by capacity in economic analysis and management, this must be introduced.

In sum, the principal positive affects of joint ventures are to be found in altering relationships with CBOs to make them more equitable and empowering. In addi-tion, there is an increase in economic and civic rooting and attractiveness for raising capital. The major negative feature is an increase in exposure to uncertainty and risk because of joint decision making. This choice is probably most akin to a develop-ment-enterprise perspective of a NGDO role.

Latin American experience suggests that forming joint ventures with local organisations is preferred for a number of reasons. First and traditionally, NGDOs have been made credible by forging links with grassroots organisations, popular movements and mass membership organi-sations: trade unions, peasant associa-tions, shanty town organisations and the like. Under the twin forces of democratisa-tion and liberalisation, these primary organisations have been weakened and fragmented, in turn undermining the social and political foundations of NGDOs themselves. Consequently, to restore legiti-macy, NGDOs are turning to what is called 'the local sphere'.

'In 1996, the Centro de Comunicación Popular y Asesoramiento Legal – CEOPAL (People's Communication and Legal Advice Center), of Cordoba, held a meeting with the participa-

tion of distinguished representatives from the Argentine social movements, called "Political parties and new social movements". One of the principal conclusions of that meeting, in which NGOs from all over the country participated, was that: *"...a strong estrangement between the political and the social is appearing in Argentina... forms of organization are arising in the whole of society that are different from the traditional forms: there is no longer a great mobilization and demand from the workers as a whole, but rather the rise of movements that address specific, short-term issues, and which give priority to the local sphere, new demands, economic survival and non-association with party politics... their purpose is to resolve specific matters that must respond to a shared ideological framework. These are forms of organization and mobilization from within civil society, based on the idea of 'citizen rights,' individual demands, taxpayer's demands, the demands of users or clients..."*[38]

In addition to establishing a 'new solidarity' or bonds with emerging grassroots and issue-based civic organisations, and hence renewed legitimacy, NGDO-CBO joint ventures also reorient NGDO finance from above (aid) to below (citizens). This reversal is partly enabled by administrative decentralisation that is making more resources available to community initiatives, to municipalities and to other local government units. In sum, joint ventures offer benefits in terms of credibility and income. It is a choice for interdependence described in Chapter 2.

Solely Owned Income Sources

Some complications of joint ventures described above can be avoided if the NGDO establishes income sources with a development impact, but owned by them alone. By and large, this type of NGDO income source provides linkages to local, primary or secondary production processes. For example, BRAC's introduction of cold storage facilities for potatoes was intended to stabilise and increase producer income by evening out the seasonal change in prices. Immediately after harvest, prices fall as the market is flooded; as prices pick up, stored potatoes can be sold at a better price. Processing of raw silk was a way of ensuring fair prices for farmers investing in sericulture, some of whom are financed by BRAC's rural credit programme and obtain technical support for the undertaking. BRAC's shops provide an outlet for finished silk products as well as obtaining other products from craft producers that may or may not be in the village organisations with which BRAC is working.

Other NGDOs operate as suppliers of inputs to and purchasers of goods from domestic producers that they then sell through shops or on contract. The Organizaço de Aduda Fraterna (OELF) in Brazil, supplies school furniture and hospital garments. In Costa Rica Clubes 4-S provide productive employment by supplying 80 per cent of hospital clothing in the country.[39] The point of these enterprises is to add an economic stage to local productive activity at fairer or more stable prices. The income stream to NGDOs provides development benefits.

Another approach is that of an NGDO operating on a fees for service basis, with subsidy for the poorest. PROSALUD in Bolivia provides preventive and curative health services in this way, while in Côte d'Ivoire, Côte d'Ivoire de Prosperité operates a private hospital in the capital and uses part of the surplus to finance its work in rural health clinics.

By uncoupling enterprises from local bases and joint ownership, NGDOs alter the benefits in terms of resource dependency. Sole ownership does not necessarily lead to greater vulnerability beyond that introduced by the organisation's own skill at making the right economic assessment and applying sound economic management. Change in sensitivity is a complicated area. Wider exposure to market interactions means that disruptions affecting economic variables increase and can be transmitted more readily in the resource base. The impact on sensitivity arising from linkage to local producers depends on their freedom to sell to other buyers. Where this is restricted, NGDOs effectively exercise a monopoly position that disempowers. Producers may not get the best deal possible. Both effects undermine development objectives and they also isolate the NGDO from the consequences of internal inefficiency.

It is unlikely that a self-generated income stream from solely owned undertakings tied to development objectives can be easily replaced by others. However, if sufficient surplus is generated, this income can be used to replace other sources that are even more critical, such as the NGDO's core costs. It comes back to the ability of the NGDO to manage well, balancing developmental and income objectives. This is not easy. Many NGDOs do not succeed, leading to displacement of management effort and internal stress.

Adopting this option should reinforce consistency in terms of mission and target groups. It should work against mission creep and goal displacement. The coupling of income generation to development impact should also make it easier to raise developmental start-up capital. Similarly, if extra income is truly generated, autonomy should be enhanced when compared with joint ventures because joint decision making is not involved. Governments are also less likely to interfere if a coupling to the NGDO's development agenda can be clearly demonstrated in terms of benefits to poor communities.

However, the success of this option is deeply associated with the issue of organisational compatibility. How does the NGDO resolve the tensions between commercial and non-profit culture, incentives, performance criteria, financial management and accounting? In other words, how well can it deal with being a hybrid?

Overall, solely owning an income source with development benefits can kill more than two birds with one stone. It can, for example, generate high quality and untied funds; maintain autonomy; keep the NGDO focused on its mission and intimately in tune and involved with the conditions of those it should serve; convince the government that it has not lost its developmental legitimacy; be attractive for development finance; and create economic conditions that enhance local sustainability. But, achieving these positive outcomes calls for complex organisational design and high management competence. This also holds true for the other self-generating option, having separate income streams that are not related to the mission.

Finally, there is the issue of raising the necessary capital. In some cases, this can be achieved through in-kind donations of professional services, equipment and materials. It can also be finance as gifts or loans from well-wishers or those who initiated the organisation, often board members. It may arise from income already being generated by the NGDO through its existing operations that is put into a reserve fund. In other instances, it depends on finance as loan or grant from governments or businesses (Chapter 7).[40]

But in all cases, the critical issue is demonstrating the link between the investment and the NGDO's mission.

Insight and Agility

Both joint ventures and separate development-related enterprises should generate new insights, but in different ways. Interdependence should also help improve an NGDO's understanding of itself and insight about unconscious paternal behaviour that become unmasked. This gives them something to work with as the old intermediary model gives way to a new one that is better balanced. Separate enterprises may or may not generate such insights: it depends on how they are structured to relate with CBOs. However, it is more likely that such ventures will sharpen NGDO awareness of how economic systems and processes operate, who are the players and how and why they act. Such insights would complement those gained through experience of commercial negotiations and market transactions.

Negotiation skills are a useful contribution to being agile. However, they are unlikely to compensate for restriction of free movement associated with local economic ties and commitment in joint ventures. On the other hand, learning to respond to market instability should promote agility. If it doesn't, the enterprise is unlikely to succeed. Joint ventures provide a tougher test in terms of responding to the ebb and flow of changes in social capital.

The Supplementing Option

Typically, when NGDOs embark on income-generating schemes bearing no relationship to development programmes they are a response to economic opportunities. Such opportunities provide a wider array of diversification possibilities. Income gained is an 'untied' profit, which effectively acts as a supplement to development-derived funds. One option is enterprises that create active and substantial organisational and management requirements. An alternative is investments, which tend to be less organisationally demanding. Consequently, they are referred to as active and passive approaches respectively. Where they also differ is in the possibility to raise the necessary capital.

An Active Approach

Choosing to establish an enterprise uncoupled from the NGDO's development work is a path chosen by few organisations. Case studies suggest that, unless careful attention is paid to commercial viability, this choice often goes wrong. There are numerous examples of NGDO non-developmental enterprises that have been a drain on, rather than a supplement to, income. For example in Bangladesh, PROSHIKA's bus company proved both uneconomic and so demanding of management time that it was disbanded. A similar story can be told for a printing press and publishing capability established by the Sarvodaya Shramadana Movement (SSM) in Sri Lanka and DESCO in Peru. Successful examples can be attributed to sound economic analysis followed up by skilled management. The following quotation sums up experience with this option.

'Non-mission-related income is probably the most controversial ... strategy. Being dominated by big

corporate interests, there are real pitfalls that a CSO has to face when dealing with a highly competitive market. Foremost is the danger of degeneration into a pure profit endeavour, and some CSOs have – rightly or wrongly – justified following this path. For this reason, a separate entity is often needed to implement this strategy. Even then, the CSO cannot wash its hands of the responsibility of ensuring a level of corporate social responsibility [that can put it at a competitive disadvantage] . Many CSOs have been criticised by constituents, [staff] , by the public, or by private for-profit competitors for venturing into non-mission-related activities.'[41]

In all cases, the NGDO faces the problem of raising the capital investment needed to do something unrelated to its mission. Commercial banks are unlikely to be forthcoming. They would look for a record of accomplishment and proven expertise. Well-wishers might be willing, but are unlikely to risk very much of their own capital. Professional development financiers – NGDO donors for example – have been the most usual source, but they often lack expertise in making the economic assessments needed.

In terms of the features of resources introduced earlier, what can be said about this mode of commercialisation? First, unless done properly, this option is likely to expose NGDO vulnerability – competition is a hard judge, always looking to exploit weakness. Unless the NGDO has reserves to buffer setbacks, sensitivity to mistakes can be very high. As for-profit organisations know, collapse can happen overnight and finding capital to replace that lost is highly unlikely – criticality is

increased. Consistency – a confusion of identity and public image – is readily threatened. However, if profits are made, autonomy can be enhanced as such income is not associated with development work or other possible preconditions for their allocation. Compatibility is the severest challenge. Unless structured to ensure no cross-interference, this option has little bearing on what the NGDO does or its culture and expertise.

A less fraught option in producing non-mission-related finance is to simply invest capital, manage it carefully and use the return.

A Passive Approach

Ask any NGDO how it would like to self-finance and the vast majority would say 'from an endowment'. The model, used by foundations, is to invest capital and operate from the interest generated, less whatever is reinvested for capital growth and a hedge against inflation. The organisations can manage these funds themselves, or give the task to professional fund managers at a fee. Instructions can be given as to the degree of acceptable risk, set against the level of returns required. Low risk, conservative portfolios are the common approach. In addition, investments can be limited to acceptable enterprises, referred to as 'ethical investment'. The management demand can be minimal. The resulting income is of high, 'untied' quality. It can be allocated in whatever way the law allows and the governing body approves – the NGDO generates grants for itself.

An NGDO considering this option needs to be realistic about how far it can go. Total self-financing from investments is both highly improbable and potentially unhealthy because it can lead to complacency and stagnation. In the words of one person interviewed, 'a little hunger is a good thing'.[42] Having to pay continuous attention to fundraising keeps an NGDO on its toes, more nimble and in tune with how the environment is shifting and why – it guards against self-satisfaction and decreasing insight.[43] A rule of thumb in an overall self-financing strategy is to aim for an income that covers the most critical costs. These can be more than just basic overheads.

For example, CDRA in South Africa sees critical internal reflection and contribution to development thinking and practice as a core process that is not a project. It is an essential feature of the organisation. Readers familiar with CDRA's annual reports will appreciate what this means. Consequently, as a non-governmental support organisation (NGOSO) part-financed by donors and from clients' fees, CDRA currently allocates half its fee income to a capital fund. Calculations suggest that a fund of some US$3 million would be needed to self-generate enough income for the organisation to allocate the needed 25 per cent of its time to reflection and dissemination. Activities for the rest of staff time would be financed from other sources, mainly fees for services. In Ghana ISODEC has established an asset replacement fund, where the purchase costs of assets is doubled and the balance is invested.

But, as we will see in Part III, there is a deeper aspect to an NGDO's 'core'. For example, on the surface, CDRA's reflection as a core process is a technical question of scheduling and ensuring there is an investment income to cover the costs of staff 'reflection' time not financed by working with clients. But, actually, systematic reflection is much more than that. It is one expression of what the organisation is all about, its very essence, its soul.[44] Taking care of the invisible elements of an organisation may require attention to money, but it cannot be reduced to it. This is an impor-tant point for leaders to consider when thinking about organisational viability and the resources required (Chapter 11).

Building up a capital reserve from fee income is one, difficult, route to follow. It takes a long time and not all donors are comfortable with such an arrangement. Indirectly their subsidy to reduce fee charges to clients is being displaced into a capital reserve.

Some NGDOs reside in countries where exchange control regulations and economic policies make it possible to swap debts. NGDOs with access to foreign exchange can capitalise on this opportunity to obtain a capital injection. However, this possibility is best seen as a momentary opportunity for a few and an option that will close as exchange controls are lifted and trade and other liberalisation policies take hold.[45]

On occasion, funders are willing to provide a capital allocation from within a multi-year grant. A common method is to allow funds allocated for annual office rental to be spent all at once on a building. This not only reduces long-term recurrent costs but, if the building is big enough, space can be sublet as an income source. In the Philippines, for example, PHILDHRRA has benefited from this type of capital support, space in its partnership centre in Manila being rented out to other NGDOs.

Another example is donors which leave a country and wish to leave behind an ongoing financial resource base for an NGDO or create a local funder for NGDO initiatives. Examples of this approach employed by the United States Agency for International Development (USAID) can be found in CR-USA in Costa Rica and the Trust for Voluntary Organisations (TVO) in Pakistan.[46]

In donors' approach to sustainability of NGDOs, capital finance is an infrequent exception to the rule. In this respect, there is a significant gap between funders' rhetoric and practice. The creation of foundation-like organisations (FLOs) in the South and East (see next chapter) are unlikely to be a substantial source of investment and hence of income either.[47] Even in the rich West, 'philanthropy' – be it giving by individuals or by foundations – constitutes only about 11 per cent of non-profit income.[48]

In terms of the six features of resource dependency, investment income – such as endowments – has very few drawbacks, which is why so many NGDOs would like to have it.[49]

Assuming wise stewardship of investment capital – with assets diverse and widely spread – all of the following are likely to hold true:

- Vulnerability will be reduced.
- Sensitivity can also be reduced, especially if NGDOs follow a prudent policy in terms of usage and not making extreme forward commitments in terms of returns on investment that are yet to be realised.[50]
- Criticality can be drastically reduced, because the income can be allocated almost anywhere within the organisation, within whatever constraints the law may pose.
- With more freedom to allocate resources, consistency can be enhanced.
- Autonomy is inevitably strengthened.
- There need be no issue of incompatibility if investments are made with sufficient attention to ethical concerns and the management task is given to

professional investment managers.

Overall, limited access to capital will be the major reason why the investment option to self-financing will not figure predominantly in the income stream of most NGDOs.

Insight and Agility

Neither of these supplementary options is likely to contribute to development insight in a narrow sense. Non-mission related enterprise can, however, expand an NGDO's horizons and diversify its economic understanding and relationships. The latter can be useful in opening up opportunities that have a development impact and this facilitates agility. If this does not happen, then it is the surplus income rather than the business that adds to agility.

Pure investments managed by others contribute little in the way of insight. On the other hand, it provides the unrestricted finance needed to respond and adapt to threats and opportunities. Untied income is one of the most important factors enabling organisational agility. However, it does not guarantee this effect. It can equally act to stifle innovation and existence of a culture which actively embraces learning for internal change. It is the potentially ambivalent effect of secure income that makes the quality and style of leadership important for agility, a topic discussed in detail in Chapter 11.

Chapter Summary

NGDOs need to be aware of the distinction between social entrepreneurship, civic innovation and development enterprise. While they have much in common, the

perspective of community engagement, social change and NGDO role differs between them. Clarity on which the organisation wants to be will better inform strat-

Table 6.1 *Overview of Self-Financing Options and Probable Implications for Resource Profile*

Resource feature	Combined approach		Supplementing approach	
	Joint ventures	Solely owned	Enterprise	Investment
Vulnerability	Shared and increased	Unchanged	Increased	Decreased
Sensitivity	Increased	Increased	Increased	Decreased
Criticality	Reduced	Increased	Reduced	Reduced
Consistency	Enhanced	Reinforced	Challenged	Improved
Autonomy	Restricted	Enhanced	Enhanced	Enhanced
Compatibility	Modest challenge	Challenge	Severe challenge	Unchanged

egy and position.

Opting for commercialisation involves becoming a complex, hybrid organisation. It invites problems in the areas of political intolerance, government suspicion, policy dilemmas, public confusion and potentially serious management difficulty. It often places NGDOs in a grey area, increasing overall risk.

Commercialisation is preferred over subsidisation because it gives NGDOs ownership of and control over their resource base, which enhances autonomy and decreases criticality. Essentially, it makes NGDOs less vulnerable than the subsidisation option.

Combining income generation with development programmes has more positive effects on a resource profile than income sources that bear no relationship to an NGDO's mission.

Choosing for interdependence with CBOs through joint ventures generates both civic and economic rootedness. It works against patronage relations and can re-establish NGDO credibility and legitimacy when this is weakened or in doubt. This option is likely to have a strong positive impact on a resource profile.

Self-owned enterprises with development benefits place significant demands on finding structural and management solutions: for example, embedding in the existing structure, creating a separate department or a separate organisation. With appropriate choices, this option generally has an overall positive impact on resource profile.

Separating income self-generation from development mission can introduce problems of public image. It demands substantial commercial acumen and presents difficulties in capital mobilisation. Problems are most acute when the NGDO chooses to generate income through its own enterprises. Problems are least acute, and the benefits to resource profile are highest, with an untied investment option – assuming it is professionally and conservatively managed. This is why endowments are the preferred choice for all NGDOs. However, both options face difficulties in raising investment capital.

NGDOs must be realistic about how much self-generation is feasible or desirable. Over-reliance on investment income can cause complacency, stagnation, reduced insight and loss of agility. A little 'hunger' and continual resource hunting can work against this danger.

Despite much rhetoric about promoting sustainable organisations, aid investment to create capital funds for NGDOs is likely to remain very modest. Initiatives to create indigenous NGDO-funding entities will have a positive, but marginal, impact on capital availability.

Chapter 7

Mobilising Finance from Other Sources

'Sustainability is when your work is recognised to the extent that you don't have to fund-raise.' (Sérgio Haddad, ABONG)

'Be an attractor for others, not a beggar.' (James Sarpei, CENCOSAD)

A resource diversification strategy for NGDOs can include gaining access to finance generated by others. This is termed a 'subsidisation option'.[1] Subsidy is not a happy connotation, especially in the current political climate, because it implies that NGDOs are not entitled to or are 'earning' support from others for what they do. It is selected because of the perspective arising from the conclusions of Chapter 4, that despite its dangers, self-generation is the preferred strategy since it offers a degree of control and protection of autonomy, no matter how modest. Nevertheless, self-generation can be usefully and rightfully topped-up from elsewhere. The choice of terminology for this strategy is not a disrespectful view about the financing of NGDO work. In fact, it is the opposite. As the quotations above suggest, gaining a subsidy on the right terms is someone's recognition of an NGDO's worth, not its failings.

In practice, it is highly unlikely that anything but a few NGDOs will mobilise all the financial resources they need through self-generation. There are also reasons why this may not, in principle, be an appropriate goal. The danger of complacency is one. However, there are other, more fundamental, issues to consider. This chapter starts by looking at what they are, together with some basic principles that a subsidy should fulfil.

Using Anil Najam's perspective of two-way co-optation, the second section looks at NGDOs gaining access to resources from government. The question is whether a mutually satisfactory situation can be arrived at, or does one party lose more than the other? The answer differs depending on how government finance is given, either as an ongoing subsidy or as a contract. The general trend is from the former to the latter.

Section Three examines raising finance from businesses, with attention to the issue of reputation for both sides. Reputation is more likely to be the agenda than expecting a direct impact on their economic bottom-line. However, issues of technical expertise and marketing play a role as well. For NGDOs, influence on corporate behaviour is as likely an agenda as is a hunt for funds to do development work.

Raising finance from other segments of civil society is the topic of Section Four. In principle, this should be both more appropriate and easier than negotiating with the other two sectors. However, this is not always the case. For professional grant makers the problem lies in the weakness of their approach to sustainability, summed up in the funders' paradox put forward by David Bonbright: 'how do you invest so that you can cease to invest?'[2]

For citizens' finance, the issue is an NGDO's capacity to encourage and deal with people's informal response on the one hand and the exclusive nature of fees for services on the other.

The final section of this chapter provides a comparative summary of these options. Part II is closed by Chapter 8, which contains an overall review of the strategic picture facing NGDOs when they seek to diversify and localise their resource base.

Justification and Role of the Subsidy Option

What justifies an NGDO to look for support from income generated by others? What should NGDOs seek to achieve when doing so and guard against in the process? Because these questions apply to each of the three paths that an NGDO can follow when hunting for a subsidy, this section looks for answers applicable to all options.

Justifying a Subsidy

Increasingly, NGDOs are arguing that the 'uneconomic' work they do for public benefit – in health care, population, education and HIV/AIDS support, for example – should be financed from public funds. Such a claim on government resources is a right of citizens however organised, not a discretionary privilege. A reinforcement for this argument derives from the fact that, to attract inward business investment, governments offer attractive tax conditions and other incentives that are equivalent to a forgone public income. A government's contention is that offering such incentives recognises, and is offset by, other benefits to the national economy in terms, for example, of employment generation and export earnings. In reply, NGDOs ask why they should not also be financially recognised for their contribution in creating the human and social capital and stability needed to make business investments productive.

In parallel, there are arguments about NGDO involvement in making good the public costs of private ownership and business operations. Such costs are often manifest as environmental degradation, especially around mineral extraction and industrial processing complexes. There can also be social costs as, in the quest for greater productivity and in response to reduction in trade barriers, businesses replace manpower with technology that causes social disharmony and family disruption. Helping society cope with environmental damage, economic adjustment and market transition merits recognition and action by companies themselves. This stance reflects the notion of a 'triple bottom line' and socially responsible business.

Politically, poverty and exclusion are argued to be destabilising forces that undermine a positive environment for national development.[3] Consequently, NGDO 'stabilising' work through poverty reduction, inclusion, empowerment and democratisation should merit public recognition in financial as well as legislative terms.

Strategically, therefore, while NGDOs – and civil society more broadly – have a responsibility to mobilise their own financial resources as circumstances permit, this should not be to the exclusion of government and business carrying out their public responsibilities as well. Part of this responsibility should be expressed through finance to those NGDOs that can demonstrate the public benefit they are generating. How this is demonstrated, and against what criteria, must be answered in a particular context – answers will evolve as society itself evolves.

National circumstances dictate the extent to which these principles can be practically applied and how. In the case of some countries, such as Mozambique and Chad, only substantial external aid enables them to approximate to their aspiration of modern statehood. They are presently not viable as modern entities without it. Consequently, their ability to respond to financial claims from NGDOs is just not feasible. However, more often, as in much of Latin America, in the Asian 'tiger economies' and in some countries of the East, such as Hungary, the Czech Republic and Poland, the problem is not lack of public resources but policy choices about their distribution.

The foregoing perspectives differ markedly from an era where NGDOs saw government and business as part of, and not the solution to, the problem they were tackling: growing numbers of poor people. This ongoing change in NGDOs' view is the product of many things. One is uneven and stumbling progress towards greater representative democracy, opening up the idea that citizens own the state and its government, not the other way round – citizens have rights, not simply obligations and discretionary privileges. Another is improvement in levels of education and communication, allowing easier comparisons and better understanding of the way things are done elsewhere – governments can no longer claim that their way is the only choice. Yet another is an NGDO shift from the welfarist notion that people have 'needs' to one recognising their potentials and right to create their own future.

While receding, the old NGDO perspectives of government leave a legacy in two ways. First is a lingering suspicion on all sides.[4] The nature and strength of distrust depends on the history of state–society relations in general and the behaviour and national role of the aid system in particular. Second is an exploration of what collaboration might mean, but with wariness of co-optation, leading to what has been termed a stance of 'critical engagement'.[5]

NGDO attitudes towards business, and vice versa, are also emerging from a period of disdain at worst to apprehension at best. Transnational corporations have been a particular focus of NGDO rejection in terms of business behaviour. Again, there is a thawing of relations with some national and international businesses that see a long-term interest in mitigating or otherwise dealing with the social and environmental consequences of their actions. Gaining a reputation for being socially and environmentally sensitive is becoming a legitimate part of corporate branding. Association with publicly respected NGDOs can help.

Relations of Southern and Eastern NGDOs with parts of civil society – people's movements, associations of peasants, workers, war veterans and people with disabilities, for example – have always been sought. On the other hand, their relations with the public at large, and the middle class as potential sources of income, have been mixed, suspicion being a common public stance. As noted in the previous chapter, the nature of civil society is undergoing change. In many countries of the South, despite enduring poverty on a large scale, the middle class is growing as are the interest groups they spawn. The nature of grassroots organisations is evolving from the traditional social movements needing help to mass-membership organisations, illustrated in Brazil and elsewhere, which are adopting civil disobedience as a necessary tactic without expecting assistance from intermediaries. The mass

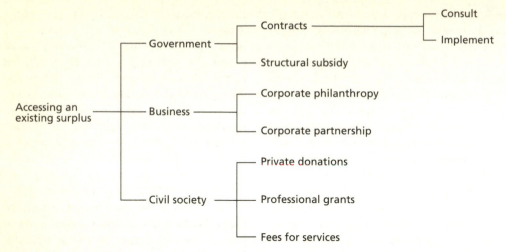

Figure 7.1 *Options in Mobilising Resources from Others*

demonstrations in 1998 of Southern and Eastern civic organisations against the WTO took place without the presence of many Northern NGDOs, who were against a confrontational approach.[6] No matter how it evolves, civil society must be part of an NGDO resource agenda.

Guides and Guards in Negotiation

Whatever the source, a subsidy should serve one or more of the following functions: reducing the economic threshold for participation, that is, enabling NGDOs to work with even poorer people and more marginalised groups; increasing outreach – doing more of what it does well; providing continuity for ongoing interventions that are not at the stage for withdrawal; and providing an opportunity to alter the behaviour of the funder – what has been

termed a 'reverse agenda',[7] or 'policy entrepreneurship'.[8] If none of these purposes is served, the NGDO is probably entering a contracting role to implement someone else's agenda and compromising its own.

On what conditions can subsidy be agreed? On what terms and within what rules of the game can NGDOs gain finance from others for their work? One answer lies in the degree of alignment between the interests and agendas of the NGDO and potential financiers. Using the options set out in Chapter 4, this chapter looks at answers in relation to government, business and civil society. As in the previous two chapters, analysis is framed in terms of six features of resource dependency. The various options for discussion are shown in Figure 7.1.

Government

Governments in the South and East raise finance in many ways. They do so from taxes, by issuing bonds, by renting out land and property and by gaining interna-

tional aid as loans and grants. How this income is allocated and spent is a question of political choice, usually set out in major policies, with budgets and laws to back them up. It has been argued in Chapter 1 that the policy-making process is a 'chaos of purpose and accident'. This confronts NGDOs with both risk and opportunity, requiring an agility to avoid the first and grasp the second.

The most important set of policies relate to how the regime in power wants to divide up roles and functions between itself, market institutions and the rest of society – civil institutions, households and individuals. Though uneven in terms of starting point and pace, the worldwide trend is towards policy frameworks and institutional configurations prevailing in the North. The fact that the North itself is not homogeneous, especially in terms of allocating social responsibility, already suggests that there is no single configuration, or model, but variations around a liberal democracy plus free market theme. In the South and East this translates into a historically conditioned movement towards multiparty politics coupled to private rather than public ownership and towards free markets and capitalist institutions as the wealth-creating force.

Our concern is how governments include civil society in the picture – by extension, will finance from government be 'a source of life or a kiss of death'?[9] As so often in life, the answer is, it depends.[10] The regime type, its ideology and history all contribute to if and how civil society and NGDOs are recognised and treated as legitimate actors in the first place and with autonomy to act in the second. Conversely, it depends on the NGDO as well. In the Philippines, partly because of their role in the overthrow of the Marcos regime, NGDOs are legitimate actors accorded recognised positions on government policy-making bodies. Their operational work is independently determined and implemented, with government being notified of what they are doing. In Sri Lanka, NGDO representatives sit on the National Environmental Council. At the other extreme, in Ethiopia, NGDOs are perceived as a sort of 'necessary evil' because they bring in urgently needed foreign funds but only to do things the government directly sanctions and monitors.[11] Without them, less foreign aid would be available. So NGDOs are reluctantly tolerated but not embraced and are not accorded a legitimate role in public policy making.

One proxy sign of government stance towards NGDOs is whether they are recognised in government budgets, as is the case in India. As part of the national five-year plan, the government sets out a role and, in annual budgets, makes state funds specifically available for them to undertake development projects. As we will see below, allocations of finance for NGDOs can also be hidden within the recurrent budgets of ministries. Another indicator of government attitude towards NGDOs is the bureaucratic location of its regulatory authority. A location in a ministry of social welfare or ministry of planning sends a different message from the department dealing with internal security. In Malawi, responsibility for NGDOs rests with the Ministry of Women's, Youth and Community Affairs. This choice is more the exception than the rule. By and large, NGDO regulatory authority is associated with departments of security and internal affairs, which is indicative of the typically political view of NGDOs described in previous chapters.

Within this political framework of recognition and division of labour are myriad policies that can affect or be of interest to NGDOs. It is also here that the institution 'government' must be examined because it is not homogeneous. Different parts of government can act in different ways with different reasons to include or exclude NGDOs from their funding. Ministries of health, education, agriculture, housing and environment are more likely to have an active link with NGDOs than are ministries of transport and communications, finance or foreign affairs.

The question both parties must explore is the extent to which they have common enough objectives for government to consider financing what NGDOs do. Paraphrasing Najam, **collaboration** is likely when government agencies and NGDOs share similar goals and strategies to achieve them; while **complementarity** is likely when a government agency and an NGDO share similar goals but prefer different strategies.[12]

Negotiation can proceed along two principal financing paths. The NGDO can seek ongoing finance for its work derived from a ministry's recurrent budget. Once agreed and included in a ministry's vote, the support can continue as a structural subsidy. This path corresponds to collaboration where both goals and strategies are sufficiently aligned, as for example, when an NGDO provides something similar to and 'on behalf of' the government. Health and educational services are common examples.

Alternatively, an NGDO can seek funding for projects that it wants to do or that the ministry or department wants done. It the NGDO's intentions fit within the policy framework and help the government achieve its goals, albeit in a complementary way, the result is usually a fixed-duration contract. The two options have different implications for an NGDO resource profile.

Negotiating a Structural Subsidy

More NGDOs enjoy a structural subsidy than may be first imagined. Where history has placed the initial burden for schools and hospitals on churches and other voluntary bodies, it is not uncommon for them to receive annual subventions in

terms of a lump sum grant or secondment of government staff. However, continuation of this convention cannot be guaranteed. Such an initial situation existed in Tanzania until the government decided to nationalise church hospitals and run them itself. At independence, churches operated some 42 per cent of the country's hospitals. As a product of the Arusha Declaration in 1977, 'The government aimed to assume an almost absolute role and control in the delivery of health care'.[13] Consequently, state finance to NGDOs declined, as did the quality of health services available to Tanzanians. This big policy shift pertained for some ten years. Now, however:

> *'Under the current economic liberalisation policies and the Structural Adjustment Programmes, private health-care services are allowed to operate. Furthermore, government health-care services are on sale to consumers under the new policy of cost-sharing, although this is against the government's populist ideological commitment to deliver essential services free of charge to consumers.'*[14]

As part of this policy reform, hospitals were returned to their original owners and a more modest subvention resumed. This illustration shows how major policy shifts can affect what might have been taken as an enduring commitment of government support, even when the regime stays the same. Other factors, like the prospect of state insolvency, can force a government's hand. The introduction of multi-party politics can be expected to have similar effects as one regime wants to differentiate itself from its predecessor. This does not mean that structural subsidy should not be sought, but that a sense of realism must prevail in terms of its reliability.

The recent adjustment-induced policy change in Tanzania is mirrored in many other countries. Generally speaking, to reduce budget deficits, governments are cutting back on allocations to the provision of public services. A different division of responsibility is sought, with consumers or citizens carrying a larger share. Cost sharing is one mechanism for implementing this shift, with safety nets for those that can prove that they are very poor.

This policy change is further reflected in a preference for contract arrangements over structural subsidy when voluntary organisations provide public services financed by public money.[15] This has been referred to as the introduction of a 'contract culture' to the voluntary sector. It is the second and, because of a privatising policy framework, growing option in negotiating a government subsidy. It signals the probable answer to the question posed in Chapter 4: are NGDOs partners or contractors? The writing 'public service contractor' is on many NGDO walls.[16]

In terms of resource dependency, structural subsidies are inclined to increase vulnerability, sensitivity and criticality. A country is unlikely to have other sources of a similar nature to tax-based income coupled to legitimate public expectations. The variables that make the difference and cause the problems are political commitment to provide the particular activity or service through public funds and sound economic management to ensure funds are available. Neither can be relied on for stability or continuity in poor countries with emerging democracies. Consistency and compatibility need not be unduly affected by structural subsidy once the ground rules have been agreed and tested. Autonomy, however, is likely to be compromised by structural dependency. The degree to which this occurs is largely a question of proportion in NGDO budgets and criticality.

The Contract Option

Adopting the contract option requires consideration of three starting conditions. These are degree of goal coherence; the room to manoeuvre; and directionality in terms of who is trying to co-opt whom. They all contribute to the nature of the negotiation and eventual impact on an NGDO's financing profile. Contracts typically reflect Najam's complementary option. Goals are aligned, but strategies and approaches may differ.

As a broad generalisation, governments are more likely to adopt technical sectoral standards and administrative planning approaches and mechanisms, while NGDOs are more likely to use thematic approaches allied to participatory methods and processes. To the extent that government is relying on aid funds, there is even more likelihood of NGDOs being co-opted into technical sectoralism rather than the other way round because that is the way governments and donors are set up and their performance assessed – strategies may differ less and less. This phenomenon has been characterised as the 'standardisation of development' or the creation of a bureaucratic 'development monoculture'.[17] It applies mostly to contracts where NGDOs act as implementers of projects and programmes that governments support or initiate.

In cases where a government agency appreciates that development work is a form of action research, they are more likely to adapt towards NGDO practice. The substantial number of government agricultural extension staff who have undergone training in rapid and participatory rural appraisal is one example. However, a common problem after training is that the institutions they work in find it difficult to adapt their procedures and culture accordingly – the institutionalisation problem.[18] In other words, there remains a gap between rhetoric and reality.

NGDOs are more likely to co-opt government into their approaches when they are in a consulting role, frequently to help design an intervention. Why? Most often because they are selected on the basis of having a different sort of useful expertise and experience to offer than 'normal' commercial firms. Consultancy contracting with government is becoming common for NGDOs like SEARCH in Nepal. ISODEC and the Centre for the Development of People (CEDEP) in Ghana both provide consultancy services to local government. A further step is exemplified by BRAC setting up a consultancy arm in Washington DC, to make its professional development services available in the North.

The extent to which NGDOs are co-opted or the other way around also depends on relative room to manoeuvre. Of primary importance is the extent to which each party has an alternative. Here, NGDOs are often, but not always, at a disadvantage, exemplified in competitive tendering for contracts. Facing an 'infinite' demand from those in poverty, the resource supplier can dictate terms and priorities. From this advantageous position, a rapid increase in NGDOs means that governments can pick and choose between them. Conversely, where an NGDO has an outstanding reputation it may be sought after and hence be able to maintain its own requirements. BRAC is one such organisation. More than once it has declined offers of support when it felt that the conditions were not right. So has CWIN in Nepal when asked to set up and operate a children's village – an institutionalised response to child destitution that it did not agree with. The organisation's governors need to stand behind such decisions. They must endorse protecting the organisation's integrity and consistency. This is not always the case, especially if it is in difficult financial circumstances.

Few NGDOs fall into this latter category, or have a luxury of choice to decline funding offers. There is also a moral pressure not to turn money away. The need is so enormous and something useful can always be done for the poor. The best must be made out of a bad compromise. Such pragmatic reasoning is understandable, as is the slippery slope of imbalanced co-optation it leads to. The question for NGDOs is the extent to which they have principles they want to adhere to. There is seldom a clear-cut case. Compromise is usual and boils down to a question of sound judgement. Ironically, perverse as it may sound, NGDOs that have principles and stick to them end up being more respected than those that do not. A reputation for being all things to all people implies a shallow or weak identity, raising questions of organisational integrity. It is just not clear what the NGDO stands for, beyond self-survival, which is not a beneficial reputation to carry.

Another dimension affecting the room to manoeuvre is pressure to get the activity done. In the case of governments and a disbursement-driven aid system, this means getting the money spent in the fiscal year or losing it. For NGDOs, pressure may stem from maintaining continuity in an ongoing activity or from impending bankruptcy. To the extent that a government agency is unlikely to disappear or be held firmly accountable for non-disbursement, the pressure can be managed. When, for an NGDO, the consequences will be rejection by communities or dissolution, the pressure to acquiesce can be very acute. Correspondingly, NGDOs are usually at a disadvantage in contract negotiations and less able to remain consistent in what they do and how. It is also a too common experience for NGDOs to be expected to make good bureaucratic delays. Once funds are approved, albeit beyond the original planned date, they are expected to start straight away – the onus is placed on them.

A final precondition to negotiation is who is approaching whom? Does the NGDO submit its own proposal to the government or does the government invite an NGDO to do what it has in mind? Where an NGDO is seeking support for its work, it usually faces competition with others staking a similar claim. Its negotiating position is weaker. It may also face dealing with corruption if gatekeepers try to misuse their position. Anecdotal evidence suggests that corruption in allocating governments funds to NGDOs is not unknown. Where an NGDO is approached because of its reputation, its negotiating position is much stronger. In fact, for some NGDOs leaders, ongoing offers of support from acceptable sources are a proxy for organisational sustainability. Reputation explains a lot, but not all, when being offered someone else's resources, and reputation stems from demonstrated performance.

Overall, contracting is more likely to lead to compromise not in the NGDO's favour. However, this depends on the starting conditions described above. Getting the right preconditions in place is therefore an important part of an NGDO strategy.

In terms of resource profile, gaining access to government funds is likely to have the following impact. Vulnerability becomes increasingly tied to political and policy stability. Changes in regime, external pressures and shifts in development priorities and 'fashions' within aid can all filter through to existing funding arrangements. Given that much NGDO funding derives from fixed-term project agreements, sensitivity need not be radically affected by a switch to government contracts. However, as with subsidy, criticality will be increased because similar sources are unlikely to be available. There

is only one government. Consistency in terms of mission and identity are most likely points of compromise. The danger of becoming a government NGDO looms large – if not in fact then still potentially in the eyes of the population. Autonomy is more likely to reduce than increase. Governments have their procedures, cycles, cultures and policies that seldom adapt to the differences between NGDOs. In addition, NGDOs are expected to comply with public audit and other standard requirements. Depending on preconditions sketched above, compatibility may or may not be compromised. But where compromise is not called for, it is more likely a sign of NGDO adoption of governmental strategies than vice versa.

Insight and Agility

A period of estrangement between NGDOs and governments has created high levels of ignorance, stereotyping and often incorrect perceptions on both sides. In seeking public finance, NGDOs can gain important insights on how government actually functions, how it can be disaggregated and how its interests can be applied to further an NGDO agenda. The interactions for this type of learning are no longer taboo. Moreover, they are expanding downwards – to local government – and upwards into policy processes. In addition, NGDOs can gain access to other government resources such as research centres.

Conversely, government insight about NGDOs can also be increased, but this by no means guarantees that governments like what they see. As noted previously, moving from the 'security of obscurity'[19] into the mainstream of national development in association with the state can bring restriction to agility – the space as well as capacity to adapt. It can also bring additional constraints to autonomy rather than improvements through greater mutual understanding. Overall, enhanced insight through gaining access to government funding is unlikely to be matched by greater NGDO agility. Whether this would be different when dealing with business is a topic of the following section.

Finance from the Commercial Sector

The commercial sector is a relatively new funding source for NGDOs to consider. The opening of this possibility is one dimension of the sign of the times spoken of earlier. It is reflected in an ongoing debate about the role of businesses in society, summed up in the question 'do they serve shareholders or stakeholders'? Is generating shareholder value the sole and proper goal of corporations where 'externalities' are addressed by government policy and law, functions for which businesses already pay taxes? Alternatively, should businesses carry a wider obligation recognising other 'stakeholders', which includes the environment? The for-profits that are adopting the stakeholder view – 'corporate citizens' or 'socially responsible businesses' are most likely to be interested in, and of potential interest to, NGDOs.[20]

The broad attraction of NGDOs for businesses is provision of technical knowledge and 'reputation by association'. Servicios para el Desarrollo (SASE) in Peru, for example, is building up a reputation for its work with mining industries, helping them be more environmentally and socially responsible. Its tactic is to use the negative publicity about industry behaviour as a point of entry and positive reinforcement for forming alliances with them. One reason SASE can do so is because its leader, Dr Caravedo, is a respected public figure, giving him access to and the trust of leaders of Peru's major companies.[21] Once one or two are convinced of the merits of corporate responsibility, they are listened to by their peers. The image and standing of a business can be enhanced by collaboration with NGDOs that already enjoy a positive public profile.

More succinctly, NGDOs have constituencies that matter – they are consumers too. Both are gaining political attention and influence. The following quotation from Shell's Chief Executive captures the business awakening to this fact.

> *'In essence we were somewhat slow in understanding that environmentalist groups, consumer groups and so on were tending to acquire authority. Meanwhile the groups we were used to dealing with (eg, governments and industry organisations) were tending to lose authority.'*[22]

There is a realisation that governments alone cannot provide the supportive and stable environment required for long-term business success – citizens' acceptance matters as well.

An attraction of corporations for NGDOs, alongside income, is to address the causes rather than the symptoms of social and other problems.[23] In transnational corporations NGDO-influence can be transmitted and enforced on a worldwide scale in a way unknown to global governance. Changing how oil, chemical, agricultural and drug companies, the steel industry and mining corporations do business can have a deep and geographically broad impact. Just as important are NGDO interactions with local firms, small- to medium-size businesses and processing plants that may, for example, be polluting the local area, causing illness amongst the wider population and in so doing creating hostile but feeble communities.

Businesses approach the issue of development financing from many angles. One of importance for NGDOs is corporate funding through intermediary mechanisms, or 'corporate philanthropy', where the business is distant from the activity. Another is negotiating a 'partnership' or direct relationship. Each option has somewhat different effects on resource profile and trade-offs.

Corporate Philanthropy through Intermediaries

The desire of corporations, or their founders, to contribute to the public good is very old, albeit not evenly spread across the world. The TATA Foundation in India, for example, was established in the late 1800s and many of America's largest foundations are the product of investment in endowments by 'robber barons' at the beginning of this century. One choice for corporate giving is, as with an endowment, to establish an intermediary creating distance from the enterprise itself. For example, the trustees of the Ford Foundation no longer include a member of the Ford family. However, for many family-initiated foundations, such as the Ayala Foundation in the Philippines or the Aga Khan Foundation, family members retain an ongoing interest, representation and sometimes direct control. What typifies this type of philanthropy is personal commitment or moral calling. A direct link to the commercial interests of the firm is tenuous and not the primary concern.

This 'old style' family-inspired corporate philanthropy is now being complemented by more business-like considerations of professional managers.

The Philippines Business for Social Progress (PBSP), for example, was established by some 50 businesses in the early 1970s. This was during the period of martial law under Ferdinand Marcos where left-wing guerrillas were making political capital out of the exploitive behaviour of foreign firms. Investing in social development initiatives (a model copied from Latin America), especially in communities around factories, extraction and processing facilities, was seen as one way for businesses to counter local support for guerrilla movements. Inevitably, opponents to business called this 'conscience money'. Times have changed and PBSP can use 20 per cent of the annual grant made by companies for development unrelated to company location. (However, the other 80 per cent is allocated by companies to initiatives that they want.)[24]

More recent corporate philanthropy can still be expected to be informed by strategic self-interest, but it is much more enlightened. It is not simply a 'look good' compensation by the rich. Corporate leaders regard it as another form of investment. The return is based on the premise that by fostering the loyalty of customers they will be more inclined to keep buying goods and services from them. Another perspective is to retain staff who would prefer to work with a company that is socially respected.[25] However, optimising a return on this type of investment calls for a clear identification between the company and the activity or event an NGDO is associated with. This requires partnership rather than contribution to an intermediary fund. Consequently, corporate investment into a common fund like PBSB is evolving less quickly and is still not a common feature either of the South or the North.

By and large, corporations want to be convinced of the viability and visibility of what their money is being used for. Jerry

Yang, co-founder of a software company called Yahoo, views philanthropy not as a form of charity but as an investment – a hand up, not a handout.[26] Such philanthropists prefer tangible, hard outcomes, not soft processes and intangible benefits, like community capacity. Even though indirect, as with most funders, they expect to see that the source of funds is known to those on the receiving end. In the South and East, they do not wish to have their support misinterpreted by government as being 'oppositional', because this may compromise business operations in the country. Hence, support is unlikely for organisations that are more activist and process oriented.

From an NGDO perspective, gaining access to finance from an 'arm's length' corporate intermediary is less likely to negatively influence their reputation. However, striking up a corporate relationship will still require a good and coherent story to be told to communities. To the extent that an intermediary can reduce the perception of an attachment to the interests of a specific corporation, such funding is less likely to create internal dissent and friction between fundraisers and developers.

Generally speaking, NGDO vulnerability is unlikely to be affected by corporate philanthropy as a source, if the source itself is derived from many businesses. The risk of poor corporate performance is spread. Nevertheless, there is no protection from the knock-on effects of a major economic downturn. Similarly, as with a switch to government funding, sensitivity and criticality are unlikely to suffer if the terms of the agreement foresee a clear end point. To the extent that approaches can be made to alternative corporate sources, unlike with government, criticality might be reduced. Consistency can be an issue. NGDOs run the risk of being seen as inconsistent with their calling by taking corporate funds, especially if they have been vehement crit-

ics of business as the cause of poverty or pollution. They will need a good 'sales' strategy to counter public perceptions of selling-out. Autonomy may be compromised less than with government because corporate funding, typically as contracts, is less allied to political interests and public policies. Compatibility may be challenged, but in a positive way to the extent that NGDOs have to introduce more economic rigour in their interventions. The problem of internal staff dissent might, however, be acute, which is akin to the problem of contending cultures in 'hybrid' organisations described in the previous chapter.

Corporate Partnership

As the title implies, corporate partnership is a direct link between an NGDO and a particular business. Consequently, the issue of negotiating a shared agenda is more prominent. It brings with it a higher profile in terms of impact on an NGDO's public image and hence higher risk. The hoped-for return is greater NGDO influence on corporate behaviour. This type of relationship is developing rapidly in the North.[27] A survey of publications suggests that the South and East have relatively few successful examples to offer so far. One example is between the Organisation of Rural Associations for Progress (ORAP) in Zimbabwe and a business in Bulawayo fabricating batteries. Debt conversion allowed ORAP to take a part share in the business. For the company, ORAP offered technology outreach to its 50,000 members as its view is that solar energy requiring battery storage is a potentially important element in community development. Discounts could be negotiated if substantial community take-up occurred. Co-ownership and access to a 'stimulated' defined market satisfies the interests of both.

In most cases, however, co-ownership is not an aspect of NGDO corporate partnership. Rather, what is negotiated is collaboration on specific initiatives of sufficiently mutual interest. Where the approach is from the NGDO, the question a business will naturally ask is 'what is in it for me?'[28] From this direction, there is no reason to assume that the business is interested in being influenced by the NGDO. What will be looked for are the returns on offer and the viability of what is being proposed. Business will be predisposed to provide support if the benefits are closer to home, in terms of geography or market strategy: geography may mean the local community providing the workforce; strategically, it may mean linking the business to a topic or initiative that shows it in a good light or improves its name recognition or market share.

An issue for NGDOs is who are they dealing with in the business? Is it a department or section set up to respond to these requests in an insightful way? Alternatively, is a request simply placed on the desk of, say, a public relations officer? In the former case, NGDOs have a proxy indicator of the degree of professional treatment that will be applied to negotiation, where a reverse agenda will be understood if it is put on the table. In the case of the latter, chances are that finance to an NGDO will be seen and calculated purely in public-relations terms.

Where the approach is from a business, it is possibly a sign of serious internal consideration of what is on offer in terms of reputation, influence on politics or consumers and technical knowledge not available elsewhere. It could also be to gain access to NGDO skills in community assessment and relations. However, opportunistic approaches to deal with a short-term public relations crisis cannot be ruled out. Approaches from businesses may or may not resonate with the NGDO's own development strategies. Where they do, the problem of dissent within the NGDO will probably already have been dealt

with. Where it has not, the NGDO is likely to enter a period of soul searching.

The critical question facing NGDOs, irrespective of the direction of approach, is what will a partnership with business mean for constituency perception, public trust and credibility? If reputation by association is a benefit for businesses, the opposite – tainted by association – may be a major handicap for NGDOs. Hence, it is important for both parties to do their homework about each other. As business-NGDO partnerships become more common, the co-optation they imply will invite more media and public interest. Any skeletons, such as NGDO financial improprieties that were settled out of court to avoid bad publicity, or asset stripping or maltreatment of workers by a corporate subsidiary, will be brought out of cupboards and embarrassingly held up for public view. Nike, a well known maker of sports shoes and accessories, for example, was pilloried in some of the media because of poor working conditions within its subcontractors. It has turned to NGDOs to help with an independent social audit to prove that it has reformed. Any NGDO involved with Nike before this event could have been tarred with the same brush.

It is of particular importance to NGDOs to negotiate terms that do not reduce autonomy. Failure to do so will probably lead to a 'lose-lose' situation, because what businesses 'buy' in the first instance is public trust in the NGDO. If a partnership erodes this valuable asset, then the business loses and the NGDO loses its independence. (This problem is similar to that of donors whose funding practices undermine the very qualities, competencies and comparative advantages of NGDOs that they wanted to support in the first place.)[29]

In addition, if a reverse agenda is part of an NGDO's motivation to form a corporate partnership, the organisation must be skilled in negotiating the changes it wants to bring about and how they will be measured and assessed. This is a new area of competence for many. Associated with it are a distinctive set of indicators and ways of looking at performance. In collaboration with the New Economics Foundation (NEF), the Institute for Social and Ethical Accountability (ISEA) has proposed a set of social and ethical accounting, auditing and reporting concepts and terms to help in setting and assessing standards.[30] It is clear that embarking on corporate partnerships demands new skills, new ways of thinking and ways of defining and measuring performance.

NGDOs have a cultural aversion to making comparisons with their peers. Greenpeace or the Nature Conservancy do not say that they deal with environmental issues better than the World Wild Fund for Nature (WWF). Nor does a child sponsorship development agency, like PLAN International, say that it alleviates child poverty better than World Vision International (WVI) or the Christian Children's Fund (CCF). It is just not done. However, entering a partnership with business can make NGDOs vulnerable to comparative advertising to be found in competitive markets. It can also create divisions within the ranks of the NGDO community between the purists and the pragmatists, leading to mixed public messages, with loss of credibility and trust. To see NGDOs at loggerheads with each other alongside their corporate partners is not an unreal danger. (Another parallel with development funding, described in Chapter 3, is the different position amongst NGDOs about aid policies. This occurred between African and US NGDOs concerning the International Development Assistance Fund (IDA) replenishment for the World Bank.)[31]

The dynamism of the market place is another factor NGDOs will have to deal with in terms of partnership-based corporate funding. Change can happen rapidly, perhaps negating original conditions within which agreements were made. Swift adaptation is not a renowned characteristic of government or donor behaviour. Moreover, in the aid system, NGDOs can become very dependent on the individual they are dealing with or the powers above. An incoming boss may have a very different view of a relationship with an NGDO and have untrammelled power to end it.

Finally, what corporate-NGDO partnerships can offer is longevity and continuity. Successful corporations continually generate the funds needed to support the relationship. Subject to mutually satisfactory performance, there is no reason why the relationship has to rest on the short-term project finance common to the aid system and much of government finance. After the exploratory years, an NGDO-business relationship can be much more open-ended and flexible than other development finance can usually offer.

From a resource diversification perspective, corporate partnership brings many interesting features, dilemmas and trade-offs. It looks likely that vulnerability will increase because of a closer tie to both market instability and the internal dynamics of the corporation and its leadership. Sensitivity would be enhanced, especially when a reputation becomes more closely allied to that of the business. It is not the resource itself – the funds – but the change in reputation of the provider that can cause rapid impact by association. What NGDO would want to be known for a close tie with Monsanto prior to its 'conversion'? Criticality may also go up rather than down because association with one corporation will probably close doors to others. Consequently, an organisation's first choice of a corporate partner can be critical, unless it strategically plays the field and negotiates non-exclusive partnerships. This is a necessary feature for corporations seeking NGDO endorsement for their product, for example, by giving a 'green' warranty. The NGDO's seal of approval is of little or no value if the organisation is limited to endorsing one manufacturer only. Its independence, and hence credibility, disappears.

By entering a corporate partnership, NGDOs face a potentially severe challenge to their identity and consistency with mission, which needs to be well explained to the constituency and public more widely. Reduced autonomy is a real Achilles' heel of corporate partnerships. If it happens, the NGDO is less good to itself and to the corporation. This is less the case with government because at least it is meant to provide public benefit. There is something less wholesome about an NGDO being subject to corporate control – a sign of a loss of soul on the NGDO's part? A further challenge is to organisational compatibility, not just in terms of internally reconciling fundraising and development departments, but of acquiring a new set of negotiating skills and assessment competencies.

In theory at least, the above discussion would not apply to civil society. This is a third source of financial surplus to which NGDOs can gain access.

Accessing Resources from Civil Society

Civil society is a fashionable term in today's development lexicon. It is also a term for a contested arena of social relations. The concept is also confused by the way it is employed. For example, some businesses say that they are part of civil society; others do not. Those that study and write about the concept cannot agree either.

For our purposes, business is not included. It has already been treated separately in resource terms. Our concern is about a political space occupied by citizens who come together to define and pursue common interests. It is a space where positive social capital can be created or eroded. The intentions of civic groups may coalesce into trust and concerted action or they may collide, producing factionalism, distrust and antagonistic pro- and anti-positions on issues. From a resource mobilisation perspective, the individuals and groupings in civil society of interest to NGDOs are those with similar values, aspirations and finance. In addition NGDOs must pay attention to the financing capabilities of the people the organisation is set up to serve.

This section looks at three types of civic actor, differentiated by the nature of the financial resources they can provide. First are donations from private individuals – the monetary complement of volunteerism; second are professional grant makers whose mission is to enhance civil society through individual organisations and more broadly in terms of a civic sector; and third are fees for services – payments by those who gain benefit from what the NGDO does. This category is not as straightforward as its sounds. For some would argue that NGDOs financed by professional grant makers to do, for example, policy advocacy are also delivering a service to the funder; albeit that the funder does not get a direct return. We will try and get around this problem by restricting the discussion on fees for services to those who get the benefit directly in return for their payment. Payments from grant makers are more akin to contracts to provide a public good.

Finance from the Citizen Base

Raising money from individuals is commonplace for much of the voluntary sector. It is less common for many NGDOs that have evolved from and are maintained by international aid. There appear to be two major strategies for NGDOs that wish to raise domestic funds from the population at large. The one chosen depends on how NGDOs read the financial capabilities of citizens. Is it just the middle class with disposable incomes that should be approached, or is there a broader resource amongst communities that can be explored and mobilised?

Most of the literature on fund-raising from individuals offers methods which will persuade and enable 'rich enough' individuals to put their hands in their pockets to make a one-time gift or, if done well, a regular donation.[32] From a sustainability perspective, the distinction between a one-off and a regular contribution is important. The former offers a cash impulse that needs to be spent rather than invested, otherwise the giver will wonder what all the fuss was about.[33] It is inherently unreliable. A regular donation is much to be preferred as are periodic fund-raising events, such as annual Christmas card sales, sponsored shows or charity dinners.

The analysis and techniques for individual fund-raising are well developed. They offer disaggregation by type of donor; different ways in which people can contribute and their motivations for doing so; how to communicate; and how to target. What is not provided are guidelines as to how much money it is reasonable to spend in order to raise money. I am not sure why this sort of useful, comparative case information is seldom available. It may be tied to the 'overheads game'.[34] Some organisations set clear ratios for costs of fund-raising set against funds raised. As a rule of thumb, when the total costs of raising a dollar exceed 20 cents, something is going seriously wrong. Not only is something going wrong internally, the wrong message is sent externally. The public is eager to know how much of its money actually reaches its intended goal or beneficiary. As a result, there are annual publications of non-profit performance based solely on reported overhead percentage. This is very misleading because different types of NGDO work, such as putting in a well, and providing family planning information and services for example, necessarily create different overhead costs. Be that as it may, fund-raising from individuals requires careful attention to the control and 'marketing' of the associated costs.

More generally, going to individuals for funds poses a challenge in terms of living up to the implied contract the NGDO is offering. What does the person have the right to expect? As Ian Smillie documents, investigative journalism by the *Chicago Tribune* into the fund-raising messages and on-the-ground practices of NGDOs concerned with child sponsorship brought much negative information to light.

'Poor as they were, none of the Tribune's sponsored children resembled the desperately sick or malnourished boys and girls whose images are a staple of fundraising appeals by child sponsorship organisations. The "magical bond" between sponsor and child proved to be mostly fiction.'[35]

What individual fund-raising creates is sharper and potentially more transparent relationship between NGDO performance and credibility – don't sell what you can't deliver or face the consequences in terms of loss of public trust. This is why honest messages with honest feedback are so vital. Without them, the organisation is always vulnerable to the reporter or critical politician lurking round the next corner.

Tapping funds from individuals to help others in a competitive market place inevitably increases vulnerability. For example, introduction of a National Lottery in the UK, part of whose proceeds are allocated to charity, had a negative impact on direct fund-raising. NGDOs also become more sensitive to bad publicity, for one scandal can mean a financial calamity. CARE Australia found this out, but has now recovered, when a case of misappropriation, in part due to escalating emergency work in the Balkans, became public. The impact of private giving on resource criticality depends on the message and implicit or explicit contract. Child sponsors typically expect every cent to reach their child even if the NGDO makes clear that this is not planned. By and large, appeals for non-specific purposes do not succeed – criticality is increased because a concrete goal or beneficiary is not specified. On the other hand, income from a legacy is untied and easy to administer – hence it is much sought after. NGDO autonomy is unlikely to be hampered by private giving beyond that which it creates for itself. To the extent that the NGDO builds up a credible base of loyal, trusting supporters, its autonomy will probably be enhanced.

For NGDOs with no history in fund-raising from individuals, this step will require major organisational adaptation. In addition to bringing in necessary skills, experience suggests that a fund-raisers' world of external interaction is so different from that of developers working with poor communities that communication is an inevitable problem. Moreover, unless tight control is exerted on fund-raising costs, ratios can get put of hand, with consequences of damaged reputations.

The title of this section corresponds to a concept and approach to raising resources from citizens being pioneered by the Ashoka Foundation, headquartered in the USA. The basic premise is that there are far more financial resources available from citizens than is commonly realised. Statistics simply do not capture the amounts of money applied locally and informally by people for things that they find important – be they cultural events, festivals, extra-curricular activities for school children, for religious expression or for recreation, for example. This is positive social capital in financial action. What statistics see is the money voluntarily donated to formal institutions – termed the gift economy. The published figures miss so much.

Of course, individuals cannot apply what they don't have. But the Ashoka Foundation argument is that the citizen base or the grassroots have more financial potential than assumed. Moreover, it is applied in ways that sustain much of what occurs within the real life of civil society – which is both broader and deeper than the formal organisations and donations one sees. In economic terms, the demand side is also its own financial resource or supply side. History shows that it is also the most secure and sustainable. Independent of states and markets, it finances what it wants to do within the means it has. It always has and it always will, even if, as in the Soviet Union, it is driven underground by the political ideology of the day.

The question for NGDOs, therefore, is how to stimulate this economic base to deal with continually evolving social and other challenges. Part of an answer is given in Part I: help expand the economic resources available at the grassroots. Another is to build the citizen sector from within, that is, to act as a civic innovator discussed in Chapter 4. The edited quotation in Box 7.1 explains one approach to such innovation: catalysing citizens as a support base.

Looked at another way, this story says that people have a capacity and 'built-in' inclination to organise themselves. It is a human phenomenon that turns homo sapiens into a social being. Formal organisations are but one expression of this innate inclination.[36] The issue is to recognise, respond to and help the further evolution of organising to deal with new circumstances, problems and aspirations.[37]

The question for NGDOs in the South and East is to what extent they can become citizen-based organisations described in the Ashoka Foundation approach; that is, where a reasonable proportion of income is derived from people who believe in and are intimately related and committed to the organisation, not distant donors whose heart strings can only be plucked from time to time.

In ways described for volunteering, NGDOs who succeed as civic catalysts are more likely to be buffered from external events, and are hence less vulnerable. Sensitivity shifts to an ability to maintain civic interest and commitment. If this falls away, or becomes negative, the NGDO will feel the effects very quickly. Criticality can be affected either way, but the chances are that civic support would allow for temporary substitution for a resource that disappears. With citizens behind and part-funding the organisation, autonomy will be strengthened. A similar story is told in Chapter 6 in relation to a move towards self-generation through joint ventures. In fact, what is described in Box 7.1 may often evolve in this way.

Much of what was said about improved insight and agility in relation to volunteers applies to citizens as a source of finance. International aid can distort an NGDO's perception about the extent to which it is understood and trusted. Conversely, through local grassroots fund-

ing NGDOs not only become woven into society but it becomes patently clear when mistrust occurs or performance is not good enough – support dwindles. Dependency on citizens is continuously educational. Rooting into a loyal socio-economic base also enhances resilience. However, such bonding may also limit agility as supporters claim a stronger hold.

The Ashoka Foundation catalyses citizen action, but is also an example of a professional grant maker skilled at allocating investments to other civic organisations or civic initiatives and innovators.[38] As an alternative civic source, how do they approach sustainability in their funding practices?

Tapping the Experts: Sustainability Finance from Professional Grant Makers

Much attention and effort is being applied to the stimulation and construction of local philanthropic organisations to expand and sustain domestic financing for NGDOs in the South and East. In other words, establishing organisations with their own local governance, autonomy in making funding decisions and an enduring resource base, usually some form of endowment. Sometimes they are referred to as foundation-like organisations (FLOs) – a term which recognises that different societies and cultures see philanthropy and the concept of a foundation in different ways – or they may be called Southern Foundations.[39] The overall purpose of these and similar initiatives is, broadly, to strengthen civil society in one or more of three ways. One intention is to finance what NGDOs do for society, ie, finance their projects and programmes. An example is debt-swap funds used by the USAID to create the Foundation for Philippine Environment (FPE) as a local funder. Similarly, Swiss Development Co-opera-

Box 7.1 Catalysing the Citizen Base

'In stimulating the citizen base, Ashoka adopts a three-tier strategy. The first tier is designed in the countries where we will have it working to tip the citizen sector in five, six, seven years. If you asked the typical Brazilian citizen organisation they will say, "Oh, Brazilians don't give, that's a quaint Anglo-Saxon custom". This is nonsense. If you look at the schools of Brazil every neighbourhood gives a ton of money and are able to organise the most amazing things, every year. For three months they write music, they choreograph, they make costumes. This is very complicated. It is nonsense that Brazilians don't give. Look at religions. They've all figured out how to build a citizen base, through trade unions or whatnot. It's just that our sector is new. So now our sector is there, there are thousands and thousands of citizens' organisations. This year we carefully selected 10,000 and sent out invitations to the competition I'm about to describe in Brazil. There are many more, this is just where we were focusing.

What we want to do six years from now is have every Brazilian working in a citizen organisation. No, but there are many ways that they can build a citizen base for themselves. Why do they know? Because all around them there are successful organisations that have a competitive advantage because in large part they have a citizen base, a broad base of support. Once we have reached that stage, if you are in an environment or human rights organisation that doesn't have a citizen base, you have competitors all around you who do. They have a competitive advantage because they do, they are more independent, they have greater elan, they have the freedom to go and do things and be less fearful than you do. You are going to say to yourself, or other members of your staff or your Board will say, if that organisation can do it, why can't you, why can't we? That's the dynamic, that's where you tip the whole thing.

So how do we get there? Every year we run a competition open to any citizen organisation. The idea is very simple. If you are a citizen organisation, come to us with a concrete, realistic, preferably interesting idea or set of ideas of how you will build a citizen base for yourself. We will help you succeed if you win the competition. We will pay half a stipend for a staff member to implement the idea; we will bring a series of specialised help – pro bono, marketing, certification, help you to become more visible, connect you with others who have done this sort of thing. Our job then becomes to help you to succeed. If we select six, eight, ten winners every year, after six years we are going to have 40 or 50 organisations which have succeeded. Twenty or thirty per cent of their income will be coming from a broad citizen base. They have found a segment of society that really cares about their issue. They have figured out how to make themselves important to those people. They have developed a servicing relation, to put it in business terms they have segmented the market and figured out how to serve it. Each organisation is going to be different: a women's human rights group is going to be different from a group dealing with rural agricultural reform. Each of them have parts of the society that care about those issues and they have got to figure out how to go and do it. It's a very simple strategy.

When we have the competition we are getting people to think. One of the first things we did in Thailand was to set up a group of successful Thai citizen organisations who have built a citizen base for themselves. For example, Crue Yoo Ee has got an amazing volunteer programme that translates into money, uses the Press all the time. He's got captive businesses, he's persuaded the leading oil company to give him gasoline stations. He works with children at risk, and some of the older kids run the stations, they hand out literature at the gas pumps. We took Crue Yoo Ee and half-a-dozen others to Chongli and a whole bunch of other cities and neighbourhoods in Bangkok. Every time you do that, light bulbs are going off. People are saying, maybe we can do that, and here are concrete ways you can do it. After maybe five or six years of a combination of the publicity, the actual practical working-through of the methodologies as each organisation struggles to segment and figure out the servicing, you have 50 or 60 organisations in Brazil, Thailand or wherever which have tasted the real power and independence of having a citizen sector. They will have figured out how to do it, and the others will copy them, especially as we will be making their successes visible.

That is a very simple strategy but it is aimed at the biggest source of money, the grassroots citizen base. It's aimed at energising the group of people who can make it happen. It's not a top-down, foundation-to-everyone-else strategy. It's the citizen organisations, the thousands and thousands of highly-motivated people whose lives are tied up in this work and want their organisations and ideas to succeed.'

Edited from a transcript of a conversion between Bill Drayton, the Ashoka Foundation founder, and Caroline Hartnell.

tion (SDC) used a debt relief arrangement to create a local endowed fund to finance environmental projects — the Foundation for Sustainable Society Philippines (FSSP). Another objective is for Southern Foundations to focus on financing what NGDOs are, ie, assist their organisational development and enhancement of capacity. Another Philippine example, supported by the Dutch funding organisation NOVIB, is a Social Investment Fund (SIF). The SIF is dedicated to financing the organisational needs of NGDOs, rather than their development projects or programmes.[40] Neither focus excludes a third option of strengthening the voluntary sector as a whole. For example, by assisting an 'apex' NGDO that represents others; by supporting NGDO networks; financing support organisations that provide services to other NGDOs, and so on. In other words, a third approach is to provide a local source of funding that extends beyond one organisation to the NGDO community and into civil society more widely.

However, we need to keep a sense of realism in terms of the significance of money deriving from professional grant makers. As we have seen in Chapter 4,

'philanthropy' constitutes only about ten per cent of non-profit income or revenue in industrialised countries. FLOs established from the development system are more likely to target their support to NGDOs that are trying to move away from foreign aid. So, in the short term, FLOs may be more significant as a domestic resource for NGDOs. But in the long term, if Northern comparative experience is anything to go by, one cannot assume that NGDOs will retain a position of privilege. Other, equally worthy, organisations will be making claims as well. In addition, we need to ask whether or not FLOs will be better able to reach out to grassroots membership organisations than their Northern counterparts. For example, only 0.2 per cent of foundation funds in the US go to grassroots groups.[41]

However, this section is not about different types of professional grant makers or their funding priorities and practices. That information is available elsewhere, much of it hidden in studies on partnership.[42] The discussion that follows is about the way that grant makers approach the issue of sustainability, specifically the sustainability of recipients' activities and of the recipient themselves.

A first question is: what theories or strategies inform civic grant makers' funding for sustainability? The short answer is that they seldom have clear or consistent theories, strategies or methods. And this is true for donors across the spectrum. For example, when interviewed, none of the major donors to BRAC could explain how they were translating into operational practice their expressed expectation that BRAC's programmes and BRAC itself should be sustainable. There were no guidelines, principles, special funds or anything similar to back up their call.[43]

In the words of David Bonbright, quoted at the beginning of this chapter, they did not have a way of dealing with the grant maker's paradox – how to invest in order to cease investing. It is worthwhile using his other insights to explore what an NGDO might face when considering sustainability with domestic grant makers.

First, sustainability is commonly treated as an add-on. Though a frequent part of the language, it is not an integral part of funders' thinking and practice. Yet, 'sustainability implies a fundamentally new way of investing in development....'[44] More importantly, this thinking must be applied at two levels. One level is citizen self-financing from micro-enterprises, elaborated in Chapter 3. The other is in terms of all the possible NGDO resource mobilisation options contained in Part II and summarised in Chapter 8. If funders don't have a handle on both dimensions of sustainability in how they provide support, then NGDOs certainly need to.

Consequently, this requires NGDOs to have thought through strategies that are integrated into the way they work. They must think beyond additions that will make good the non-sustainability of what they are doing.

The gap between donor rhetoric and practice towards NGDO sustainability reflects the psychological problem of 'letting go' described in Chapter 3. It is not easy to give up power and influence. It is not comfortable to do oneself out of a job, even though this should be a sign of success. Consequently, by way of compensation and self-defence, donors ask probing questions about sustainability for which they also have no answers. This is true for some of the most experienced funders to NGDOs.[45] The challenge for donors is to adopt a systems view of the problem by recognising that they are not dealing with one-off cases but a vital feature of the development to which they must adapt or lose credibility.

So, one NGDO strategy is to sort out ideas and discuss them openly. It is simply not good enough to say 'we will try to do our best' in some vague way. Options need to be well thought through and presented for discussion. Sustainability – in all its dimensions – should be an agenda item in any negotiation. Funders' humility and acceptance that they do not have the answers would help. It would create a precondition for joint problem solving in a complex and difficult area.

This requirement is especially important for NGDOs that do not directly work with CBOs. Typical examples are apex organisations, such as the Urban Sector Network (USN) in South Africa, established to help co-ordinate the efforts of NGDOs with common interests, or national bodies set up to represent the NGDO community, because by being one step removed from citizens, they are in a poor position to develop a civic base for their functioning. They may be able to sell services, but if they do not have a strategy to sustain the core, they are very vulnerable. In addition, apex bodies may end up competing with their members for funding. One strategy to avoid this calls for an agreed complementary division of labour and skills that are combined in funding proposals and contracts. An alternative is for the apex to charge out for services members use, which in turn they must include in their budgets.

Funds from grant makers within civil society are generally of higher quality than from the other sectors. There is seldom an issue of corporate tainting or becoming more subject to political control. Though there is old evidence to the contrary,[46] the bureaucracy of grant makers within civil society tends to be less than government, but not necessarily giving as rapid or responsive behaviour as businesses. More importantly, foundation-type finance can and often does seek to be more innovative, less tied to oversimplified outputs and impact measures, more amenable to supporting processes and more concerned about the organisation itself. An important potential in this type of resource is one of organisational learning (Chapter 9). This objective is usually less possible with other types of funding that want guaranteed, tangible outputs to show to tax payers and shareholders. Some professional grant makers also have an eye on their funding coming to an end and methods, such as 'tie-off grants', to help in transition. Their strategies may include support for investment for self-generation, but this is not so common.[47] Nevertheless, overall, gaining access to foundation type funds is usually an aspiration for many NGDOs.

However, because this type of high quality resource is in relatively short supply, NGDOs with access become privileged, which has its dangers too. By and large this type of funding reduces NGDO vulnerability to external shocks and events that are often politically driven. If the foundation's own financial management is in order, general economic downturns are buffered in terms of continuity by grants already made – neither vulnerability nor sensitivity are increased. Criticality, however, casts a potentially dark shadow. Foundation-type money cannot be easily replaced or substituted with sources of equivalent quality. On the other hand, foundation money can enhance consistency, partly because foundations are usually very careful about who they support in the first place. Once a commitment is made, there is a concern to ensure the NGDO does what it wants to do.

Autonomy is a complicated area. On the one hand, like all donors, foundations have their own agendas and programme priorities. Consequently, there is a natural tendency for applicants to tailor their own ideas and agendas accordingly. However, once allocated, there is less of a tendency to interfere. The degree of impact on compatibility is difficult to judge. Civic funding is seldom more administratively demanding than other sources and tends to reinforce rather than challenge the voluntary norms and values of staff. Overall, it tends to support rather than change existing process, structure and function.

This type of funding probably has more positive impact on agility than insight. To the extent that foundation staff provide a specialist professional technical resource during negotiation, they can fulfil an 'educational' role. But it is the relative reliability and other qualities of this source that offer room for experimentation, adaptation and adjustment, that may be positively encouraged.

Fees for Service

A third option in financial resourcing from within civil society is NGDOs charging for what they do. This is becoming commonplace, albeit not without causing some anguish. A common source of discomfort with this option relates to the issue of access and exclusion. Any charge sets a threshold that may be a barrier for the poorest that an NGDO wishes to reach. Solutions lie in both organisational strategy and overall resource profile.

In terms of strategy, NGDOs are often charging more to those who can pay, in order to underwrite or provide a free service to those who cannot. The example of PROSALUD in Chapter 6 indicates how this is being done for health services. A similar arrangement is used by May Day in Ghana. May Day uses commercial fees to private clients to cross-subsidise its rural health clinics. The categories of those permitted a reduced fee – for example pregnant women, children under five and emergency cases – can be made public.[48] This leads to the second issue, an NGDO's capacity to determine who really can and cannot pay.

In community-based interventions, participatory wealth-ranking techniques are used to help identify the poorest strata of society. Where interventions are more institutionalised, like health clinics and schools, this detailed knowledge may not be available. Though the potential for abuse is always present, local informants and leaders can be asked to assess cases that say they are unable to meet a fee.

In industrialised countries, fees are a substantial proportion of non-profit income. One reason that this occurs when commercial services are also available stems from a sort of 'trust premium'[49] – clients are attracted to pay for the service of a non-profit-making organisation because they think that they will be treated better and that there is no intention to make a profit out of their need for water or education or out of their illness, for example. Owners and staff are, it is assumed, motivated by the idea of serving others, not just making as much money as the market allows. This is a different way in which trust, an aspect of social capital, can effect NGDO income. Even poor people, if they trust the provider of the service they are getting, will be more inclined to pay at least something. So, once again, an NGDO's reputation is a feature of this resource mobilisation option.

In terms of resource profile, if it forms a substantial part of operating costs, fees for service is an option likely to increase vulnerability and sensitivity. The effects of drought, floods, crop failures and price instability can all feed rapidly through into people's disposable incomes and NGDO cash flow. The effect is made worse if the organisation has made expensive investments that create an ongoing demand for cash to do maintenance or to re-stock consumable items. It is unlikely that fees for service can be replaced by an alternative. Criticality is increased. Consistency is challenged by the problem of access by the poorest, discussed above. NGDO autonomy shifts from funders to the behaviour of the market and the alternatives it offers potential clients. Freedom to make decisions becomes conditioned by the likely response of fee-payers – if they can go elsewhere, that is. In addition, depending on the service, the NGDO may also face constraints on autonomy because it is obliged to satisfy national standards, in terms say of types of medical staff or teachers' qualifications. Finally, compatibility may only be moderately affected to the extent that new financial systems must be introduced to deal with processing fees and generating economic performance information for effective management.

A major insight gained from fee paying is the real demand for a service, as opposed to the demand expressed when something is free – market conditions and financial thresholds are sources of information about people's real needs and preferences. Where choice exists, it is an important source of feedback about organisational performance. Though not necessarily improving agility, it can also indicate if the NGDO is being agile enough. If not, the signs quickly appear in the cash-flow figures.

Chapter Summary

This chapter examines implications for an NGDO's resource profile for three potential sources of 'subsidy' for its work: from government, businesses and civil society.

A subsidy should lead to one or more of a lower threshold for people's access; greater outreach and scale of operation; improved continuity to ongoing work; or reverse influence on the funder.

Finance from government is a legitimate claim for NGDOs to make. In negotiating agreements, NGDOs can complement or collaborate with government agencies.

However, the nature of government funding is shifting from structural subsidy to competitive contracts.

Government finance often leads to imbalanced compromise not in the NGDOs favour, with a negative impact on autonomy and ways of working. It may also threaten an NGDO's comparative advantages.

Finance from business pivots on an NGDO's reputation and constituency, and to a lesser extent on its specific skills. Corporate partnership can place

NGDO reputation and public trust most at risk.

Access to funds from intermediaries owned by a number of corporations carries less risk than partnerships, but offers less in the way of reverse influence on corporate behaviour.

Access to funds from civil society creates least problems for NGDO identity and better economic and civic rooting.

Finance from individuals creates a stronger demand on NGDOs to demonstrate adequate performance in relation to fund-raising messages. It also calls for cost control and good 'marketing' in relation to the issue of overheads.

Strategies which catalyse people's self-organising potential and link to the citizen base are more likely to generate long-term sustainability.

Finance from professional grant makers in civil society has many positive features. However, the relative shortage of this type of high quality funds often creates a shadow side in terms of criticality; exacerbated because donor strategies towards

Table 7.1 *Overview of Subsidy Options and Probable Implications for Resource Profile*

Resource Feature	Government		Business		Civil society		
	Structural subsidy	Contracts	Philanthropy	Partnership	Donations[a]	Grants	Fees
Vulnerability	+	+	=	+	—	—	+
Sensitivity	+	=	=	+	+	—	+
Criticality	+	+	=	+	—	+	+
Consistency	=	—	–	–	*	*	≠
Autonomy	—	—	=	≠	*	=	•
Compatibility	=	—	≠	≠	≠	=	—

+ Increased; — Reduced; = Unchanged; – Compromised; ≠ Challenged; • Constrained; * Improved

a Citizen-based approach

sustainability are weak or non-existent.

Fees for service poses problems of access for the poorest and requires adoption of more market-oriented behaviour. Nevertheless, it helps NGDOs pay attention to real as opposed to expressed needs and provides rapid feedback on performance. Under conditions of choice, this option's success is conditioned by public trust as much as by quality of service.

Chapter 8

Strategic Choices for Sustaining Financial Resources

'The fastest way to succeed is to look as if you're playing by other people's rules, while quietly playing by your own.'[1]

One way to summarise the major messages and some of the detail described in Part II is by looking at the choices an NGDO leader or manager faces between alternative options. What priorities for resource mobilisation would make most sense? An answer depends on responses to at least two important questions, which relate to the organisation itself and to its environment.

In terms of the organisation, two factors are important. First, using frameworks from previous chapters, where does it want to position itself in relation to Figure 4.2? How much autonomy does it aspire to and what role does it want to play in society? If an NGDO has not worked this out, it is effectively casting its fate to the wind. Moreover, if the big trends set out so far are true, then the wind is blowing it towards public service provision on contract to government, with perhaps a modest amount of income from fees and the occasional grant – the lack of definite choice is, in fact, a choice to become another ladle in the global soup kitchen.[2]

Second, at what stage of development is the organisation? Resource strategies in infancy are likely to be different in maturity. Early stages lack proven experience; they probably rely more on voluntary effort and may nestle within a host institution which offers moral and material support. Later stages have resource history, record of accomplishment and credibility to build on and the dangers of complacency, inflexibility and growing bureaucracy to deal with.

Both position and stage of growth need to be set against an assessment of potential sources within the country. What national circumstances prevail? For example, how dependent is government on aid and its conditions, or on external investment and its volatile demands? What is the state of government domestic revenue and ideas behind big public policies? What is the condition of state–society relations? What is the NGDO history and public perceptions of its values and functions – is it credible? What legal conditions exist? How does civil society express itself? What is the state of social capital? Who trusts who, and who helps who and why? How big is the middle class? Is it informed by a tradition of mutual support and obligation to those less well off? Is this expressed mainly formally through intermediaries, or informally through social and family networks? What is the nature and distribution of poverty and its gender dimensions? What is the profile of for-profit enterprise – for example, locally or foreign owned – and what is its relation to politics? Is there a fair and stable political culture, which ensures regimes are legitimate?

This chapter does not explore the multiple combinations of variations in the answers to these questions. Readers can use them to create their own profiles of resource potentials. Instead, by way of a concluding summary to Part II, we will look at resource mobilisation strategies in relation to positioning and stage of development.

Resource Mobilisation and NGDO Positioning

It is highly unlikely that a single option presents itself as 'the' answer to resource mobilisation. Indeed, if one guiding principle for sustainability is resource diversification, then leaders will inevitably need to come up with complex strategies employing multiple options. The chapters making up Part II describe 14 reasonably distinct possibilities covering all resources. Each has been assessed in terms of six features of resource dependency, summarised in Tables 5.2, 6.1 and 7.1. With these tables as a guide, an NGDO should be able to sort out what combination of options would be best. However, a precondition for preparing a strategy is to be clear about what position it wants to have in society, simplified as the four quadrants in Figure 4.2.

Table 8.1 is an example of priority options for an NGDO that wants to retain reasonable autonomy, civic rootedness and credibility, and act for long-term reform in systems that create poverty and injustice, while dealing operationally with the problems these systems cause – that is to locate itself in quadrant 'A' of Figure 4.2.

The top priorities are designed to create self-generated income to cover core costs as a requirement for autonomy. This is aided by mobilisation of volunteers. Credibility is attained by rooting into society through joint ventures with CBOs. Autonomy is complemented by solely owned development enterprises providing linkages and economies of scale. Government consultancy contracts, informed by experience of working with CBOs, provide links to government and policy processes, creating opportunities to pursue a reform agenda. Private donations help establish a constituency that government and business will need to take notice of. It also reinforces NGDO legitimacy. Non-development enterprise is used to increase insight on market conditions and corporate behaviour that, in its turn, makes it a more credible and knowledgeable corporate partner. Government subsidy is applied to reduce costs and thresholds for access, complemented by fees for service. Finally, corporate philanthropy is used to interact with business and communities to help solve causes and effects of local problems.

The table is only one illustration – NGDOs differ. One choosing to be a service provider on its own terms would situate itself bottom left in Figure 4.2. To be sustainable at this position probably means concentrating on fees for service, backed up by volunteers and financial self-generation in other ways. Another wanting to do as much as it can for people who are poor, with no worries about substantial autonomy or systems reform, would actively pursue government contracts and subsidies, placing itself in the bottom right of quadrant 'C'. In addition, to protect against change of regimes and policies, it might establish a parallel enterprise offering similar services for those who can pay the full cost.

NGDOs that do not work directly at the grassroots, such as support NGDOs,

Table 8.1 *Strategic Preferences in Resource Mobilisation*

Rank	Option	Comments	Enabling condition(s)
1	Self-generation through investment	Professional (external) fund management	Endowment capital available
2	Volunteers	Avoiding political patronage ties and strict selection.	Culture of voluntarism
3	CBO members	This can be both non-financial and financial by catalysing the citizen base	Tradition and examples of civic cooperation
4	Joint ventures with CBOs	Manage spin-off and withdrawal	
5	Solely owned development enterprises	Problem of linkages and financial transparency to ensure economic viability	Legal possibilities and taxation policy
6	Professional grants	Used for innovation and learning	
7	Government consultancy contracts	Emphasis on reverse policy influence	NGDOs accorded a legitimate policy role
8	Private donations	Problems of fund-raising costs and media vulnerability (link between explicit contract and performance)	Ease of public communication
9	Non-development enterprise	Problems of managing a hybrid (opt for a legally separate entity if possible)	Legal possibilities and taxation policy
10	Corporate partnership	Emphasis on reform of corporate behaviour	Corporate citizenship or social responsibility accepted and endorsed as policy by owners/shareholders.
11	Government subsidy	Danger of being a government NGDO	Still part of government policy
12	Fees for service	Resolve problem of access by the poorest	Detailed information on poverty distribution, stratification and households
13	Corporate philanthropy	Emphasis on tangible outputs and local problem solving between business and communities	Businesses prepared to collaborate and pool finance

probably have fees for service and professional grants high on their list, while those that only wish to pursue reform, are probably tied to grants from Foundations with a hope of self-generation through investments. In addition, they would target consultancy contracts with governments and partnership with businesses as preferences.

Whatever the position chosen, quietly playing by its own rules calls for a conscious selection of appropriate resource options. However, different options are unlikely to be equally appropriate at all stages of organisational evolution. This is illustrated in the next section by BRAC's stages of resource mobilisation over the past 25 years.

Resource Mobilisation and Stages of Organisational Evolution

The exploration of financial sustainability requires attention to the stage of organisational evolution. Young organisations with unproven ideas are less likely to attract domestic financial resources, but may have more luck with volunteers and material support. If credibility comes with proven experience, attracting finance becomes easier and the organisation may have managed to save money as a source of investment. CDRA's experience suggests four phases or stages of financial growth as follows.[3]

The Voluntary Phase

In the beginning it is an impulse to human action. Whatever its origins, people get together to do something they care about. Resourcing in this stage is informal, highly personal, often 'subsidised' by a host institution or venue that provides space and communication facilities, for example. Success brings new demands and increasing pressure to become more reliable and formal, typically translated into recruiting staff. Even if only part time, the organisation crosses a resource threshold. It has an obligation to pay someone. It finds informal 'making do' no longer adequate and starts to invest in its own infrastructure.

The Programme Phase

In this phase, voluntary effort gives way to strategies that must find a way of financing the gap between what the service or activity costs and the fact that the beneficiaries cannot fully, or even partially, meet that cost. This is a financial and organisational turning point. Voluntarism gives way to professionalism. Free resources from the founders and host institution are insufficient; this means finding other sources further afield that will have their own policies and criteria against which to allocate funds. The organisation becomes more complex and financial negotiation with third parties becomes a necessary skill.

The Organisational Phase

This phase is characterised by further formalisation of systems and procedures now complemented by increasing internal differentiation of skills into specialist departments, coupled to the establishment of seniority and hierarchies. People also become more concerned about job security. Consequently, the type of finance needed must be longer-term and more reliable. This means greater attention to raising money from professional funders. The coupling of money supply into donor funding cycles brings demands for better accounting and reporting. It also brings a growing proportion of money required for overheads. Consequently, criticality is increased and with it vulnerability. By this stage, what the organisation does has probably become an established part of the landscape and a public expectation. People, including staff, cannot imagine life without it.

The Institutional Phase

Assuming that it has become a fully fledged organisation, growth in size, which is still considered to be a measure of success, brings clearer authority lines, firmer procedures and stable systems. These are needed to ensure a smooth work flow and reduce task uncertainty between staff that seldom meet from day to day. The organisation starts to stiffen up. Expectations of continuity in employment and pressure for greater financial security require more attention to long-term resource strategies. The choices made here will be critical in determining its future position. CDRA sees this moment as a fork in the road, towards either state subsidy and grants, or towards active fund-raising, that establishes itself as a core professional activity. Moreover, from an organisational development perspective:

> *'It is false to think that organisations should move as rapidly as possible through each phase, skipping as many as possible and reach the institutional phase – the ultimate level at which self-sustainability is achieved.'* [4]

In a nutshell, resource options chosen need to be both consistent with the current stage while also helping with evolution to the next.

BRAC

BRAC is at the institutional stage. Its resource strategy over the past 25 years shows the importance of a commitment to sustainability from the outset (Table 8.2).

The 1970s saw BRAC as a volunteer initiative to help in the resettlement of refugees in Sulla, in the Sylhet District of Bangladesh. Finance came from a core group of supporters. Within a short space of time, it was clear that relief work was not the answer to building a newly independent nation. Supported by foreign aid, development programmes were introduced and expanded beyond the north-east of the country. One of eight guiding principles in the original BRAC development approach was the need for sustainability, locally and of BRAC itself.[5] In recognition of the enormity of the country's problems, two other principles were recognising the importance of a market perspective and entrepreneurial spirit.[6] From the outset, staff were expected to have a business outlook.

Consequently, within the first decade commercial activities such as the Arong shop and BRAC Printers were undertaken. The 1980s saw a continuation and expansion of this type of resource mobilisation through a potato cold store and investment funds, together with a credit-based development programme. The 1990s again saw expansion of investment to generate income. However, there was a stronger development of enterprises such as the production of milk, seeds, chickens and prawns, for example, being financed through the credit programme. All these programmes are owned and run within the legal framework of BRAC as an NGDO.[7]

The resource options chosen, particularly the many types of programme-support enterprises, are one example of BRAC's development principles being applied in practice. They also reflect the

Table 8.2 *BRAC – Evolution of Resource Mobilisation*

	Sources of finance	Mobilisation initiatives
1970s	Donor finance	Initiate BRAC commercial activities • Arong shop (programme-related) • BRAC Printers (non-programme-related)
1980s	Donor finance Credit income Commercial income	Increase local commercial activities • Cold store (programme-related) • Investment funds (non-programme-related)

1990s	Self-financing rural credit programme
	Donor support
	Local financing, gifts
	Intensification and cost reduction
	Income from programme support
	  enterprises
	• milk, seeds, chickens, prawns
		Sale of BRAC development services
		Expand foreign commercial activity eg
		  Arong shops, UK
		Expand non-programme enterprise, eg
		  Internet
		Expansion of programme-related
		  commercial activity.

2000	Rural credit programme surplus used
	  for cross-financing as internal
	  programme subsidy
	Non-formal education and health
	  programmes:
	• government support/subsidy
	• cost sharing
		Non-programme income diversification
		• University
		• BRAC bank
		• BRAC US development consultancy
		• Programme support enterprises

Source: Adapted from Fowler and Young, 1998

fact that BRAC does not aim to play a significant policy role, beyond the use of research on its own programme experience, to alter specific areas of government practice. BRAC is known more as a technically competent development organisation than an activist reformer.[8]

The immediate perspective is that BRAC will not require foreign finance for its rural development programme. Complementing existing income sources, the recently authorised BRAC Bank will take over the credit programme. It will provide core income and finance for selective subsidy of other development programmes. The intention is to claim a subsidy from government for BRAC's non-formal education and health programmes, as well as to introduce cost sharing. For the rest, BRAC will be self-financing with

outreach to about one third of the national population of 120 million. To further increase income, there will be additional expansion of programme (consultancy) and non-programme (fee-paying private University) income streams

BRAC is a good example in that it shows what can be achieved in terms of complex resource mobilisation strategies and what commitment to sustainability from the outset can do for an organisation. It is a bad example to the extent that it is unrealistic for many NGDOs operating in different political and legal contexts where size is seen as threatening. Important as they are, aside from the strategies and techniqwues, it shows the significance of early clear sightedness about the organisation itself – its development agenda and its identity. Eventually, BRAC would be an

NGDO that did not rely on foreign aid. It took almost thirty years to achieve. Nevertheless, it was a consistent and enduring self-image that guided resource decisions and what flowed from them into the future.

Institutional Stability – Regeneration and the Viable Organisation

'Sustainability means continuing to answer the question "how do we ensure our relevance?"'

(Marleen Ramirez, Asia-DHRRA)

Part III concentrates on the least well developed perspective of sustainability, that of the organisation continuing as a viable entity. As we will see, it is not that there is no thinking or writing about the topic.[1] However, it has been given relatively less attention when compared with impact and resources.

The concept applied to organisational sustainability is labelled 'regeneration'. It is chosen for a number of reasons. For a start, it is consistent with the function of agility that is a theme of the book. Regeneration is one way of being agile. Further, it is an active concept. It is something that must be consciously attended to: it seldom simply happens on its own. This requires insight – the other part of the guiding theme. Finally, it captures the essence of what is required to remain viable. Organisations that do not regenerate themselves are unlikely to survive.[2] Simply put, regeneration implies feeding and reinvigorating a life force.[3]

A question that needs to be asked about regeneration is: 'regeneration for what?' Put another way, what keeps an NGDO viable in a changing context? A consistent, timeless answer from interviews, and previous chapters, is reputation, allied to public trust. What builds reputation? The answer from the CCR, and many others, is relevance and quality.[4] While the question belongs to the organisation, the judgement that finally matters belongs to society. Relevance means that the organisation is continuing to produce something of social value. Quality means that the organisaton stands out, not just by what it does but by how it does it. Quality is judged by stakeholders from their own standards and by comparison with other organisations.

Individual reputation is important for individual survival. However, it is seldom enough. NGDOs also need a positive collective character. One errant organisation can tar the rest with the brush of public mistrust. Recognition of this fact has led many to create codes of conduct for mutual improvement of quality and agreement on standards for judgement by their peers.[5] Difficult as they are to agree on, the real problem with such codes is enforcement, even when they are backed up, as in Kenya, by legal statute.[6] In some countries codes of conduct are being superseded by more formal systems of accreditation. The Philippine Council for NGO Certification is a response to a tax reform plan that would withdraw exemptions for NGDOs. The initiative is intended to convince government of the merit of a self-regulation system that ensures integrity at no cost to the government. To be certified, an NGDO would have demonstrated transparency, proper governance and professional competence. Certification gives legitimacy as an 'approved recipient'. This status should assist organisations in their corporate and public fund-raising efforts. It would also be used to support applications for tax exemptions. The broader goal of the initiative is to maintain the credibility of the sector as a whole.

Similar concerns about legitimacy and the merits and dangers of introducing formal accreditation are being expressed elsewhere.[7] The arguments for accreditation hinge on giving greater confidence to supporters and others that resources are well spent. The arguments against pivot on the danger of entrenching a system of unequal relationships. It is in the competitive interests of those already accredited to make it difficult for others to obtain this status. And there are also complicated issues about the technicalities of criteria and peer judgement. This debate is unlikely to be resolved in the near future. However, growing pressure and self-interest to improve the image of, and public trust in, the sector are likely to lead to a growth in accreditation.

However, the primary concern of Part III is regeneration of an NGDO, not the sector as such. In theory anyway, a sector made up of organisations that are renewing themselves should regenerate the sector. Interviews point to three factors that feed such regeneration: learning, adaptability and leadership development. Chapters 9, 10 and 11, deal with each in turn.

Learning is propagated and promoted as the solution for almost every organisational ill, which it is not. Some writers go so far as to equate learning with institutional sustainability itself.[8] In as far as this means insightful agility, I would have to agree with them. It appears that different authors see a similar dynamic involved in learning.[9] There is a general consistency in what is understood by NGDO learning, how it happens and why it is blocked.

It is not that NGDOs do not learn, but a common problem is forging a link to necessary change in organisational behaviour. Chapter 9 begins with a brief review of why NGDOs have learning disabilities.[10] It then proposes a set of basic learning principles explained as a 'learning spiral'. From this foundation, the rest of the chapter draws on a framework built up from a three-stage process of generating information and personal learning; gathering this into 'tested' collective knowledge and a 'constructed' organisational reality that is then translated into the wisdom needed for organisational change.[11] Team approaches are shown to be an important element in this process.

Learning must also be tested by the question, 'for what?' From the perspective of this book, the goal of a three-stage learning process is to generate the insight necessary for sustainably-oriented regeneration – change that increases agility. Five features of agility are identified and then employed, in Chapter 10, to examine how organisations are regenerating themselves. Different approaches are illustrated. A key issue is the extent to which change results in an organisation not just being different but becoming more agile, so that change is easier next time around. One answer lies in human relations and in working in teams; another lies in people feeling comfortable about addressing failure; and yet another is generating a wider 'comfort zone' and personal security when dealing with uncertainty and complexity. Trust is an essential component in achieving this organisational condition, particularly the trust between leaders and followers.

There is relatively little written about leadership of NGDOs and how leadership is reinvigorated. What is passed off as 'leadership development' often boils down to corporate managerialism with a human face. This occurs in part because of a lack of NGDO-derived evidence and knowledge. It also reflects the growing dominance of social entrepreneurship as the frame of reference (Chapter 6). Chapter 11 therefore explores various dimensions of NGDO leadership and looks at recent initiatives to help form successor generations.

Finally, as a concluding summary, Chapter 12 focuses on the nature of the 'Virtuous Spiral'. What does it look like and how does it work? How can it be made into a continuing spiral – not behaviour for a moment, but as a way of organisational life?

Chapter 9

Regeneration Through Learning

'Regeneration has to do with fine tuning excellence to new substance.' (Laurie Nathan, CCR)

Today's conventional wisdom is that future organisational survival will depend on an ability to learn and apply learning to alter behaviour.[12] This argument has been picked up and applied as a new truth and solution to dealing with growing instability, complexity and increased competition. This chapter looks at learning applied to NGDOs and sustainability. It begins with a brief review of what have been identified as common difficulties for such organisations to learn in the sense of using information and new knowledge to alter how they function. This sheds light on what they need to do to in order to become more competent at learning for regeneration.

From here, we look at what has been learned about learning in NGDOs. A common theme is that learning arises from ongoing processes of personal action and reflection that are located in an organisational learning system, not in a department or an event. Together they form a 'learning spiral' that becomes a core dimension of organisational culture. This way of looking at the topic is then applied to learning about and adapting features of sustainability described and analysed in previous chapters. A guiding framework is one of information being turned into knowledge that is then transformed into regenerative wisdom.

The concluding section identifies factors that are particularly relevant to wisdom that will make the organisation more agile and hence more sustainable.

NGDOs as Learning Organisations: Obstacles and Disabilities

NGDOs are generally not happy with their ability to learn. This conclusion can be found in numerous studies, publications and meetings dedicated to the topic.[13] Inevitably, the question posed is why such a common problem exists. The answers lie in historical, psychological and deep-lying structural conditions. They can be summarised as follows.

Historically, these organisations have emerged from and been driven by action, activism and deep belief in doing practical things with and for people. Belief is accepted as sufficient foundation for action, with knowledge generation as a plus. A direct operational orientation has put less value on, and effort into, indirect processes such as reflection and learning. They are seen as 'desirable luxuries' that will be introduced if there is time.

One important consequence is that an investment in learning is seen as part of the overhead costs, not a core element of being effective. And because overheads must be kept low (Chapter 4), learning is the easiest budget line to cut – no one will miss it anyway. So there is chronic under-investment in learning systems and processes. This stance indicates that 'development as action-learning' (Chapter 2) is not being taken seriously.

NGDOs promise much. To fund-raise they have to portray themselves as organisations that have mastered simple solutions to complex problems. This message is too seldom justified by performance, particularly in relation to sustainability (Part I).[14] Consequently, many generate false expectations and an abiding fear of media exposure. This creates a disincentive to thoroughly investigate experience and an incentive to cover up and move on. As a result, error and failure are denied rather than embraced as potential sources of learning. Together, activism and denial contribute to an organisational psychology and culture that are not learning-oriented.[15]

Denial is also allowed to survive, if not perpetuated, because of the disbursement foundation and pressure of the aid system. There is such a loose coupling between the performance of aid and the amount of money allocated to it that there is more incentive to prepare for the next allocation than to look critically and learn from the past expenditure. This generates a culture that does not make learning a central task.[16]

There are also structural barriers to learning that worsen as organisations grow, differentiate and formalise (Chapter 8). Vertical barriers can arise between disciplines and departments. Horizontal barriers can grow between management and staff. Resource insecurity, fed by project-based development, keeps staff on edge, on short contracts and focused on producing the time-bound outputs needed to get the next project grant. Typically, no one is interested in funding an NGDO to stand back to see if all its project building blocks – usually evaluated one by one – are actually adding up to be a useful, well designed wall or other structure. Despite best efforts, evaluation still operates as an instrument for control rather than learning, feeding insecurity further.

Barriers, for example in information sharing, can also arise between domestic NGDOs because of political or other alignments, especially where competitive bidding is a significant factor in resource availability.[17] In addition, divisions along North–South lines can occur because of different perspectives on issues of policy or NGDO–state relations,[18] as well as because of resource competition.

The above set of conditions is seldom found everywhere, all the time. The combination of learning disabilities varies between NGDOs and across the sector. What they point to, however, is the fact that difficulties in learning are not superficialities amenable to easy reform. Overcoming learning disabilities requires a change in mind-set as much as change in procedures or investment strategies. The problem cannot be solved by simply throwing money at it, although this would be a temporary help. The root of the solution lies in deeper organisational features. As will be seen in Chapter 11, promoting deep reform is an important task for tomorrow's leaders.

Be that as it may, at this stage we can turn to what NGDOs are doing to improve understanding and practice in organisational learning.

Learning Principles and Application

All organisations and people within them learn. It may be haphazard, it may lead to nowhere, but daily encounters with life continually generate new experience. Sometimes it is absorbed as conscious knowledge or fact. Other times it is unconscious – a tacit realisation or understanding rather than concrete data or information. Whatever the level of consciousness or awareness, most principles of organisational learning start with a simple interplay between action and reflection. The product is 'a learning' that is then applied to new action with an intention in mind – new action is planned, not random.

The Principle of a Learning Spiral

This basic learning process occurs everywhere in an organisation. The basic sequence is action, reflection, learning and planning, leading to new action. This sequence applies to individuals, to an intervention and to the organisation as a whole. It should form a spiral, not a circle that feeds back on itself.[19] Why a spiral?

Because the next reflection after action has the benefit of being able to look back and 'down' on the previous reflection and learning – the process should be cumulative, not circular. There is movement to a new level of understanding and awareness that builds on those before. Figure 9.1 illustrates the learning spiral.

The content of each lesson varies with each individual in relation to past experience and particular setting. For example, a field worker's task and setting differs from that of an accountant or a technical adviser located in the head office. Correspondingly, their learning will differ. But, as importantly, their perspectives on the learning of others will differ as well. For example, competent field workers learn the detail of the setting, its actors, its systems and their processes. They learn who is poor and why. What vulnerability is and how it is built up and expressed. What the fault lines are between groups. Their location gives detailed insight, but insight may be blinkered by personal relations. After all, the person has to live there.

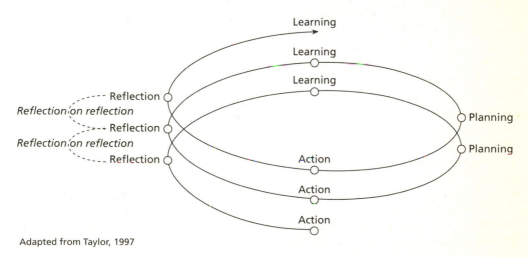

Adapted from Taylor, 1997

Figure 9.1 *The Learning Spiral*

Technical specialists tend to look with sharper eyes on issues in their field of expertise. They also are likely to have a wider comparative experience to draw on. They are positioned to look in a different way at someone else's learning. They have less detailed understanding of a particular situation, but may be less blinkered. Hence, they can apply more rigour than a field worker. So, field worker and specialist may see the same thing in different ways. A study by Noaki Suzuki shows why there is a common difference in perception between headquarters and field offices of international NGDOs.[20] The basic dynamics can be found domestically as well. Consequently, it is necessary to 'construct' the organisation's understanding not just by adding up that of individuals, but also by testing them with each other.

A challenge in creating a learning organisation, therefore, is first to bring together facts and personal learning as primary information sources, then collectively make sense of what they mean and then translate the result into greater capacity to be agile – to transform information into organisational change

Learning and its Organisational Application

Everyone in an NGDO generates and processes information. The task is to bring this together in a way that contributes to change that makes the organisation more relevant and with improved quality. A three-stage process can make this happen.

1   Gathering information. Collecting raw data in a systematic way from both inside and outside the organisation.
2   Generating relevant knowledge. Through dialogue and negotiation, generate an interpretation of information and primary learning that makes organisational sense. In other words,

create meaningful organisational knowledge, ie, construct the organisation's reality.
3   Applying organisational wisdom. Use past experience to translate knowledge into organisational implications and actions for change.

Gathering Information

By and large, NGDOs have well-developed systems for gathering factual data. Work plans, monthly financial and narrative reports and participatory surveys, for example, produce copious amounts of raw information. However, non-literate sources are difficult to deal with. Some organisations are innovating in this area by, for example, giving communities still or video cameras so that they can record and express their images of poverty, illustrate their problems and record and express their opinions.[22] However, a presentational problem is that charts and pictures mean more to those that produce them than to those who read them.

Other sources of basic data are financial and narrative reports. A frequent deficiency of such reporting is that they are primarily used to explain variance between goal and actual achievement. These documents are seldom employed to reflect on what has been learned. For this, meetings, internal workshops and periodic planning and budgeting processes are required.

There is a tendency to report on projects at the expense of reporting on the behaviour of the organisation itself, for example the state of staff motivation, inter-personal relations and conflict management. It is as if the project is an external entity that is uncoupled from the organisation's own deeper functioning.[23] Often, such insights and learning from organisational 'readings' need to be used in other ways.[24]

Another source of learning and comparative information comes through networks, attending courses and from other exposures and 'training' activities. These methods were a common response to an interview question: 'how does your organisation learn'? Which, in the light of the above, is more an answer to the question, 'how do you gather information'

Two more fundamental issues arise from gathering information about sustainability. Chapter 3 suggests that many of the indicators of relevance to sustainable impact are personal proxies. They do not lend themselves to straightforward observation and 'documenting', especially when, like spontaneous adoption, they are outside of project parameters and maybe the geographic area.

Narrative reports can capture some of these intangible aspects, if the NGDO values them and actively seeks them out. In other words, if the organisation inculcates the idea that intuition is legitimate knowledge. Put another way, active seeking depends on the extent to which an NGDO has an 'enquiring frame of mind' associated with an action-research view of development tied to systems thinking. It is less likely to be found in NGDOs tnat see the development task as one of efficient delivery.

A second issue about sustainability information is that it must show a direction of change. This requires either the use of dynamic measures – such as a rate of change in infant mortality – or comparisons with previous static measures, like gender representation on a local council measured each year. Interpreting differences means that personal learning must contain an element of systems appreciation. The required learning will not come from descriptions of how things are.

In sum, learning for sustainability makes particular demands on information gathering and interpretation. In addition to traditional data collected from and interpreted towards projects, the organisa-tion must also collect the type of predictive intuitive information described in Chapter 3. It must seek out information about the internal state of the organisation itself. This would include intangible conditions such as mutual trust, strength and spread of understanding about the organisation's mission and values and the state of staff motivation. All of these sources must then be interpreted in relation to the systems described in Chapter 1.

Generating Relevant Knowledge

How can NGDOs generate relevant knowledge from raw information and personal learning? A direct answer is through dialogue and negotiation to test and interpret what is placed on the table. In technical terms, it is through a process of collective consideration that constructs a reality that is meaningful for the organisation. There are various ways of doing so, which depend, in part, on the size and complexity of the organisation. Some methods are procedural, others, such as teams, are more structural. As described below, they can all be applied to learning and changing in relation to sustainable impact and continuity in resource mobilisation as well as to organisational change.

A positive way of looking at frequent meetings is that they are a necessary function enabling internal participation to continually construct the NGDO's reality. Each person's opinions are important to them and valuable to the organisation. The issue is, through collective encounters, to form a sufficiently shared understanding on which to base future action. As we will see in Chapter 11, meetings are one expression of a contract between leaders and followers that makes 'directive' leadership styles and imposition of one person's knowledge and learning inappropriate.

For small NGDOs, dialogue and negotiation to generate shared knowledge often happen on an ongoing, informal basis, aided perhaps by retreats. The organisation consciously creates a moment when everyone can stand back and reflect on what they have learned both internally and from external exposures. Such moments are also provided by scheduled, periodic gatherings of staff. Common examples are weekly planning and review meetings that bring together field personnel or management committees made up of senior staff. Information and communication exchange are therefore vital if the 'realities' created at different levels are to be compared and tested against each other. However, too often in bigger organisations realities are constructed as a pyramid.[25] The task for NGDOs is to create webs rather than pyramids of learning and reality testing. Moreover, to fully construct the organisation's reality and reading of itself, the webs must be both horizontal and vertical.

More extensive and intensive forms of NGDO collective dialogue and negotiation are visioning and strategic planning exercises. For big NGDOs, this may involve commissioned studies, academic inputs, comparisons with other organisations, evaluations of past performance and experience and stakeholder interviews. These activities feed into a schedule of internal encounters which compare various outputs. Strategic planning workshops are a typical way of bringing everything together to negotiate the organisation's future.

NGDOs are also adopting structural changes to help overcome learning barriers, most commonly by a team approach.

Adopting a team approach creates an ongoing process of dialogue and negotiation to challenge and combine personal information and learning. It brings to bear multiple perspectives and tests of personal learning to produce shared knowledge. It is purposefully intended to break down disciplinary barriers, not just between development professionals but also towards staff providing supporting services. They can be found in accounting, logistics and human resources units – 'those that stay at the office'.[26] For example, ISODEC have formed eight 'matrix teams' that cut across all organisational units. Teams deal with advocacy, fundraising, networking, gender and other themes which are important enough to be recognised and formalised. Each team has a focal point selected because of its specific interest and expertise

An additional feature of teamwork is that it can more easily take a client's situation as the starting point for learning rather than the specialist discipline of a single staff member. This supports the integrated approach to sustainable impact described in Chapters 2 and 3.

Budgets can also be used to steer organisational learning. For example, simply allocating staff of different departments to teams is unlikely to achieve a more comprehensive way of sharing information and learning from it unless resources are allocated to enable their regular interaction. Team functioning can be greatly improved if budgets are adjusted accordingly.

Teams are, in the words of Dinky Sullivan, social places to build, reinvigorate and nurture 'the individual and collective soul': they are a way of generating collective learning, but also a way of caring for each other's vision. Resonance between the soul of the organisation and that of the individual is an important part of their motivation (Chapter 11). A 'soulless' organisation is more likely to be fragile than agile: it does not inspire, but simply employs.

Teams can transcend organisational boundaries. Often as a part of inter-NGDO and wider alliances, teams are constructed around a specific advocacy issue. The team remains until the task is completed. NGDOs implementing COCOBREAD use teams made up of relevant staff from participating organisations that have different contributions to make.

Team testing, sharing and collective knowledge creation applies to resource mobilisation as well as for sustaining impact and organisational change. For example, it is particularly important when an NGDO chooses to become a hybrid organisation combining for-profit and non-profit activities described in Chapter 6. Somehow or other, the lessons learned from both types of activity must come together in ways that help manage the inevitable tensions between them and maintain a common understanding. This can occur in teams at management as well as at lower levels. For example, CEDEP in Ghana has invested in a farm for income self-generation, demonstration and outreach through its field programmes. A management team is responsible for making this difficult combination work well in terms of its multiple goals. The complex knowledge generated by the group comes from their respective areas of learning. It is within the team that trade-offs are made between the costs and benefits of different options to enhance reputation and sustainability.

The success of a learning process described above cannot simply be assessed in terms of generating ideas, collective knowledge and decisions about what has to change. It must also ensure that conclusions are actively shared and supported, not just tolerated. Achieving this quality of organisational learning depends on the way that power difference is handled; the way that dissent is dealt with and how participation is structured and takes place.

Typically in NGDOs, power difference is handled through inclusive consultation (ie even more meetings!). The value of the outcomes depends on the leadership style and, ultimately, in the trust that a leader enjoys. When consultation is perceived as a ritual and trust is weak, the knowledge generated is less likely to establish a foundation for action to change the way the organisation works.

Realistically, some types of change – reducing staff for example – are hardly ever likely to gain agreement of those affected. This fact leads to a general issue of how dissent is expressed and dealt with. To a large extent, this is a function of the culture of the organisation and of the society in which it is embedded. The watch-word in dealing with dissent is 'respect'. Dissenting views can be positively dealt with by showing that the changes introduced actually work as intended. For example, in the 1970s, BRAC faced dissent from some staff about the creation of a programme-related investment in potato cold stores. They felt that this commercialisation would erode its soul: some staff left; others remained. The test posed by dissent was one of BRAC remaining loyal to principles (Chapter 8). While evaluation suggests that BRAC is achieving much but not all it aspires to, adopting different methods does not mean that it has lost its way or principles.[27]

Disagreement about resource mobilisation strategies is not uncommon amongst NGDOs as they deal with a changing context described in Chapter 4. A common issue is whether or not the organisation is losing its soul. Treating dissent as a test to be successfully completed is one way of showing respect to such concerns.

The value of collective knowledge depends on the process and quality of participation. For many organisations planning, reporting and budgeting cycles and systems are the track along which internal participation is timed and structured. While this method is useful and stabilising in its regularity, it is not enough. Why? First, because it is insufficiently able to draw out the tacit as well as the factual sides of learning. It does not necessarily tap into people's hearts as well as their minds. Second, it is insufficiently nurturing and caring. Put another way, it does not adequately create deeper human conditions required for the next stage, creating the shared wisdom to change and regenerate.

Finally, all of the above can be looked at in another way suggested by one theme of the book. If all has gone well, the (spiralling) product of the various ways of generating collective knowledge and an updated appreciation of organisational reality is renewed, tested insight. In other words, when it is 'captured' into collective knowledge, a continuous flow of information creates a new 'reading' about the organisation, about the world it is living in and what new 'substance' will give it excellence.

The next step is to move from this stage of reflection to the wisdom of planning for the implementation of organisational change.

Creating Organisational Wisdom

To choose how learning can best be translated into new organisational behaviour, collective knowledge must be married to past experience. Unfortunately, past approaches to change may not be an adequate guide. A reason for this is that the depth and rate of change in the world makes stronger demands on depth and speed of change in the organisation. Old, proven, incremental methods may not be appropriate any more. The spate of major restructuring exercises observed across the NGDO community, particularly those originating in the North, suggests that this fact has found its way into their consciousness.[28]

Change can be planned and introduced to make any number of improvements that enhance relevance and quality. However, previous pages have stressed that, from a sustainability perspective, the most important changes are those that lead to greater agility.[29] This section looks in more detail at what this means as a lead into the next chapter on how NGDOs regenerate themselves.

Wisdom is about applying knowledge into change – it means deciding how to move an organisation from its present operating state to a new state, that combines being more agile with an enhanced reputation. Improved agility means greater capacity to respond to change with greater speed and adaptiveness.

The starting point is an assessment of the present operating state which involves a 'reading' of five factors: power distribution, resource profile, culture, learning process and relationships.

Power distribution concerns the degree to which staff at different levels and locations can take initiatives and reach decisions themselves consistent with stated values and goals. (Typically, power distribution is framed in terms of centralisation versus decentralisation.)[30] Continual referrals up and own a decision-making chain reduce speed and introduce stiffness rather than flexibility. So, how many links or steps have to be made to get a decision taken? How many layers have to be involved for what topics? What range of discretion do different types of staff have? Is this narrow or broad? How long does decision making take and why?

The six factors in Part II show the relationship between resource profile and agility. Generally speaking, resource diversification coupled to a reasonable level of self-generated income should enhance responsiveness to change. It can speed and expand freedom of choice as well as the resilience to catch up after learning from mistakes, rather than being slowed down by them. The question then, is how far does the resource profile enable agility, and in which direction on Figure 4.2?

There is a strong relationship between culture and agility. The problem is that the concept is difficult to grasp. Moreover, culture is often used as a term for anything that is intangible or cannot be placed somewhere else, like a skill, a system, a plan or a mission statement. NGDO culture is dealt with in a general way in *Striking a Balance*.[31] For our purposes, the task is to home in on the dimensions of culture that affect agility. One that often appears is trust between leaders and followers that decisions are made fairly for the good of the organisation rather than because of 'untested' personal prejudice or for personal benefit. If trust is mutual and strong, decisions are not continuously questioned. Simply put, are leaders and the leadership trusted and do they trust the staff? Is the atmosphere one of them and us? Is there a feeling of being a family? A leadership that does not live the values it articulates, for example the respect of others, is one that breeds distrust in itself.

Another cultural dimension is a 'spirit of enquiry' that pervades the NGDO.[32] Is it a curious, enquiring organisation? Are new initiatives and experiments welcomed or killed at birth? If culture is based on worship of abiding truths that cannot be re-examined – we have always done things this way – preconditions for agility are less likely to be in place. This cultural dimension is one of attitude that starts at the top.

Finally, culture sets the norms and conventions through which dissent and dissonant information are used constructively. For example, are seeds of resistance sown by belittling or disregarding dissent? Recycling old, unresolved disagreements expressed in new ways is hardly like to increase flexibility or trust.

The learning process, discussed above, determines how new – potentially discomforting – ideas or learning are picked up, collectively tested and then moved into organisational consciousness or discarded.

How quickly does this happen? How are good ideas recognised and accelerated? An example is dealing with an external observation that many NGDO credit programmes benefit the organisation more than the borrowers. How does a credit organisation respond to such a charge – shrug and say it is not us, or quickly embark on serious soul searching?

Fifthly, NGDOs are not islands – they are part of a web that they have constructed. This creates expectations, relational ties and commitments that bind. For example, expenditures may be committed far into the future. The NGDO is 'mortgaged' with less room to manoeuvre and adapt. However, past transactions can also create levels of 'relational capital' that can help with release and movement. For example, joint ventures with CBOs are strong ties. But, if the NGDO has built up sufficient trust, it is more likely to be able to persuade the CBO to alter its way of working or the existing relationship without its motives being deeply questioned, So how much relational capital does the NGDO enjoy? Do, for example, communities suspect its attempts at agility to be a cloak to hide rejection and breaking of agreements, or do they assume that what is intended has their interests truly at heart, a way of serving them better?

A different aspect of the relational web is that of conditions set by law. For example, how easy is it to change staff, or to stop one activity or start another without violating registration requirements? In short, the relational web reminds us that NGDOs are not free agents where agility can be applied in any direction of their choosing. How tight is the web of existing commitments, expectations and legal constraints?

A third, crucial aspect of the relational web is where an NGDO's reputation is to be found, strengthened or eroded. It is through relational transactions that an

NGDO is understood and appreciated. The transactions can be intimate and direct, for example, with CBOs, governments and donors. They can be more impersonal and indirect through publications, advertising, media commentary and peer behaviour that catches the public eye, for example. The combination shapes the NGDO's reputation and room to manoeuvre.

To these factors could be added agility issues such as the relation between internal procedures and organisational stiffness or flexibility; the tightness or looseness of structures; or the contract arrangements that guarantee job security. But, these and other components affecting agility are derived choices. They reflect the more fundamental factors listed above that determine, first, what an NGDO wants to be. Then come items like systems and structures that translate being into doing. If an NGDO does not want to be agile, it will not make appropriate resource choices. It will not develop a responsive culture, or

delegate power within its systems and structures.

A number of assessment tools capture elements of these five factors. One example, dedicated to an NGDO's learning ability, has been prepared by Bruce Britton;[33] another by Lisa Cannon is a practical guide focusing directly on NGDO sustainability. It contains a set of questions that enable an organisation to read the condition of its sustainability.[34] However, the focus is not specifically on learning for agility. Whatever the tool or method, the task is to ask the right question about each of the five factors described above.

Let us assume that NGDOs have used some form of learning process and now have the insights required to improve their adaptability. How then, do they go about reorganising and regenerating themselves to be more agile, and hence sustainable? With the help of the five factors described above, the next chapter looks at examples to answer this question.

Chapter Summary

This chapter establishes a number of links between an NGDO's and its own sustainability.

Organisational sustainability depends on reputation, which in turn depends on producing social value in terms of relevance and quality. Stakeholders, not the NGDO, make ultimate judgement of these achievements.

The credibility of the NGDO community can weaken or enhance an organisation's reputation. Accreditation is one response to this fact.

Sustainability in unstable environments requires an ongoing regeneration of an NGDO's 'life force', through learning, adaptation and leadership.

The task of learning is to create insight about the environment and the state of the NGDO itself.

Learning occurs in everyone throughout the organisation. It does not happen in one place or department. To be a learning organisation calls for a 'spiralling process' of action, reflection, learning, planning and new action that can be applied to an individual, to an intervention and to the organisation as a whole. The spiral is achieved by consciously learning from previous reflection at a new vantage point of additional experience

Basic information and personal experience have to eventually translate into regeneration. This can be achieved through a three-stage process of generating information and personal learning; gathering and testing to form collective knowledge and a 'constructed' organisational reality that is translated into the wisdom needed for organisational change.

The success of this process is determined by the way power difference is handled; the way that dissent is dealt with and how participation is structured and takes place.

Team-based ways of working and information webs are important for the collection, testing and generation of knowledge.

Sustainability requires knowledge to be translated into changes that increase organisational adaptability. This corresponds to bringing about agility-enhancement in one or more of the following five areas:

- Power distribution.
- Resource profile.
- Culture.
- Learning process.
- The relational web.

Chapter 10

Regeneration through Organisational Change

'Are we still innovating ourselves?' (Maria-Christina Garcia, CINDE)

Organisational change is where learning and insight should have their effects. Much is written about the practice of introducing change into NGDOs, often under the heading of 'capacity building'.[1] Sustainability is a common intention of altering the way an NGDO functions. This chapter makes such a goal more explicit by using the five agility factors identified at the end of Chapter 9 as lenses through which to look at practical examples.

An introductory summary about organisational development helps set the scene. The first section reviews current understanding about initiating organisational change. Important features include understanding the 'trigger' for change as well as assessing the conditions already in place. These activities help estimate the likely depth of change in relation to method, motivation and resistance. From here, the review discusses three guiding principles for change and ways of managing the process.

Section Two contains descriptions and analyses of how NGDOs go about regenerating themselves. They vary by history, size, age, the social value they generate, their contexts and other variables. They are illustrations, not models, of approaches to change. What they have in common is a desire to be more relevant and sustainable after the change, with an enhanced reputation built on relevance and quality.

All types of change are likely to involve adaptation by existing partners. As we have seen in Chapter 3, this may create problems for partners that are used to the organisation before any change in its behaviour. Recognition is needed that organisational change is a relational as well as an internal affair.

The concluding section uses material from cases and other sources to specify what constitutes agility-enhancing change in each of the five factors identified in Chapter 9 – a set of recommendations with greater organisational viability as their goal.

Organisational Development

How does an NGDO know what should be changed in order to be more sustainable? The answer from previous chapters is that it is thinking and acting strategically.[2] This ideal starting situation, however, cannot be assumed for all organisations. Trapped in complacency, some are simply caught out by events: they have not anticipated; they have not invested in insight; they have not been curious enough. Whatever the case, regeneration needs to be based on an awareness of initial conditions.

Knowing Where you are and Why Change is Necessary

An important starting point for regeneration is understanding the impulse or 'trigger' for change. For example, is it poor performance, internal discord, death of the ideal, a funding crisis, new ideas, building on success, new leadership or recommendations from strategic review or assessment? Triggers are not always traceable to a particular moment or event. Often, they arise from a growing appreciation that all is not well, leading to a capacity assessment for which a number of NGDO-related tools exist.[3] Although they do not use the concept of 'agility' in their design, they offer a structure and process for understanding the operating state.

Most capacity assessment tools are somewhat mechanical, relying on an 'inside-out' perspective. They assume a logical set of organisational components which should be checked to see if they exist in sufficient quantity and quality. More sophisticated tools take the organisation's complexity or stage of development (Chapter 8) into account.

An alternative approach is an 'outside-in' approach where important stakeholders set standards of performance that are then used as capacity measures and criteria. From their assessment, internal features of the organisation's functioning can be identified. Here, the client leads.[4] Given the importance of reputation for sustainability, the latter approach is to be preferred. Regular socials audits, explained in Chapter 3, are one way of gaining stakeholder assessments.[5]

Triggers and assessments should give an idea of the 'depth of change' and processes required. Depth means the extent to which change gets to the organisational core of mission and culture.[6] The deeper the change, the greater the time needed and degree of difficulty involved. Changing knowledge and skill is easier and quicker than changing organisational behaviour or values. Kelleher and McLaren make a distinction between first- and second-order change. First-order change occurs within the organisation's existing framework of self-understanding – its 'paradigm'. Second-order change alters the framework itself, for example core principles and interpretation, if not the definition of role or mission.[7] The former may be a localised, incremental alteration affecting a few. The latter affects everyone and almost everything.

Looked at another way, change can occur along a continuum from local internal innovation to organisation-wide transformation. Any change along the spectrum can work for or against increased agility. For example, a team-building exercise in a unit or department can loosen-up routines, reduce segmentation of work and get people to trust the judgement of colleagues more than before. Introducing more flexible working hours can improve motivation and people's willingness not to 'watch the clock' but adjust their tempo in response to fluctuations in demand. Moving from a resource centre full of poorly accessible books and papers to a management system using electronic communications can have widespread impact in terms of increasing organisational speed. Conversely, adding signatures to authorisation forms for purchases, travel or other expenditures, slows procedures, but the effect of this must be set against the lesser chance of malfeasance.

Changes at the transformational end of the spectrum – for example, a shift of role from service provider to facilitator – can be expected to raise more questions and deeper misgivings than adjustments to procedure. Queries and demands for stronger levels of justification are to be anticipated, not just from staff but also from clients, local government and governing bodies. The latter are particularly important if they believe that one of their functions is to protect the organisation's integrity and soul and to continue to work in the image of the founder. Recent change to the constitution of the African Medical and Research Foundation (AMREF) – intended to make governance more local, to change board tenure from open-ended to fixed-term and to make the flying doctor service more economically viable – occurred because it was endorsed by the Founder's widow. If she had acted to defend her husband's memory, rather than arguing that he would want AMREF to adapt to the future, board approval of their own regeneration was far from certain.[8]

Appreciation of the 'trigger' and the likely depth of change that learning calls for is important for at least two reasons. First, it is necessary in order to select and design the change process, discussed below. Second, its gives an idea of likely commitment to change. Human resistance to losing anything is normal. This applies not just to possessions but also to that which is familiar, such as tried and trusted ways of doing things. Resistance is a natural reaction to threat of loss; particularly in extreme situations where regeneration will cost employment. Though awkward, resistance is not a human aberration, but is a response to be expected and constructively managed.

In sum, it is important that those designated to introduce change understand the preconditions. These are:

- What is the spread and level of forces for and against change?
- The level of overall commitment to seeing change through. Is there conviction amongst leaders and governors that change is necessary?
- An anticipation of how deep change has to go which creates different degrees of threat. Is there consensus about where change must lead and that negative consequences are legitimate?
- The stance of external stakeholders. How will what is proposed affect them and the organisation's reputation? Will outsiders aid or hinder change?

From this appreciation change must be introduced and managed.

Making Change Happen

One sign of turbulent times is the mushrooming of books about managing change, aided and abetted by management fashions propagated by consultants. Analysis of publications shows that there is approximately one new management fashion per year.[9] Leaders and managers of NGDOs are at the point of having to manage the fashions of management in order to decide what regeneration process is appropriate for their circumstances. With this forewarning in mind, conventional studies suggest some basic principles are needed to introduce, manage and consolidate change.[10]

Principles

One of the most important regenerative principles is to lead the process from a positive appreciation of achievement, not from a negative approach of solving problems.[11] Establishing a desirable, shared vision or image of the future organisation, or part of it, serves many functions. One is to give security that change is actually directed somewhere: it instils confidence that trauma or discomfort will end up in something 'tangible'. This has motivational and communication benefits – valuable ends will justify painful means when there is something clear to communicate about.

The sustainability perspective adopted throughout this book complicates the common idea of a vision as a fixed, stable distant endpoint. If agility is the key to sustainability, the vision becomes one of an organisation comfortable with and effective at continuous, insightful change. An agile organisation lives its vision everyday. The appropriate image would be one of an organism that remains true to itself and its mission while thriving on whatever the environmental change has to offer. In this scenario, instead of re-visioning and renewing strategies, the organisation is continually adjusting its milestone, the benchmarks provided by comparison with others and its own measures of insight and agility.

A second principle is to shift the organisation's attitude from complacency to one of urgency. Urgency will arise if leadership is prescient, has correctly read what future viability means and is able to instil a prevailing sense of necessity and that the status quo is not an option.

The third principle is to empower staff to help to create the future and not simply follow instructions on how to get there. Directed change can of course occur: it is usually much quicker. However, the roots of support will be shallower, change will be fragile and consolidation will often take longer. The participation framework and criteria set out in Chapter 2 are one way of looking at how staff can be empowered. The issue for change-oriented leaders is whether they can put the genie back in the bottle once regeneration has occurred. Unless greater staff empowerment is part of the future vision, simply using it as a means of staff support for change may backfire later. To disempower after empowering invites lack of motivation and loss of trust: conditions that work against agility.

Managing Change

There are various ways of introducing and managing change. In terms of process, NGDOs can typically choose to:

- implement by directive at any place, layer, system or group;
- trickle change down from the top through the different layers of authority;
- approach change by working with or through all those who must effect and will be affected by the change;
- adopt a comprehensive, coordinated approach.

In addition to the specific content of change – a skill, a procedure, a policy, the infrastructure, authority levels and budget allocations, for example – the process will also depend on factors of depth and cost.

An organisational development intervention is typically considered to go through three stages: initiation or start-up; transition to a new operating state; and integration and consolidation where what is 'new' is simply seen to be 'normal' – it becomes culturally embedded as 'the way we do things around here'. However, from an agility point of view, what is 'normal' becomes less static. Conceptually, 'normal' will mean 'always different, but directed towards sustainability through a reputation of relevance and quality'.

Management, accountability and oversight of regeneration can be allocated to:

- a leader or leadership team, which may include governors;
- a multi-functional team representing those most concerned;
- a manager with authority to see change through and then retire when the task is done.

The choice depends on many factors, including, for example, the profile of likely resistance; coherence in management conviction; the speed required; and the opportunity costs of management and staff time. For example, where senior management or the leader are not convinced, but have to be seen to be doing something, they are likely to set up and later ignore a multi-functional team of lower-level staff. Because the leadership has kept its distance, it can always later pick and choose what it wants to support. Where speed is needed, for example when the 'trigger' is a crisis, the power of a leadership team is often the likely way forward. When consensus is vital for movement, a multi-functional team may be the way ahead, but with management included.

Whatever the combination of 'trigger', depth, preconditions, process and management, our concern is with the sustainability dimensions of regeneration. A reasonable working assumption is that organisations always want to increase their viability and enhance their agility. The following examples highlight the various ways it is done.

Regeneration in Practice

Case examples and other information gathered through this study suggest that there are five or six reasonably distinct ways that NGDOs reinvent themselves. They are distinct to the extent that there is a dominant regenerative feature, not that they exclude other dimensions of change. They are termed: continuous improvement and tinkering; reflective evolution; process reform; role change; structural reform; and transformation. In very broad terms, they reflect different depths of change described above. As will be seen, there is no particular relationship between the five areas of agility enhancement and an approach to regeneration. Different types of change can affect any or all of them.

Continuous Improvement and Tinkering

Unless they are totally rigid, NGDOs always adjust in minor ways as a response to experience. The question is whether continuous improvement becomes a creed that is actively and consciously lived.[12]

Established in 1968, the Centre for Conflict Resolution gained a sound reputation for its work within and beyond South Africa. However, with success came expansion and problems of quality. Staff competent in conflict resolution became managers as well, but without being necessarily skilled for a such a role. These combined functions and high work loads led to sloppiness – for example, late arrivals for meeting clients, late reports and invoicing and lack of attention to detail – and reputation started to suffer. Consequently, a range of changes was introduced aimed at re-establishing and retaining a reputation for excellence.

In addition to employing a finance manager and updating internal systems, a staff reorientation took place that made the client's appraisal of a CCR consultant's work central to the notion of quality. Now, client appraisal of the service provided is a standard practice from which personal and organisational adjustments are regularly made. This is backed up by a staff development programme that provides for annual upgrading.

For many NGDOs, the usual source of information from which adjustments are made is the project monitoring system. It is an overt source of the tiny spirals of learning and action that modify practice – 'fine adjustments to the substance of excellence'. It is where reputations for sensitivity, and ability to listen and respond, are made or broken. The issue about using this source is whether or not the organisation's curiosity takes it beyond monitoring to questioning what is happening within the underlying system.

Continuous improvement is not simply a technique but a way of thinking: a stance; an aspect of culture.

Reflective Evolution

Regeneration can be an evolutionary product of reflection as a way of being – here the 'trigger' is not a crisis, or product of a periodic strategic review or other learning instrument.

In South Africa CDRA was established in the mid-1980s to provide organisational development services to CBOs and other NGDOs.[13] As explained in Chapter 6, from the outset, when this type of approach was not particularly fashionable, CRDA saw systematic reflection to improve development practice as one of its main functions. Today, CRDA is known throughout and increasingly beyond southern Africa for its contribution to thinking and practice in what is generally known as capacity building. For CDRA, periodic introspection and reflection is part and parcel of what it is, not just what it does developmentally.

In addition to learning from reflection, to help chart a course for the future CDRA undertook a leadership evaluation. This highlighted the need for internal reform to match its internal and external readings. Consequently, a number of courses of action were agreed.

1   The financial system was improved and reoriented away from accounting for grants to costing and managing the services provided to clients.
2   An investment was made in a building both as an asset and to reduce future recurrent costs.
3   A proportion of fee income would be placed in an investment fund. It will eventually provide the income needed to sustain the reflection component, which is very difficult to finance from other sources. Though self-financing is

being enhanced, fees for services is regarded as a way of keeping the organisation in tune with the context – one way of preventing complacency.

4   Through its annual reports and greater attention to publication and dissemination, CDRA is actively widening and sharpening its identity as a 'brand'.
5   More systematic attention would be given to the concept of development practice.
6   To complement client-responsive tasks, CDRA is working more strategically by building a cadre of professional organisational development practitioners for NGDOs.
7   A new leadership form is being introduced that will eventually function as an interaction between three spheres. One focuses on strategic development and evaluation; another on the development of practice and core methodology, including institutional learning; while the third is responsible for organisational management and administration. The explicit intention is to reduce hierarchy and spread leadership throughout the organisation. There will be no management team, but a 'holding group' as '… the beating heart of a living organism, a sense organ that can assess and regulate the flow of organisational processes'.[14]

Spurred on by the review, these changes are to some extent a more formalised recognition of what had been happening intuitively. They have emerged organically. The core of regeneration is thoughtful evolution. In other words, if an NGDO is already in a reflective learning mode, it is less likely to need the impulse of periodic strategic planning events or crisis to prompt regeneration. Regeneration is more likely to be proactive and prescient than reactive.

Process Reform

One form of regeneration is to alter how an NGDO goes about what it does – its core practice – without necessarily altering its role or position. An example of this type of regeneration is the Triple Trust Organisation based in Cape Town.[15] Established in 1988, TTO's objective is to provide opportunities for the poorest to become financially self-reliant through self-employment. Winner of the Ithemba Award for 'givers of hope' in 1997, TTO can be considered a 'blue chip' NGDO. TTO's 'trigger' to regeneration was an increasing sense of vulnerability at being over 90 per cent dependent on donors for its finance. The end of the Mandela era, coupled to donor fatigue, withdrawal and redirection of funds from NGDOs to the government, brought the prospect of unsustainability sharply to the fore. What TTO was doing in terms of its social value was not the problem: its public profile and reputation were well established. Nevertheless, while reputation helps, it is no guarantee of support when the profile of NGDO funding in a country radically alters. Regeneration therefore had a strong element of financial reorientation and income diversification, tied to a fundamental reform of TTO's way of working, but not of its role or development contribution. The TTO response has involved:

1   The establishment of an Institute for Development Services as a separate company selling professional services in its area of expertise. For example, this acts as a consultant to others and implements the VENTURES programme for entrepreneurship development in schools. In addition, TTO's invention – a board game called BEST – was given to the Institute for marketing and sale.[16] TTO also runs entrepreneurship training for prison inmates. The Institute's memorandum and arti-

cle of association specify that any surplus must be distributed to TTO.

2   TTO is attempting to move from external donors to the government, stressing its self-acknowledged responsibility for employment generation and contribution to this amongst the poor.

3   TTO is also investing in potentially lucrative businesses, such as low-cost housing. It has a 15 per cent stake of a parent company that owns a building firm and gains income from a training levy.

4   An equally important cost-reducing shift is from retailing to wholesaling as the basis of its work and outreach. Before 1998, TTO employed trainers to run courses. This has now changed to a community-based approach where TTO staff live in a village for a month and act as trainers for trainers. They select individuals with sufficient aptitude who are then paid for the training courses they undertake. This move has sharply reduced the costs of outreach, but also the number of staff TTO need. Rather than redundancy, TTO is opening up in a new province to create continuity in staff employment.

Item 4 above is the crux of this type of regeneration. TTO's goal and type of impact has not changed. What has been radically altered is its internal process – from retail to wholesale. This shift cuts costs while permitting faster and wider outreach. The other changes described above spread income and hence risk. Initiatives for self-generation of income give greater control and reduced vulnerability.

Formally, TTO operates on a five-year strategic plan that rolls over yearly. The yearly budget process 'weaves up and down' the organisation, but the related dialogue often shows up weaknesses which lead to revisions. Consequently, there is an ongoing tinkering with structure and systems that is both highly adaptive but also potentially destabilising. One cannot rely on today's organisation chart to reflect today's situation. Continual adjustment is tied to a leadership style that seeks innovation and renewal. The 'shock' of vulnerability gave a new reason to tinker some more, but with a clearer purpose – to ensure viability.

Finally, TTO's national reputation allows it to promote and lobby for big ideas. For example it is proposing to run a micro-credit programme through post offices, almost all of which are computerised. This may prove more appropriate than labour-intensive methods devised in countries, like Bangladesh, which have far higher population densities. TTO is determined to 'tinker' externally in the big picture, as well as internally.

Role Change

NGDOs can regenerate by altering the role they play. There can be various reasons for this. It can be a response to growth and diversification within a sector, which creates new needs, niches and scales of operation. It can be a product of success and reputation that creates both its own demand and stresses that are best solved by a role change.

One example of a three-stage role shift can be seen in the evolution of the Village Development Resource Centre located in Gaidakot in the Nawalparasi District of Nepal.[17] VDRC started life some 15 years ago as a community-based self-help organisation. The group used money contributed by members for village projects that were predominantly welfare in nature. Over eight years, an informal arrangement evolved into a system for implementing community development projects. To play this role it was better to be formally registered as an NGDO. In this position, VDRC then started to act as an intermediary between national and international NGDOs and local communities. Typically, this involved design and implementation of basic projects in health, water and credit. Over a five-year period, support for human resource development and organisational infrastructure created professionalism and a good reputation.

From this foundation, VDRC adopted a strategy that would move it from a role as intermediary to one of a support organisation for others – the second shift in role. VDRC's leadership saw that political reform of the early 1990s opened space for civic organisations, many of which were attempting to be NGDOs but did not know how.[18] There was both need and opportunity for an experienced organisation to assist others. By mid-1999, VDRC was working in a support role with 40 local organisations and 66 cooperatives. However, sensing that the donor bubble would burst, it also took steps to be more financially self-reliant. In terms of resource mobilisation VDRC:

- has leased 4.2 hectares of land as a sisal plantation to generate income;
- is gradually constructing a development resource centre whose facilities and services can be hired by other organisations;
- is selling consultancy services; and
- with the original members of the self-help group, as a separate organisation, has created a savings and credit cooperative that now has 2100 clients. In time, the cooperative may be converted into a savings bank.

VDRC attributes its ability to change its role and to the maintenance of a positive local image to committed, innovative leadership; attention to strategic thinking and planning; financial discipline; a philosophy with its roots in community self-mobilisation and ownership; and attention to ongoing investment in human resources.

Another type of role regeneration is exhibited by the Society for Participatory Research in Asia, in India. Founded in 1982, PRIA's original agenda was two-fold: promoting and doing participatory research and capacity building at the grassroots.[19] Both were seen to be sound expressions of a philosophy of empowerment. Based, in part, on results of participatory research, the late 1980s saw a shift to embrace more development themes. Currently, PRIA has five themes, each of which is designated a centre within the organisation.[20] The early 1990s, saw a conscious strategic shift from direct development action to the adoption of a supportive role for an emerging set of other sub-national organisations. In addition, PRIA started to pay more attention to requests and opportunities within and beyond the South Asia region. A new entity, PRIA International, was established to provide a platform for wider outreach.

These role shifts required a reorientation of grassroots groups away from PRIA to a set of intermediaries that were themselves in an early state of evolution. This has led to the charge that PRIA detached itself before a reasonable alternative was in place. It poses a question of whether PRIA can stay rooted in India if it is semi-detached from the base and work that gave it domestic legitimacy and credibility in the first place. Will it be able to reach out without replenishing its local relational capital and standing?

'In general, a powerful perception that came across from many inter-actions was that the role PRIA played during the eighties was sterling and very highly valued, that this role was not being played, or at least played as well; that there seemed no compelling reasons for PRIA to withdraw; and overall, that PRIA might have thrown away

a bird in its "local" hand in chasing two in the "global" bush'...[21]

PRIA, largely through the person of its executive director, has consciously helped create an international civic agenda and sought to alter the links between and beyond international development institutions. There has been a dedicated expansion in terms of geographic view and choice of role from local, through national and regional to global. Though not without its challenges, PRIA's progression is one of regeneration. The recent evaluation from which the above quotation is drawn is one sign of an action-learning stance in relation to the organisation itself and openness to ideas and perceptions of a range of PRIA's stakeholders.

Role shifts can also occur by stealth. They lead to organisational change that may not regenerate but, with hindsight, degenerate. This perspective characterises regeneration by Centro Internacional y Education y Desarrollo in Colombia. Started in the late 1970s, CINDE's mission was to test and demonstrate innovations in child education and health to improve the living situation and life opportunities of Colombia's most disadvantaged groups. CINDE elected to work with the black population in Choco, one of the most marginalised and isolated states. The approach adopted was first to work with parents and households, increasing their abilities to look after their children. From household improvement, parents naturally turned to communal problems, such as mosquito breeding grounds and malaria. By the mid-1970s CINDE had a proven approach to promoting child-centred health, education and environmental improvement. It was working with 800 families organised into PROMESA ('hope') groups.

In collaboration with and funding from an international NGDO, CINDE expanded its work within the state and the city, and its role expanded into 'doing and delivering projects' directly with communities, to providing consultancy services linking community and local government. These included programmes for better health, education and living conditions; running post-graduate programmes; and working on local leaders who could act as promoters and multipliers. A further role shift occurred when CINDE helped establish a local NGDO in the region to take over its work and localise its efforts. CINDE is able to concentrate on systematic learning from experience, results of which are incorporated into its postgraduate and programmes as well as applied in the development of children's learning material, such as educational toys. One important factor prompting the more recent shift has been an internal assessment that, because of its reputation, CINDE was taking on things that made it lose focus. Innovation was overtaken by expansion, repetition and delivery. Expansion was not the right path. Helping to create a new NGDO with a more operational perspective and competence allowed CINDE to refocus on what it was good at – innovation and learning.

In all cases, the shifts in role have been essentially self-chosen and not forced. They are mainly products of success. However, success has its problems too: it can lead to distraction and loss of focus; it can create tensions in relationships; and it can stretch an organisation too far as it tries to respond to new expectations and demands. From an organisational development perspective, working through the shadows into a new light is an important part of regeneration – a little along the lines of 'no pain, no gain'. A regeneration process that has not caused some discomfort has probably not altered very much of substance.

Restructuring

One of the more common terms used for regeneration is 'restructuring' – altering the inner form and tasks of the organisation to make it better able to carry out the functions it wants to perform. Unfortunately, in this type of change the means are mistaken as ends. Structure should be the outcome, not the beginning, of critical consideration of identity, role and culture. Creating structure is the final grounding of intangible and tangible aspects of organising into a set of competencies, responsibilities and internal relationships that make new sense. Restructuring should emerge from processes of assessment, environmental scanning and negotiation, for example. A better term may be re-organising, of which structure is one part.

What can go wrong when structure is seen as the answer to an organisational problem, in this case a financial crisis, is reflected in the next illustration from Costa Rica. Centro de Capatación para el Desarrollo (CECADE) is an NGDO founded in 1975 by a combination of grassroots organisations and intellectuals.[22] The initial philosophy was to work with communities on all aspects of rural development primarily through training.[23] Experience led to an expansion of services from training. CECADE's services grew to include technical assistance to rural producers; collaboration in agro-industry and commercial sectors; financial management; and development initiatives with local government. A growing reputation created demands for its skills beyond national borders, for example assisting in regional integration and local development work in Nicaragua.

From the outset, CECADE's services and organisation were almost wholly financed by international aid. The end of civil conflict in Central America saw the region lose its geopolitical importance and with it the interest of the international aid system. Consequently, in the early 1990s CECADE faced an impending funding crisis.

The first response was to restructure CECADE into three independent units to operate as legally separate enterprises owned by the CECADE governing body, the General Assembly. Using capital provided by a donor, a centre was established to produce videos on issues of sustainable development. Another venture was established from an existing department to produce and sell publications on sustainable development and to provide editing services. The CECADE development department was reformed into another profit centre. This construction did not work well. CECADE's core functions still relied on external aid. Each enterprise had its own financial and administrative organisation that duplicated costs. In addition, the components of the organisation began to move apart, at the cost of a common identity and philosophy. It reached a point where CECADE faced financial collapse and an identity crisis.

Consequently, the structure was reintegrated managerially and its three operating units brought back to one location with shared common facilities. Each unit sets its own remuneration levels and is required to be self-financing, which includes paying for common services and a proportion of core costs through a charge for space occupied in CECADE's building. Duplication is reduced and economies of scale have been gained. Two of the for-profit ventures that were legally registered remain so and pay taxes. The development unit is shifting from project funding and implementation to consultancy and facilitation of local groups and local government that raise development finance themselves. This is demanding extensive and sometimes difficult negotiation with communities who simply see

that CICADE is changing the rules of the game.

Throughout these transitions, membership of the general assembly governing the organisation remained the same. It was still a combination of grassroots representatives and intellectuals. They remained the guardians of the original non-profit philosophy, but now overseeing three 'commercialised' entities. They 'recalled' the organisation back to its original purpose, insisting on an arrangement that ensured complementarity of effort.

The Ecumenical Centre for Documentation and Information (CEDI) in Brazil is a similar example of restructuring by splitting an existing organisation into separate legal entities. CEDI was established in 1974 during the military dictatorship with an agenda of protecting human rights. Over time, it grew into five programme areas that offered both mutual protection and an enhanced ability to make itself heard.[24] Each programme had similar strategies for fund-raising.

Political change in Brazil in 1994 altered the landscape in many ways. It became clear that strategies for each programme would have to be radically revised in terms of how to reach out to society, how to get involved in building democracy and how to raise funds. It also became clear that the progressively strong neoliberal view of projects would lead to internal friction. Therefore, as a pre-emptive strategy, CEDI restructured itself into five legally separate entities with no overlap in their governance.[25] Collaboration occurs on a functional basis depending on the tasks to be done.

Transformation

The sixth and most far-reaching type of regeneration is transformation, which signals major reappraisal and organisational reorientation, but not necessarily a shift in purpose or mission. One example of an organisation undergoing transformation is DESCO in Peru.[26]

In 1996, DESCO completed a self-evaluation. The exercise stemmed from the organisation's realisation that its relevance was diminishing, attributed to a complex interplay of factors. One was the rapidly changing environment involving President Fujimori's politics of 'democratic autocracy'; another was the effects of economic liberalisation as well as the weakening and fragmentation of unions and peasants' associations – DESCO's traditional partners.[27] In addition, foreign aid was downgrading Peru as a recipient, calling into question the reliability of the source it substantially relied on. Coupled to this change was a movement towards performance based on 'deliverables' – the capacity to critically reflect was being replaced by a capacity to deliver. DESCO did not see itself as part of the 'defeated' left but did see the need to regenerate itself as a new actor in new politics.

Consequently, with the help and guidance of a firm that had reorganised big Peruvian companies, DESCO staff were elected to an organisational re-engineering team. Its income source was reoriented away from aid towards a holding company owning development enterprises, some jointly with people's organisations, others solely.[28] This source, together with consultancy income, was considered sufficient to cover financial requirements.[29] Organisational regeneration was made complete by change in five other areas.

1 Administrative systems were computerised, linking planning, budgeting and monitoring.
2 Working procedures were simplified and two specialists were appointed, one dedicated to finance and credit, the other to gender.
3 Authority was decentralised, giving intervention teams and projects greater authority.
4 With scholarships and bilateral support, substantial investment was made to develop human resources. Seven young professionals were placed on degree courses in Europe and the US. A total of 42 field staff went on courses out of the country to upgrade their skills, reorient their practice and expand their horizons.
5 Efficiency gains were sought by reducing staff. DESCO reduced employees from 114 to 71 without labour conflicts. This was handled in three ways. First, professionals were assisted to find other work, often at substantially higher salaries. A performance-based assessment system was introduced. This led to the forced removal of some 14 people that were using the organisation for their own purposes, such as consultancies. Finally, support staff such as secretaries with more than 15 years' service were offered redundancy payments above the legal requirement. Computerisation allowed more staff to do more of their own secretarial work.

The whole regeneration process cost about US$100,000. Unfortunately, in 1998 a currency crisis caused a substantial financial loss. By a vote of 52 to 1, staff agreed to forego a 'thirteenth month' salary as well as accept a reduction in health insurance benefits.

Working with DESCO is still a personal, political option – a particular way of doing things with and for the disadvantaged of Peruvian society. These aspects of its core identity and principles have been consciously preserved.

Alongside its development interventions in agriculture and credit, for example,

DESCO has redefined its future agenda around three goals. First, by building space for dialogue amongst young people – be they in universities or the slums – about the society they want in the 21st century. Second, by creating linkages to build pluralistic politics from below through local governance. Third, to actively work on the development of social leadership, focusing on citizenship, economic and social rights and participatory methods. DESCO's original agenda in society is maintained, albeit expressed in an updated way.

Finally, transformation has brought an intended generational change to DESCO leadership from Jesuit-trained social democrats of the 1960s to a governing board of younger professionals.

Conclusion – Organisational Change to Enhance Viability

The purpose of this section is to focus on organisational features that strongly condition an NGDO's agility.[30] Five features – power distribution, resource profile, culture, learning and the relational web – were identified towards the end of Chapter 9. It is important to be clear that these are not the total of the many things that can be done to make an organisation more viable. For example, cost-reduction measures, team approaches to work, new technologies, and new communications or accounting systems, for example, can all play a role. However, in keeping with one theme of this book, our concentration is on areas of regeneration that better equip an organisation to adapt to turbulence and instability as normal environmental conditions.

This section examines what positive change in each of these areas would look like. The intention is not to find 'the' answer to regeneration for organisational viability: there isn't one. Rather, the task is to identify lessons to help in the design of interventions that have a specific goal of enhancing sustainability through improved agility.

Regeneration for Agility – What Should be Aimed For?

Sustainability is about organisational adaptability. In order to make an organisation more adaptable, an intervention should aim to achieve the following types of change.

Power Distribution

The goal is to increase the scope of authority downwards and outwards so that, for example, most operational decisions need only be approved at the next higher level of authority. Only issues that have an effect beyond the operational arena, such as a policy towards local government or gender, move further up. To ensure confidence in how authority is being exercised, its redistribution should be complemented by negotiated performance standards. This provides both a boundary to authority and criteria for behaviour that can protect those in authority, especially field staff, from untoward pressure.

The cases examined show different ways that power can be distributed. For CINDE, PRIA, and to some extent TTO, power is shared by delegation to others. With CINDE and PRIA, tasks and responsibilities are devolved to other organisations that they themselves helped to establish. For CRDA, a new leadership style should give everyone authority to be a leader in their own realm. DESCO also reflects empowerment coupled to greater personal responsibility in consulting, and sharing risk and authority in joint ventures.

Resource profile

The goal is to protect core functions through self-generation of income and to spread income risk as widely as possible across sources. Unless it is a conscious decision, resource change should not reduce autonomy or alter position and role in society. Obviously, change in role and position can be important strategic choices as an NGDO matures or seeks to become more agile (see relational web).

Where the 'trigger' for regeneration was financial, NGDOs alter their resource base with an emphasis on self-generation. TTO, DESCO, CECADE all introduced self-owned income sources, complemented by others, such as consulting and contracting, but not solely dependent on them. For VDRC and CDRA, attention to resource mobilisation has been strategic – to prevent a funding crisis if donors tire of Nepal or NGDOs or both – or to protect a core element of organisational identity. One observation is that enjoying a relatively secure funding source with continuity or growth and with people asking for services, as in the case of both CINDE and PRIA, also has its downside – it can lead to loss of focus or rootedness. Secure funding from others is not an unmitigated blessing. As noted previously, 'a little hunger helps'.

Culture

The goal is to increase trust, willingness and the ability to communicate widely: to inculcate a sense of the organisation as a living community or a family, not simply an employer; to promote space for curiosity and enquiry.

Cultural elements of the cases are less easy to trace. For CINDE, regaining its mission, identity and culture of innovation was an important part of its strategy after losing focus. For CDRA, enquiry, introspection and reflection are such an innate part of what the organisation is about as a living entity, that securing this function is almost a question of cultural life or death. DESCO has tried to ensure that its process of transformation has reinvigorated trust and commitment.

Learning

The goal is to achieve balance between formal reporting and exploration of personal learning and intuition. Proxy indicators should be better recognised and used as an acceptable part of managing. Learning should be understood as an unwritten part of everyone's job description. The notion of development as action-research should become stronger, underpinned by procedures, budgets and new approaches to practice. Curiosity must be a watchword and be seen throughout the organisation.

In the case of CECADE and TTO the source of learning for regeneration was a threatening event or coalition of trends and forces. Good reputation is no guaranteed defence against 'big picture' trends such as the politics of aid. Internal triggers in CCR, CDRA, VDRC, CINDE, CEDI are a sign of prescience or of learning processes working adequately, albeit in the case of CINDE later than they would have liked.

Relational web

The goal is that resource dependency on the NGDO of communities and local government, for example, should be reduced. Structural claims on the organisation's presence and expertise should be replaced with 'continuous' negotiation and reappraisal of role and function.

In a number of cases, regeneration can reduce structural demands and alter old expectations. For example, a role as an intermediary typically creates a web of grassroots groups who cannot pay and expect the NGDO to act as a resource supplier. This is how they raise project money in the first place. For VDRC and

PRIA, becoming support organisations moves primary attention to other NGDOs who are more able to pay. Unlike the past conditioning of CBOs, these do not immediately assume that costs will be met by the support organisation. DESCO had to embark on a major process of negotiation with old partners as well as establish new relationships. It has moved from an intermediary funder to a 'development investor'. This calls for a very different set of relational arrangements.

Regeneration is one vital component in organisational viability. It needs to be part of an NGDO's genetic make-up. It cannot be an add-on, like an energy pack pulled out of a cupboard. It cannot be applied like a dose of pure oxygen, the tap being opened when the organisation gets tired and falls behind. Regeneration as a way of being is a question of organisational stance or attitude, which is not located in a think-tank or strategic planning department, as useful as they can be. Segmentation is not the answer. Culture and leadership is.

The difficult challenge for leaders and managers is to instil energy for continuous change without this leading to incoherence, instability and burn-out. This type of decision – balancing the need for change with reasonable stability – is one of the many aspects of sound judgement that NGDO leaders must employ, alongside their own ability to inspire. Regeneration of quality leadership is the third vital element in achieving organisational sustainability and the topic of the following chapter.

Chapter Summary

Regeneration for greater sustainability means making conscious organisational adjustments:

- Appreciation of the trigger involved; where does the impulse come from and why?
- A reading of existing preconditions against criteria that may be internally of externally derived; whose measures count?
- Insight on how deep and broad change needs to be and how deep this needs to go; local and limited or deep and broad?
- Estimates of the forces for and against change; how strong are they and how are they aligned?

Change processes should be led by and towards a shared future vision, not solely justified by solving existing problems.

Change should be informed by a sense of urgency.

Empowering staff is a necessary but risky part of change processes that consolidate themselves quickly.

Regeneration can have different characteristics related to the 'trigger' and primary organisational change being addressed. Six possibilities are:

1 Continuous improvement.
2 Reflective evolution.
3 Process reform.
4 Role change.
5 Restructuring.
6 Transformation.

To increase agility, organisational regeneration should aim for the following goals.

- *Power distribution:* increase scope of authority downwards and outwards

complemented by negotiated performance standards.

- *Resource profile:* core functions
protected through self-generation of
income. Income spread minimises risk
and vulnerability.

- *Culture:* increased trust, willingness
and ability to communicate widely.
Appreciation of the NGDO as a
community or family. The existence of
a spirit of enquiry as a living part of
the organisation.

- *Learning:* balanced between formal
reporting and exploration of personal
learning and intuition. Proxy indicators are recognised and used in
management. Learning is not compart-
mentalised. It is understood to be an
unwritten part of everyone's job

description. The notion of development as action-research is strong,
underpinned by procedures, budgets
and approaches to practice. Curiosity
is the NGDO's credo, seen throughout
the organisation

- *Relational web:* no resource dependency relationships exist. Claims on
the NGDO's presence, resources and
expertise rest on 'continuous' negotiation and reappraisal of appropriate
role and function.

Regeneration for sustainability is not an
add-on but an integral part of an NGDO's
life, its culture, the way things are done. It
is instilled, guided and moderated by
sound judgement and inspirational leadership.

Chapter 11

Regeneration Through Leadership

'I never wanted to be a machine attendant.' (James Sarpei, CENCOSAD)

'An organisation kills its prophet at its peril.' (James Thomas, TTO)

A frequent observation in the preceding pages is that leaders make a difference to many aspects of NGDO life, including viability. This maxim holds true across the world for all sorts of organisations. Peter Drucker goes so far as to assert: 'In all human affairs there is a constant relationship between the performance and achievement of the leaders, the record setters, and the rest.'[1]

This chapter focuses attention on leadership as one critical factor in NGDO regeneration. The vast amount written about leading organisations relies on experience derived from for-profit enterprises. Therefore, care must be taken before applying this knowledge to other types of organisations.[2] Consequently, this chapter explores our relative level of ignorance about answers to three significant questions:

1 What makes an NGDO leader effective in terms of organisational performance?
2 How is quality of leadership assured over time?
3 Who will be tomorrow's leaders?

Looking for answers to the first question moves through three stages. The first stage briefly reviews and compares what drives studies of leadership in other sectors, particularly politics and business. Their focus is different and cannot simply be assumed to apply to non-profit-making organisations. The second section examines an argument that leadership in such organisations is more determinant for organisational performance than is the case for government or business.

Section Three moves from leadership of non-profit-making organisations in general to NGDOs in particular. The approach is to draw on general theory and writing about leadership and then relate this to NGDOs. For example, it is necessary to be clear about the difference between a leader and leadership; to understand the relationship between leaders and followers and between leadership and management; leadership in relation to gender; and the origins of leaders, for example.

Section Four concentrates on the issue of leadership development for a successor generation. It examines short-term initiatives to accelerate the formation of potential leaders, pointing out a necessary shift from training to a more holistic approach of forming and mentoring. In addition, it considers the longer-term problem of attracting young people to civic leadership as a career choice.

Section Five pays attention to the issue of leadership transition with particular attention to stages of organisational growth, succession from the founder and the 'halo effect'. A common succession problem is of a weak second level cadre and lack of succession planning. Why this occurs is reviewed.

The concluding section summarises what must be learned about leadership effectiveness, transition and succession as the preconditions required to move beyond generalities and platitudes to insightful

decision making. In other words, there is a knowledge gap, which must be filled by observing and drawing on how exemplary leaders keep their organisations viable; how continuity in leadership quality has been assured – of particular relevance to governing boards – and on how best to invest in leadership development. In short, the chapter ends more with an agenda for necessary study than firm proposals for regenerative action.

Leadership Study from a Comparative Perspective

Leadership is everywhere in life. Some leaders are better than others; some stand out from the rest – they excel. These individuals are a common focus of attention and learning. However, the nature and purpose of enquiry tends to differ between leaders and leadership in politics, business and the non-profit-making or civic arena.

Political leadership is typically the terrain of historians and biographers, who tend to investigate and explain leaders' success in terms of their socio-economic origins, psychological characteristics, life-shaping experiences, significant relationships, personal behaviour and ideology. Political leadership may emerge from social and labour movements and reactions against oppression. Nevertheless, just as frequently leaders emerge from hereditary elite, professional classes, party-political machines and military takeovers. Analysts typically seek to explain how these elements contribute to political leadership in terms of person in context – why such a person stands out at a particular time and place. In essence, they ask why and how some individuals excel in acquiring and applying *political capital*. The recent study of Nelson Mandela is an example within contemporary politics.[3] James' work about Toussaint L'Ouverture is a similar study in

an era of colonialism and slavery within the context of the French Revolution.[4] There are many more, typically in the form of biography. Nevertheless, the examination of political leadership seldom leads to prescription in terms of dedicated programmes of individual formation and political advancement or selection. In this sense, political leaders 'arise to the moment'; they are seldom formally trained for such roles.

The study of leadership in corporate activity, on the other hand, typically serves utilitarian purposes. Biographies of exemplars, such as Lee Iacocca, and Bill Gates, are meant to illuminate and instruct how leadership can ensure corporate success. Underpinning studies of corporations is the desire to explain the relationship between a leader, or leadership, and the economic performance of the organisation he or she leads. In doing so, investigations of business leadership – and of management as its symbiotic counterpart – also draw on the human elements and processes described above. However, the task in these studies – by academics, business schools, consultants and management 'gurus' like Tom Peters and Peter Drucker – is to identify desired leadership attributes in order to better select or train the individuals that embody them. The goal is to find and develop people and leadership systems that can improve competitiveness and generate economic value in complex environments and increasingly international and dynamic markets. The objective is to know why and how those who are pre-eminent stand out in the creation of *economic capital* and financial wealth. The quest to analyse and prescribe models, methods and oversimplified 'How To' guides of corporate leadership is a business in itself. As the shelves of bookshops testify, it is an enterprise that dominates existing theories of leadership.

Outside organised religion, relatively little – beyond anecdote and the notion of charisma – is known or understood about the nature of civic leadership. Measured in terms of academic investment and practical application, study of this domain has been neglected. For example, the number of journals dedicated to leadership and management of non-profit-making organi-sations can be counted on one hand. It is difficult to find studies of renowned civic leaders across the world who have not had a political impact, but are exemplary because of what they have achieved for society in other ways. Yet, recent data indicate that such organisations make a more substantial contribution to society than is commonly assumed. This is demonstrated in tangible terms, for example, in employment, in contribution to gross domestic product and in size in comparison with industry groups.[5] This sector is also argued to have significant influence on social relations, norms and values, such as trust, reciprocity, tolerance and inclusion. These are all critical features of *social capital*.[6] If this new data and arguments are correct, investment in understanding the leadership of non-profit-making organisations is both grossly deficient and urgently needed.[7] From comparisons, what do studies of such leadership tell us so far?

Is Leadership of Non-Profit-Making Organisations Different and Does it Matter?

Many studies on leadership of non-profit-making organisations are disappointing. They suffer from a number of common weaknesses. First, they are dominated by North American and, more generally, Anglo-Saxon conditions and experience.[8] This tends, secondly, to mean that the organisations considered are fee-paying hospitals and schools and, to a lesser extent, trade unions and other membership bodies, such as neighbourhood associations. The sample seldom includes organisations dedicated to civic and social change. Second, the distinctive features of leading non-profit-making organisations are only weakly demonstrated, if at all. Much of the analysis and conclusions would equally apply to business.[9] Third, leadership is seen to be as much, if not more, the function of a governing board. This perspective does not commonly reflect the situation in the South and East of non-profit-making organisations as leader-centric organisations[10] – an important cultural point to which we must return. Finally, many writers pay attention to management, rather than leadership, and use different distinctions between the two. Consequently, language and categories become confused and sound comparisons are difficult to make.

With these limitations in mind, comparative study suggests that leading a non-profit-making organisation is indeed different, exemplified by the fact that the leader has a more significant influence on performance than for organisations in other sectors. Two reasons are put forward to explain this: one is psychological and the other has to do with the nature of the organisation's design.

Probably the most significant factor is the role of a leader's values and personal behaviour. These are important in fulfilling the moral and psychological 'contract' with staff and volunteers – the followers – who choose to forgo a full market return for their labour.[11] (In a study of leading 'innovators for the public', the Ashoka Foundation found that some 70 per cent of individuals selected as potential social entrepreneurs could identify with a family member who had exceptionally strong values.)[12] The leader is a critical element in generating and satisfying this component of personal incentive and reward.

For Peter Drucker, the successful leader of a non-profit-making organisation embodies the organisation's mission[13] – personal resonance with followers is critical for organisations that rely on motivations that are not principally informed by competition and money (business) or conformity and power (government).[14]

Consequently, non-profit-making organisations are especially vulnerable to a leader who does not show consistency between rhetoric, practice, organisational calling and vision. Such leaders undermine internal trust and necessary personal conviction. Unlike in profit-driven enterprise, a follower cannot find compensation for such a leader's shortcomings by working harder for material reward. In addition, competition suggests that business leaders will think of themselves first and others second. Therefore, expectations about trust are not so high to start with. The social and emotional dimensions of a leader and leadership,[15] become more performance determinant than in bureaucracies or businesses.

Another, more contestable, argument is that non-profit-making organisations tend to work with looser structural arrangements that allow power to be used in more flexible, leader-dependent ways.

'While unofficial power arrangements certainly exist in work organisations, they appear to be more fully developed in the voluntary organisation, since the latter is characterised by looser structural arrangements. And this looser structure would appear to be related to another important consideration: in voluntary organisations, the leader is more likely to have a strong impact than in more structured organisations, because there are more possibilities for variation in the voluntary setting.'[16]

The problem with this assertion is that the few non-profit-making organisations under consideration in Hall's study are member-based to provide mutual aid, often with an elected leader.[17] It is doubtful that service-providing organisations are, a priori, looser structured when compared with business or bureaucracies. For example, some ten years ago observers already noted the bureaucratisation of NGDOs.[18] However, to the extent that NGDOs rely less on formality and attribute more value to the person than to the function he or she fulfils, his assertion may have some merit.

The most plausible argument for the differentially high impact of leaders on non-profit-making organisations when compared with other sectors lies in the realm of organisational psychology. The general point, however, remains. The nature and quality of voluntary sector leadership is more likely to determine achievement than in other organisational types. The question, however, is does this matter?

The relative inattention to leaders and leadership in civil society has negative consequences for development thinking, policy and practice. In terms of thinking, it sets unwarranted boundaries around the concepts, frameworks and theories employed to understand how societies generate, appreciate and distribute leadership. Second it limits, and hence distorts, the picture of leadership that gives rise to the actual configuration of civic institutions and organisational behaviour to be found across the world. Such distortions can lead to highly questionable policy recommendations, expectations and programmes of external assistance.[19]

Third, by default, perspectives from the corporate sector become the reference point for analysing what leadership in society is all about and how it can be improved.[20] More dangerously, it can lead to denial or neglect of non-economic values and norms that are intrinsic to culture, civic life, state–society relations and national stability. Non-economic, moral, spiritual, social and other values may be claimed, validated and propagated by political processes, but they are not owned by politics as such. They are already located somewhere within civil society. Consequently, ideas about promoting or strengthening civic leadership are overshadowed by how for-profit organisations would go about doing so. Correspondingly, interventions intended to accelerate the development of civic leadership become too narrowly framed.

If, as argued above, a leader of a voluntary organisation is a more significant factor in effectiveness than his or her equivalent in business, we surely must look within the voluntary sector to see and learn what this means. In Peter Drucker's terms:

> 'There is thus a real need among the non-profits for materials that are specifically developed out of their experience and focused on their realities and concerns.'[21]

This observation is of special relevance to a current concern within international development, namely to improve organisational capabilities and performance of NGDOs in the South and East. Moreover, as previous chapters show, it is also relevant to NGDO viability.

A recent global initiative to enhance NGDO capabilities is the International Forum for Capacity Building (IFCB), formerly known as the International Working Group on Capacity Building (IWGCB). One conclusion from an IFCB multi-continent study of NGDO capacity building needs is that:

> 'Leadership development programmes for both existing and "second generation" leaders was a matter of interest in several regions and a top priority in South Asia and southern and eastern Africa'.[22]

A consultation of NGDOs in South Asia was even more explicit in what it says about the content of leadership development initiatives.

> 'Leadership development: [This] would include developing a less leader-centric NGO functioning, democratising organisations, developing second generation leadership, as well as balancing leadership and management.'[23]

This chapter argues that, though useful common-sense steps can be taken, we do not know enough from within the sector to do well what this quotation calls for. We are not on firm ground when it comes to making sound investments in NGDO leadership development. From a sustainability perspective we do not know for sure how successful leaders go about making the many resource trade-offs described in Part II. How do they exemplify and inculcate a spirit of curiosity, or use proxy indicators in decision making, or adapt as the organisation evolves, for example? Consequently, a starting point has to be the wider understanding of leadership translated towards NGDOs. This is the task of the next section.

Leadership Effectiveness and NGDOs

This section reviews the nature of effective leadership and its application to NGDOs. It does so from many interrelated perspectives, beginning with what it means to be a leader in relation to followers. Leadership is further examined in terms of where leadership should be located in organisations; the relationship between leadership and context, particularly in relation to culture; differences between leadership and management; the origins of leadership; specifically, can it be nurtured and developed; and gender perspectives, including the gender-balancing role of NGDOs in society and in enhancing the values associated with positive social capital and civility. These provide the grounding for a summary review of what characterises effective leaders and leadership.

Leaders and Followers: Looking Beyond Organisational Boundaries

There are almost as many definitions of leadership as people who write about the topic. The perspectives informing definitions vary. They pivot around gathering and intelligently using power; setting a personal example; 'holding' and projecting a valued vision; enabling others to act together and to excel; possessing and applying multiple intelligence as a human quality that simply 'triggers' 'followership'; and communicating the basic rules that make organisations effective.[24]

Two things are implied in all perspectives. First is a leader's gift to awaken, but not to impose, behaviour in others. Second is an ability to align and coalesce individual and group behaviour in the required direction for the organisation to be successful.

In relation to the first, much effort has been expended on looking at a leader's personality traits and practices that followers respect. The 1997 study by Kouzes and Posner is a classic example. Their research found 20 ingredients of leadership that are admired. Possessing this combination enables an individual to excel in terms of human relations and interpersonal transactions. Logically, once these ingredients are known they can be selected or trained for. However, other evidence suggests that this is not enough. In addition, leaders must also provide a valued purpose, a direction that people aspire to. This 'direction-giving' quality creates what has been referred to as transformational leadership.[25]

Expanding on this second point, Alistair Mant argues that wide intelligence and a deep practical understanding of the world underpin outstanding leaders.[26] These attributes, coupled to an undamaged psychological make-up, generate both trust in, and followers of, goals and ideals.[27]

The dimensions of inspirational guidance and value-based goal setting are particularly important for leadership of organisations dedicated to social change. Why? Because followers respond not to economic incentives and market rewards but to a less tangible foundation of socio-political values and associated aspirations. NGDOs must therefore be concerned about transformational leadership, but with an added twist.

The additional complexity is that leaders of NGDOs envisage a direction or goal that requires the development of capacities, relations and values within client communities and local leaders outside of the organisation itself.[28] This is the creation of positive social capital. Taking this step rests on a leader's unshakeable conviction that the self-development and self-empowerment of people is possible. For example, Shaob Khan, the founder and leader of the Aga Khan Rural Support Programme (AKRSP) was able to develop strong personal loyalties with villagers as well as staff. His conviction extended beyond the organisation's boundaries. He is still spoken about with awe.[29] For this extension of leadership to come about we must answer the question 'where does leadership lie?'

Leaders and Leadership in NGDOs

There are contrasting views of where organisational leadership is located. The 'pyramid' view locates leadership at the apex of the organisation embodied by a single leader or 'top-team' recognised as having this position. The team variant is not considered a dominant feature of NGDO leadership in the South and East – an individual normally has primacy. A common, sometimes pejorative, observation is that an NGDO is known by the leader, not the organisation as such – it is 'his' or 'her' NGDO; it is personally owned. Isagani Serrano of PRRM, has called this 'the halo effect'. The image of the NGDO leader is a reflection of and

statement about the organisation itself. As will be seen later, the halo effect can have an important influence on succession.

The 'deep' view sees leadership as a quality distributed throughout the organisation. As limited as it may be, everyone has a leadership role to play as part of his or her function – 'leadership is a social or collective phenomenon.'[30] This perspective is seen to be particularly applicable to rural development.

'Thus the concept of leadership should be expanded to one fixated on the most visible individual to a more collective vision…'[31]

The relevance of this distinction for NGDOs is premised on the proven need – in good development practice – to empower staff in their work with communities.[32] The link between an NGDO and those it serves is, in effect, the bond between a leader's vision of social or civic reformation and its practical application.

It is vitally important that NGDO staff working with communities nurture the local leadership needed to enhance and sustain social capital and civic change. Differences in context and people's participation for ownership of change all demand the flexibility that internal empowerment of staff can bring about.

'We would thus focus the discussion on leadership for successful rural development on the contributions made by personnel who are called on to exercise varied but continuous leadership at headquarters and in the field, by proxy and in their own right. This concept of diffuse leadership needs to be taken more seriously than journalistic accounts of rural development successes suggest.'[33]

Hence the leader must appreciate and bring into existence webs of collective leadership that empower within the organisation.[34] Moreover, he or she must also see how the organisation can tap into the social and civic energy and potential for leadership that exists in communities. This means enabling front-line staff to act as facilitators and catalysts, rather than gate-keepers to NGDO resources.

Leadership in Context

Another perspective on leadership relates to 'contingency'. This is the view that appropriate and effective leadership depends on: the context of the operation; past experience that has become part of organisational wisdom; the current operating state; resources; and the future goals of the organisation. Contingency was a reaction to an assertion, prevailing in the 1960s, that there is one best way of leading. The alternative view is that no one 'best' type of leadership exists. What is most effective cannot be determined unless environmental conditioning factors are known.[35] It is probably true to say that the 'one best way' of managing or leading is no longer a tenable position.

An important facet of contingency – acknowledging the influence of a particular time and space – is leadership in relation to culture. Do cultural norms, conventions, standards, expectations and socially ascribed status have a significant bearing on leadership? Work on culture in relation to business organisations shows that it does.[36] Drawing on this work in relation to NGDOs suggests, indeed, that culture counts, but that the situation is made complex by overlays of culture from different sources: from without, from within and, often, from abroad.[37] This implies that leadership must be aware about and take readings of the cultural dimensions to leadership, both externally and internally, as for example removing prejudice towards women or altering paternalism in state–society relations.

This latter agenda is proving to be both important and difficult in a country like Malawi. Thirty years of autocratic rule by Hastings Banda has effectively cowed the population. One consequence is an expectation that leadership, including that of NGDOs, is authoritarian, coupled to an assumption that personal initiative will be stamped on. In such a context, NGDOs must be agents of cultural change, showing that other leadership styles are both valid and effective. For a newly appointed NGDO leader to come from government, insist on being called by his surname and introduce a new format for internal memoranda, may not be the way do so.[38]

A further implication is to locate leadership in the context of other factors as well. Most salient are the configuration of civil society; the trajectory of state–society relations; the nature and distribution of poverty and exclusion; the evolution of NGDOs; and the policy and practice of international aid. It is vitally important that a leader can read the context properly in order to reach sound judgement on organisational implications. In this sense, reading is not a one-off or periodic event, but a continuous process of sensing as well as knowing what is going on in the world outside the organisation's formal boundaries. The process is akin to a radar antenna continually scanning, separating out and assessing the significance of important objects and their movements from all the background noise and clutter.

Leaders and Managers

In addition to context, studies have grappled with the issue of the difference, if any, between leaders and managers of organisations. Conventional wisdom suggests that they can be differentiated by their primary orientation and tasks.[39] Leaders concern themselves with inspiration, purpose, organisational positioning, strategy and the future. Managers focus on resources, processes, people and getting things done. There are arguments against this implicit separation between thinking and doing. It is essentially divisive and reinforces an old-fashioned dichotomy which adequately reflects the need to integrate both.[40]

Studies of NGDOs suggest that if they are internally empowering – which tends to mean operating with significant delegated authority – the distinction between the essential features of leaders and managers should not be drawn too sharply.[41] For example, to work across the meeting point with communities, frontline staff must be able not just to convey the leaders' inspiration, but hold it themselves. They must grasp and articulate the image of a changed situation to those who must similarly aspire to and eventually embody the change. This requirement also applies to relations between managers and staff. Conceptually, the inspirational dimension of leadership must act as an energy source directing within and beyond the organisation.[42]

Correspondingly, NGDO leaders must not ignore different degrees of emphasis in the functions carried out between themselves and managers. The issue is to recognise how they create and spread energy and a guiding image of development throughout the organisation, particularly to field staff. They must diffuse the message so that all staff, managers included, can express the potential for leadership within them.

Origins of Leadership and the Next Generation: Nature or Nurture?

Up until the 1950s, studies on leadership were dominated by the search for personal traits that singled out leaders from others. This emphasis was premised on the assumption that such characteristics were inborn, innate and hence not amenable to dedicated development or training. Such a view was superseded by research into leaders' styles and behaviours. Once these traits were identified, they could be trained for. Associated with contingency theory, the approach to leadership evolved further to examine 'situational leadership'. In other words, what makes a leader effective is determined by all sorts of pre-conditions and contextual factors. There was no one, uniform and universal set of leadership characteristics beyond, perhaps, the ability to fit into a particular setting at a particular time. This corresponds to one theme of this book.

Current thinking would suggest that the nature–nurture view of leadership and its development is, in fact, a false dichotomy. There are inherited, innate predispositions – such as intelligence and intellectual capacity – which offer greater or lesser potential for leadership. They are not very amenable to development by dedicated action. But there are also many mediating factors in life's experience and formal education that can bring out leadership qualities to a more than sufficient degree from a less strong innate basis – much is learnable, but a strong intrinsic potential is a definite asset.[43] Peter Senge formulates an answer to the nature–nurture question in the following way.

'The ability of people to be natural leaders is, as near as I can tell, the by-product of a lifetime of effort – effort to develop conceptual and communication skills, to reflect on

personal values and to align personal behaviour with values, to learn how to listen and to appreciate others and others' ideas. In the absence of such effort, personal charisma is style without substance.'[44]

Peter Drucker answers the nature–nurture question in a similar way.

'Most of the leaders I've seen were neither born nor made. They were self-made.'[45]

The critical issue is, what process of personal development and learning do leaders undergo from birth that reinforces whatever level of potential leadership capabilities exist? Making good 'deficiencies' stemming from innate weaknesses and personality problems is difficult. To do so requires continuous effort, dedication and cost. The point about successful leaders is that they do not need to demonstrate their power or authority or to bathe in public accolades or to be known for their charisma.

'To make a programme succeed and to expand it certainly requires unusual talents for organisation and communication, supplemented by a good sense of human psychology and how to use incentives. But the characteristics usually associated in the public mind with charisma – a dominating personality, a spell-binding speaking style, a demeanour of utmost confidence – are not evident prerequisites for leadership of rural development endeavours.'[46]

Consequently, recognising and investing in demonstrated potential is a sensible element of purposeful leadership development. Unfortunately, few NGDOs have well-developed schemes to identify and invest in the necessary exposures for their staff: what business would refer to as career planning and development. There are many reasons for this. One is financial. Leadership investment is typically treated as a cost that must be covered by overheads. However, overheads must be kept low: hence low or no investment. Coupled to this are uncertainties of organisational continuity stemming from project-based development finance. NGDOs are wary of entering into commitments in terms of career development when the future is insecure. Another reason concerns attitudes. People are expected to be capable of doing the job they are hired for and then 'learning by the seat of their pants' as opportunities for personal growth present themselves – individual leadership capability evolves or it does not as the case may be: a form of 'natural selection'. This could be considered the common approach to NGDO leadership. Finally, there is fear of 'poaching'. Lack of adequate investment in leadership, when set against rapid expansion of the NGDO community, is creating a large gap between supply and demand of competent people. These factors give rise to a perception that leadership development is a high risk, negative-sum game militating against investment.

Overall, therefore, as noted above, it is not uncommon to find a good leader without a strong potential successor.[47] This is an unwelcome situation when it comes to leadership transition and organisational regeneration. Be that as it may, as we will see below, there is growing attention to investment in a new generation of leaders.

Leadership and Gender

Gender aspects of leadership and management are significant features of contemporary organisational thinking and practice. A common perception – and complaint – is that women must be better than men to achieve the same status. Furthermore, in organisations women have to play by men's rules in order to succeed. These, plus negative culture-bound attitudes, create a 'glass ceiling' for women as managers and as leaders. There is corporate evidence to support the notion of an implicit barrier. As well as obstacles to upward mobility, there is also evidence that women are not rewarded for the same work as men at the same organisational level – there is something about corporations that disempower women.

The study of gender and organisations has moved beyond overt features of numbers, positions and rewards to female employees. Significant as they are as indicators of the problem of male-dominated systems, more attention is now given to deeper lying psychological foundations of organisational behaviour that generate gender-specific disempowerment.[48] What can be done about this is also being explored in the development context.[49]

There are numerous reasons for concluding that women and men are different. Distinctiveness stems from physiology and from a long process of socialisation, or domestication, and from a mode of modernisation that has not, in most societies, produced gender-fair or balanced outcomes or relationships.[50] The task for today's organisations is to recognise and value the complementarity of what women and men have to offer at all levels and in all facets of organisational life.

At a societal level, complementarity is also needed between the 'genders' of organisations and institutions. By this is meant between organisations that exploit, compete, acquire and accumulate; those that collaborate and share; and those that regulate and mediate. Social capital is premised on relational values of reciproc-

ity, non-exploitiveness and trust. Similarly, the civil nature of society relies on values of tolerance, inclusion and fairness. These are not common attributes of corporations in competitive markets. They are, supposedly, the attributes of the non-profit-making sector. NGDOs would offer a gender-balancing element within society because of a disposition to reflect and promote female strengths. However, if the relative paucity of women leaders of NGDOs is anything to go by – outside of the women's movement and women's NGDOs – this contribution may not be realised in practice; nor does gender balance appear to be borne out by studies within NGDOs.[51]

A recent study shows how embedded the problem of gender equality is in NGDOs.[52] Consequently, any change of strategy to 'engender' an organisation must address deep-lying issues using both power and participation. The organisational development process must change the rules of the game rather than simply help people play by the old rules in a genderised way – like sustainability, gender equality is not an add-on. They are both ways of thinking about organising.

> *'Trying to "add gender" into the structure and work of an organisation is like trying to add the idea that the world is round to the idea that the world is flat'.*
>
> *'We need first to re-conceptualise what an organisation is, then we can re-invent organisations and institutions of all kinds in line with our vision of gender justice and racial equality integrated with sustainable development.'*[53]

Overall, NGDO leadership remains male-dominated, yet intentions and contributions to social change can be characterised as female. This implies that, while male leaders are predisposed to female values, this seldom translates into an organisational ability to counter unequal gender opportunities.

Successful Leadership of NGDOs – to be a Social Artist and Artisan

What does all of the foregoing suggest about a profile of a successful leader? A number of things stand out.

First, a successful leader is driven by and committed to a conviction that self-development of people is possible and necessary. This steadfast belief is allied to a value-set that gives primacy to achieving public good with and through others, not individually. However, here lies a paradox. The paradox is that the individual's drive towards doing things for others is also the source of self-realisation and satisfaction. Balance between the two drives must be properly managed lest there is slippage into self-aggrandisement. Consequently, humility is an important part of the value-set as well. For example, Fazle Abed the founder-leader of BRAC, is not known as a public figure – he intentionally wishes BRAC to be known, not himself.

Second, is an ability to communicate values of a motivating agenda. However, communication is not just through the written or spoken word. It is also conveyed through how people read the integrity of a leader's commitment. Followers must sense that the implicit psychological contract of working with the NGDO will be honoured and not abused. They must have deep reasons to trust. In parallel, a similar message must be communicated to the outside world in ways that affirm honesty of purpose. Often this calls for political insights and contacts, built up without patronage or loss of principle.

Third, aspects of personality structure mean that caring and respect are second nature, complemented by a conviction that

power is best employed and 'enjoyed' when it is shared. The point is that an effective leader has an inner self-confidence that is not dependent on possessing power but, in contradiction, is expressed by a willingness to share it. For example, Dr Manibhai Desai, the founder of the Bhartiya Agro Industries Foundation (BAIF) in Pune, India, was very exacting in his demands. However, this was not just tolerated, it was embraced as an integral part of commitment shown in his hard work and personal sacrifice: '...my life is my message'.[54]

Fourth, exemplary leadership requires deep knowledge of and insight into the nature of social processes and systems. It calls for a capacity to read environments with accuracy, care and speed. It demands the mental capacity to understand information and select viable points of intervention: the agenda in action.

Fifth, by nature effective leaders are curious and adaptive. Curiosity is fed by a continual search for opportunities that will keep the organisation relevant and respected. The first response of an effective leader to a new idea is 'why not' rather than 'why'? This is a positive, appreciative stance. Adaptiveness is expressed in a willingness to experiment and take calculated risks.

Finally, effective leaders are good readers and redesigners of their organisations. They can readily see, for example, how the organisation fits into its environment: they see where a 'misfit' is right, because the organisation is trying to change things outside, and quickly realise where a 'misfit' is wrong because it shows that adaptation has not occurred quickly enough.

In sum, exemplary NGDO leaders are both creative artists and competent artisans. Artistry equates with inspiration to see society work in a different way and to communicate this vision to others so that they are motivated to act. Artisanship requires the skill to create an organisation through which those motivated to act can do so effectively and honestly, and once created it requires skill to remain respected and viable – to be insightful and agile.

Previous discussions suggest that such people are both born and self-formed. If this is the case, what can be done to accelerate the growth of potential leaders? This is the topic of the following section, after which we look at how organisations make the transition from one leader to the next.

Leadership Development and Preparing the Next Generation

There are both short- and long-term challenges to leadership development and the preparation of successors. The short-term challenge is to find and apply better ways of developing the sort of leadership characteristics identified above. The long-term challenge is one of wooing and attracting young people into the sector. Modest progress is being made in each of these areas.

Problems in Leadership Development

Sound and proven processes for leadership development of NGDOs are in their infancy. A lack of detailed and systematic insight about successful leadership, a supply-driven pressure to quickly expand the NGDO community, plus attrition of candidates because of poaching by official aid agencies, have worked against serious investment in getting it right. Fortunately, things are changing.

Past Approaches

By and large, leadership development has followed two tracks, the strategic and the managerial. The first approach has often relied on strategic planning as the theoretical and practical means to get aspiring leaders to reflect on the 'big picture' issues and then deciding how best to position their organisations within them. Leadership development programmes have tended to take present or future leaders out of their organisations and, in interactive ways, get them to explore the future together.

The alternative track has been in the helping of leaders or senior staff with project planning, monitoring and evaluation, financial management and human resource development. Conceptual issues of NGDO position and role, and the nature of social and civic change, for example, are less evident. Much that is termed capacity building is premised on better delivery, with more specialist courses for those wishing to be 'advocates'. It is more the exception than the rule for capacity building to happen in-house. Training courses are still seen to be a suitable way of improving organisational performance through individual, rather than group, development. The limitations of this approach are documented elsewhere.[55]

In recognition of the limitations of these tracks for leadership development, there is a move towards experiential, rather than course-based, personal forming coupled to individual mentoring over an extended period. This is necessary because the nature of the NGDO leadership problem is not simply amenable to past approaches for its solution.

The Generational Problem

The problem of the preparation of successors is sufficiently articulated from the Philippine experience to merit an extensive quotation.

'One of the challenges that face NGO leaders today is the problem of successor generation. During the PHILSSA-sponsored focus group discussion ... one of the participants lamented that some of the present crop of second liners lacked the fiery idealism and commitment of the pioneers in social development work. To which another replied that the second liners could not be clones of the first, that they must and will chart their own paths.

Briefly, the problem with successor generation is the task of wooing, keeping and mentoring the next generation of development workers to have the necessary commitment and vision to, not only continue the work, but also bring to it the originality and creativity the present situation requires.

Preparing the next generation is an important task because the pioneers of development work are overworked and overextended. The NGO pioneers were trailblazers, armed with the writings and thinking of the 1950s–1970s on organizing and poverty alleviation, tried and tested by their grassroots experience and their ranks swelled by the young conscientized by the Marcos era of repression. The pioneers of development work built one of the most developed NGO communities in the world. But the problems that they faced are still present. Fresh faces and new approaches are necessary to find solutions to some of the more intractable problems of development.

The NGO second-liner is besieged on two fronts – in his/her external and internal environments. Externally, the second-liner now operates in an uncertain ideological environment, unlike the pioneers who found comfort in the dogmas of the past because of their prescription of a clear set of convictions and options. With this comes the precariousness of doing development work without a clear framework or a distinct set of "enemies". As a result, social development work has gradually focused plainly on "what works" rather than on any ideological agenda.

Internally, second-line social development workers face the problem of dwindling resources of foreign funding which has natural implications on NGOs' financial sustainability. Without a steady income, NGOs cannot make long-term plans for their staff. This forces NGO workers to hop from NGO to NGO to gain a wider breadth of experience.

In order to keep a good staff, NGO leaders are trying to strike a balance between defining NGO work as a career which provides a traditional career path and benefits, and trying to define NGO work as a career that preserves its reputation as a vocation for volunteers.

The dilemma of NGOs is how to preserve the voluntary spirit that is necessary for NGO work while providing the right working conditions for NGO workers to make a long-term commitment. Nurturing senior people is a particular difficulty in NGOs, hence the propensity of NGO workers to leave their original NGOs to become first-liners in new NGOs, or worse, to leave the development field altogether for *work that is more secure, challenging, or lucrative.*

While there is a need to look for the same commitment and idealism in the second-liners as there was in the pioneers, the second-liners will need to be different since they will face a different development task.

NGO second-liners face the challenge of organizational maintenance rather than organization building. Secondly, they must maintain the vision and momentum while confronting practical issues like dealing with national and local government. Moreover, second-liners must find creative strategies for advocating reformist policies. In addition, they will have to develop new forms of partnerships with more independent people's organisations requiring them to withdraw in certain areas and carve new niches in others. Finally, second-liners must be pioneers and fiery idealists.'[56]

It is obvious that 'training' is not going to get to the heart of the issues sketched above, nor, for that matter, will training deal with the more general issue of developing leaders of social entrepreneurs, civic innovators or development enterprises. What, then, might work?

A New Style of Leadership Development

Approaches to leadership development and the preparation of the next generation necessarily differ, but relate to each other. How is explained from two examples. One illustrates leadership identification, the other succession preparation.

The Ashoka Foundation has set out to identify 'innovators for the public'. David

Bonbright has documented who they are, what they look like, and the nature of their innovation.[57] The process hinges, in the first instance, on rigorous selection. Ashoka Foundation selection focuses on four criteria – creativity; entrepreneurial quality; the social impact of the idea; and ethical fibre. They are looking for a first-class idea in the hands of a first-class entrepreneur – someone who is self-formed and with social commitment.

Once selected, the Ashoka Foundation provides an income to create the space required for the person to pursue the idea, but not funding for the idea itself. A good entrepreneur should already have this worked out. Additional support comes from members of the Ashoka Fellowship: individuals with similar dispositions and potentials – people who want to change society as a system and have a good idea of how to make that happen. The Fellowship is organised locally and globally and offers mutual support, not dependency.

On the other hand, preparing the next generation differs in that the individuals concerned have already 'pre-selected' themselves. In the quotation used above, they are 'second-liners', that cannot be clones of the founder. They must work out how to address old problems – poverty, exclusion and abuse of rights, for example – in the new contexts of democracy rather than dictatorship, globalisation rather than protected nationalism and open communication rather than closed indoctrination. Nevertheless, not being a clone does not mean that experience of founders is not of use. The issue is, how can it best be tapped?

In association with Co-Multiversity, an NGDO committed to leadership development, the Caucus of Development Non-Governmental Organisation Networks (CODE-NGO) has devised a certificated successor-generation programme based on an action-reflection sequence with structured content. Over a one-year period, participants spend one week per month together in a course setting with materials to systematically examine and reflect on internal features and the external role and relations of NGDOs. The weeks between these sessions are spent back in the NGDO. This period would contain tasks to test and substantiate the formal material, guided by a mentor or coach assigned to the participant. Many of the mentors are existing NGDO leaders. Mentoring, documenting and sharing leadership experience are emerging as important elements in preparing successors.[58] It is akin to the 'accompanying' approach used in process consultation.[59]

In my view, this approach has the right foundations. However, it may be too limited in terms of ensuring sufficient exposure beyond the confines of NGDOs into the world of other social, political and economic actors as well as into the international arena. Secondments, exchanges, conferences are all ways of fostering an expanded view and network of personal contacts.[60] It is also important to ensure that participants have been exposed to rural and urban deprivation. It cannot be assumed that NGDO staff have had much depth of such exposure either

More generally, an experience–reflection process, with or without mentoring, is being adopted not just for leadership development, but also for formation of organisational development consultants by CDRA and by the German Agency for Technical Cooperation (GTZ).[61]

It is too early to say how successful this approach will be. A longer-term issue is who will be interested in working in an NGDO, a social enterprise or in civic innovation anyway?

Going Fishing

In many countries of the South, the inspiration for social action and forming or joining an NGDO was a product of living under repressive regimes. In America, reaction to repression was often fed by Jesuit teaching and education. Links between academe and NGDOs were often strong, in part because the latter offered a refuge for scholars expelled from, or not at home in, a university subject to political control. In other places, schools of social work were imbued with an emancipatory fervour and involvement in real politics of post-colonialism and left–right rivalry.

This type of formative environment for young people has ebbed away, leading to political disengagement and concern for a career that ensures a good life. In addition, links between NGDOs and schools, colleges and universities are weak or non-existent. As a consequence, knowledge about and interest in NGDOs or voluntarism is not being nurtured in young people. In other words, NGDOs are not going fishing for new recruits.

In a few countries, dedicated effort is being put into stimulating youth volunteering as a possible precursor to an NGDO type of career. The Ayala Foundation in the Philippines organises a National Leadership Congress. The event brings together some 70 to 80 young people in their third year of college who have been nominated as best student leaders. The purpose is to give public recognition to voluntary leadership, reinforcing the idea that this is legitimate and a good extra-curricular activity to be included on CVs. It makes career sense.

On the other hand, in other countries, such as Bangladesh, the NGDO sector is large, well profiled and reasonably remunerated. In India the Gandhian ethos of voluntary work is so ingrained and levels of educated unemployment so high that NGDOs face many applicants. The leadership problem, here, becomes one of selection for the right motives, not attraction for the wrong ones.

Another path is to make youth volunteering in an NGDO much easier. For this, NGDOs are contacting schools and colleges, and providing information on what they do and why. However, this remains an activity that happens in any spare time available, and is seldom viewed as preparing the next generation.

Whatever is tried, in many countries NGDOs remain with the problem of financial and job insecurity and low pay. Nevertheless, this is still not a reason not to more actively propagate the ideas and ethics of NGDOs to today's youth.

Pass the Halo: NGDO Leadership Transition

There is a disturbing lack of writing and knowledge about leadership transitions in NGDOs.[62] The processes involved are seldom investigated or published. Hence, they remain mysterious and obscure. Leadership profiling, identification and selection seem to constitute a private domain that cannot, or must not, bear the light of day. Consequently, there is little evidence from which to draw conclusions or recommendations on how to ensure that transition is successful.[63]

There are complementary ways of approaching the issue of leadership transition. One is from the perspective of necessary change in features of leadership as an organisation evolves. Another is from the perspective of board responsibility and strategic choice. In both, transition from the founder-leader is a special case.

Organisational Stages

Chapter 8 suggests that there are stages of organisational maturation.[64] Logic suggests that each requires a different shape of leadership because the operating state at each stage creates different types of demands. The initial, or pioneer, stage calls for creativity, dynamism, attracting followers as volunteers and exploring the unknown. Relationships are highly personal and warm; decision-making fast, intuitive and informal. Success brings growth and the need to formalise activi-

ties, shift from voluntary to more formal and stable arrangements and a more secure resource base. The professionalism of staff may exceed that of the founder in specific areas, and the need for greater predictability and structure of work reduces the appropriateness of informalism and personal relations as the basis of work and decision making. The question is whether or not the leader can make the transition to a new style and content of being. If not, a crisis of confidence in the leader may occur.

Subsequent stages push towards hierarchy, consolidation and rigidity. Typically, this movement detaches the leader from the critical link with communities. Hierarchy insulates, and translates, information, introducing a growing element of organisational and institutional self-interest in interpretation. Lacking first-hand knowledge of everything going on and being fed pre-processed data, the leader must identify proxy indicators of the NGDO's condition. The leader also needs to find ways of continuing to communicate the vision and spread the inspiration down and out to staff he or she may seldom if ever meet. If the NGDO has gained a substantial profile, political suspicion or jealousy of other NGDOs makes increasing demands on political reading and intelligent use of relationships. Growing responsibilities for continuity of employment increase demands for more complex resource strategies. The list goes on.

The final challenge, in and beyond the institutional stage, is to keep regenerating the organisational fire, through learning and adjustment. Beyond consolidation, stability and security lies the challenge of the continuous leadership of change – what Peter Vaill refers to as a life of rafting in a world of turbulence and white water.[65] The leadership challenge at this stage is for learning to become the way of being. This condition is highly demanding and tiring and unless the leader finds a way of recharging his or her batteries faces the '…problem of individual burnout, which is so acute in non-profits precisely because the individual commitment to them tends to be so intense.'[66]

The issue is the extent to which founders can adequately adapt and adjust to the demands that they have helped to create. If they can, as in a number of NGDOs in South Asia whose founder leaders are still present after 20 years or more, all well and good.[67] If they cannot, who decides that it is time for a change and how does it occur? Is there a successor lined up to take over?

Transition in Practice – Passing or Changing the Halo?

Two strategic issues stand out in terms of the path to transition. The first relates to the halo effect. The second arises from the choice between an insider or an outsider, which in turn depends on whether or not a successor has been groomed and why change is needed.

There is a *prima facie* case that the process of transition is likely to differ from the founder leader and for subsequent changes. Why? Firstly, because there is no precedent to be followed, the process must be created from scratch. Who decides how to go about it is an important issue. Subsequent changes in leadership will have experience to draw on without the emotional features associated with a departing founder. Second, the founder often handpicks governing boards. In deference to him or her, the outgoing leader may have the most influence, if not implicit veto, on what the board decides. Third, founders are seldom, if ever, on fixed-term contracts. Their hand in their own departure – outside of unexpected death – can set important preconditions for the profile and process of the new person sought.

Inevitably, as the organisation grows, the leader or group initiating the NGDO remains significant and powerful. Where leaders stand out, as is commonly the case at the start, they wear the 'halo' that spreads its effect on how the organisation is seen and sees itself. Three important choices present themselves. First, transition can be used to reaffirm the organisation's image by selecting a successor with the same credentials. This reinforces what the NGDO stands for, reconfirming the psychological contract. An alternative is to spread the halo around, or try and uncouple a tight association between the individual and the NGDO. The third option, discussed later, is to make a public statement about regeneration by discarding the old halo and getting a new one.

The first option is illustrated by PRRM. Once released from prison in the mid–1980s for being a member of a left-wing movement trying to overthrow the Marcos regime, Boy Morales took up the reins of the moribund PRRM and his popularist credentials and political alignment became the watchword for the movement. However, this image was balanced by a board composed of individuals in business and government. Consequently, PRRM was seen as a reformist organisation run by a radical. On Boy Morales' appointment to a ministerial post in the new Estrada government, a successor was needed. The choice was for Bobby Tañada, an outsider with similar credentials dating back to his father as a renowned leader of a nationalist, but non-communist, movement. He embodies a similar principled compromise of PRRM as a radical organisation using reformist means to satisfy an agenda with broad support, the eradication of poverty and overcoming of civic inertia.[68] No internal candidate offered this possibility. It was important for PRRM that the halo was sustained and handed on. Reflecting back to a quotation at the start of the chapter, a new prophet was needed and found.

In the second option, founder-leaders take steps to reduce the halo effect and profile the NGDO rather than themselves. Typically, this is associated with a conscious process of distributing leadership into a collective arrangement and investing in potential successors from within. It is not that the halo necessarily disappears, but it is earned through service and internal respect, not from external profile. This has been the strategy adopted by some NGDOs, such as BRAC, which is currently initiating a second generation of leadership. PROSHIKA in Bangladesh started this process in the late 1970s when the founder-leader took sabbatical leave in order for the next level to carry the load. Leader sabbaticals are a common feature in building the next generation from within. In the case of CINDE, the founders spent a substantial amount of time and effort in identifying and nurturing an internal candidate as a successor. Gradual withdrawal from hands-on leadership to a more advisory role was a way of doing so.

Whether for external or internal consumption, the halo effect is taken into account because it expresses continuity through change. An alternative, however, is to use leadership transition to signal a break with the past. This usually means bringing in an outsider. A question is: from how far afield?

Governance and Strategic Choice: from Inside or Outside?

What happens if the founder-leader cannot make the transitions needed as the NGDO matures? Alternatively, for example, what is to be done if the NGDO's reputation slips and crisis looms? In terms of this study, regeneration is required whether the incumbent likes it or not. These are moments when someone, typically the governing board, takes power over the process. A potential complicating factor in board control is the role of staff and donors and, in some settings, the government.[69] Part of the calculus motivating NGDO staff is their right to participate in organisational decision-making. This can extend to an acknowledged role in leader profiling and selection. Though they vow not to, donors can and sometimes do express their satisfaction with a leader or indicate their concurrence with a proposed replacement.

Whatever the case, the boards are ostensibly in charge and responsible for regeneration in a sustainable direction. The boards need to reach the right judgement about a number of things. First, they must consider if a successor from within is to be preferred and available or inappropriate even if available. In other words, is it time for fresh perspectives and fresh blood? Second, what message do they want to send about their reading of the future? What statement do they want to make? For example, boards of some international NGDOs have signalled a shift to a more business-like approach by recruiting from the private sector.[70] Appointing from outside the NGDO in the first instance and from outside the NGDO community in the second instance (be it from government or business) sends a massage about whether or not the old psychological contract and rules of the game will apply in the future. To signal a break with the past, the old halo is exchanged, hopefully, for a better one.

What emerges from these trade-offs in terms of people is known. We can see who new leaders are and where they come from. Unfortunately, this information is not systematically documented or analysed in relation to an NGDO's evolution. Therefore, we do not know what is going on in different settings and at different stages of organisational life. Consequently, there is little advice that can be given about what works and what does not work in terms of leadership transitions under different conditions. In addition, there is little public insight about how readings are arrived at and strategic decisions are reached; nor about the role departing leaders play in making them.

On occasion, one hears of boards complaining that they are treated like rubber stamps – the outgoing leader and staff have it all sewn up. In addition, tussles sometimes arise between local governors of an NGDO and distant owners who may exercise a final veto.[71]

Overall, the content and process of NGDO leader selection and transition resembles a black hole in a star-filled sky. Many forces play themselves out. New and brighter stars emerge, others fade away. However, the information and learning about why, how and when disappears inwards. Consequently, it is difficult to shed much light on this vital feature of organisational regeneration for sustainability: it is a knowledge gap worth filling.

Chapter Summary

Regeneration through leadership suffers from lack of firm knowledge in a number of areas. First, what is it that makes an NGDO leader effective and outstanding? Second, how do NGDOs ensure an optimal match between leader, leadership, the stage of organisational development and future needs?

General theories suggest that to be pre-eminent NGDO leadership requires:

- to be driven by and committed to a conviction that self-development of people is possible and necessary; allied to
- a value-set that gives primacy to achieving public good with and through others, not individually; with
- a balance between the two that prevents slippage into self-aggrandisement;
- an ability to communicate values tied up in an inspiring, motivating vision

or agenda, conveyed through how people read the integrity of a leader's commitment or moral fibre;
- good political insights and contacts, built up without patronage or erosion of principle;
- a personality structure where caring and respect are second nature, complemented by a conviction that power is best employed and 'enjoyed' when it is shared;
- deep knowledge of and insight into the nature of social processes and systems. It calls for a capacity to read environments with accuracy, care and speed. It demands the mental capacities to understand information and select viable points of intervention: the agenda in action;
- a nature that is both curious and adaptive; and
- a capacity to be a good reader and redesigner of organisations.

Successful NGDO leaders are both creative, inspirational civic artists and competent organisational artisans.

Leadership development and preparation of successor generations is in its infancy. In terms of identification, the Ashoka Foundation's approach merits greater attention. In the short term, fostering succession calls for less reliance on training and more on extended processes that give structured reflection on experience allied to mentoring and personal guidance. In the long term, it means getting young people interested in the values NGDOs hold and the agendas they aspire to. Greater interaction with schools and opportunities for the placement of volunteers within NGDOs would help.

Too little is known about leader selection and transition – what triggers the process; what role do founders or departing leaders play and what regeneration is needed for future viability? Nevertheless, of importance is attention to the psychological contract which followers rely on. A critical choice is whether the contract is to be sustained, albeit in different ways, or regenerated to something new. Leader selection from within or without, and from how far without, sends a strong message about what regeneration is thought to be needed. Selection from outside the sector typically signals a break with the past.

Chapter 12

The Leader's Legacy – Creating a Virtuous Spiral

'What leaders are called upon to do in a chaotic world is to shape their organisations through concepts, not through elaborate rules or structures.' (Margaret Wheatley)[1]

Sustainability is about insightful response to change. But, how does an NGDO know that it is being insightful or is changing enough? The simple answer is 'society says so in a variety of ways'. The 'secret' of a virtuous spiral lies in a system tying together this question and its answer in a dynamic way.

By way of closure, this chapter provides a summary linking the two major themes running through the preceding pages. It does so by describing what a virtuously spiralling system is made of and looks like. Creating a virtuous spiral is the most important legacy a leader has to offer.

The Virtuous Spiral

A virtuous spiral of NGDO sustainability comprises four elements that should feed positively into each other. If they do, the NGDO, literally, goes upwards from strength to strength. Its longevity is more assured as the sequence repeats itself from a new vantage point of accumulated wisdom. However, if one element is weak or falters, the others can, perhaps, cope for a while but, in the end, the spiral takes a descending turn for the worse. The NGDO passes over its peak of maturity and declines into institutionalised bureaucracy and inertia – a living death. Recovery to peak performance is then only possible with major trauma. A virtuous spiral can prevent and arrest such a decline. Figure 12.1 shows the spiral and its major elements.

In concept, the virtuous spiral is an interactive process bonding the NGDO with its environment. The starting point is performance in relation to the organisation's mission. Has it read the environment correctly and is it contributing something of enduring social value (Part I)? Recognition of this achievement creates a positive reputation, public support and feedback in terms of demand or other expression of appreciation, such as positive media coverage which, together, enhance opportunities for resource mobilisation (Part II). In its turn, coupled with its own performance assessment, public expression and critique feeds into the learning process, creating new knowledge that incorporates past insight. And, if the organisation is agile, renewed insight translates into organisational change and regeneration (Part III). In other words, the organisation adapts to produce better impact and

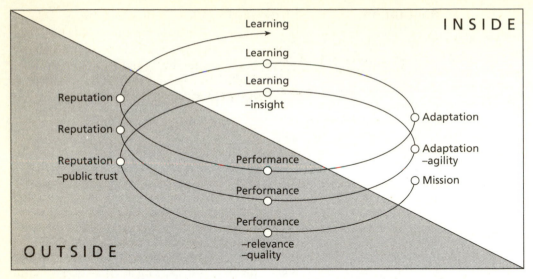

Figure 12.1 *The Virtuous Spiral for Sustainability*

enhanced social value, which reinforces a positive reputation, which feeds resources, and so the spiral continues.

Performance

In the last analysis, aside from the few NGDOs whose endowments ensure sustainability irrespective of performance, what is achieved for society is the foundation for a sustainable future. It is also the focus of the question, 'what am I and the organisation accountable for and to whom?' On what will my personal and our collective credibility and legitimacy rest? Answering the accountability question is particularly important for NGDOs in many countries of the South and East because their intentions are subject to so much public doubt.[2] However, it is equally important for NGDOs that take up policy positions on public issues, especially those in the North that speak in the interest of the South. In fact, it is true for any organisation that speaks on behalf of those who are less able to do so for themselves.

The significance of the accountability issue, highlighted in Chapter 3, is becom-

ing more acute and public as NGDOs, and other civic groups, book success in influencing inter-governmental gatherings and negotiations. Civic impact on global negotiations started in earnest at the 1992 Rio conference on the environment. More recent examples are NGDO pressure on negotiation of the Multilateral Agreement on Investment (MAI), which was subsequently postponed, but as good as abandoned; and more graphically, civic impact on the WTO at its meeting in Seattle in November 1999. These achievements invite the question 'Will NGDOs democratise, or merely disrupt, global governance?'[3] A continual self-questioning of 'who are we, what are we here for and where is our mandate?', will be a healthy and more necessary stance in the years to come. If NGDOs do not have their own well-considered answers, others will provide them to suit their own purposes. The dimensions and criteria of relevance and quality should help in continuing to find an answer.

Reputation

To a greater or lesser degree, the viability of most organisations – apart from business monopolies and government agencies – depends on their reputation. The degree of dependency on reputation increases where people have, and are able, to choose between alternatives. However, NGDOs of the South and East are in a complicated position when assessing their reputation. First, unlike business or government, they lack a reasonably direct or transparent feedback mechanism that acts as a measure of reputation. Businesses have market share, profitability and share price as direct indicators. Politicians and governments have votes and civic protest as signs of satisfaction or dissatisfaction. Reputation is reflected back directly by clients or citizens.

NGDOs infrequently obtain much of the resources from those they serve. As a result, the nature and direction of reputation become confused and multiplied between the funder and the beneficiary. In addition, the content of feedback is seldom unequivocal and is open to diverse, interest-based' interpretations. Out of this confusion must emerge that nebulous quality called trust. Moreover, for sustainability this quality must be present throughout the NGDO's major stakeholders.

However, NGDO beneficiaries are seldom able to fully exercise choice. Hence, the mere fact that they participate with an NGDO intervention is not a clear signal of what they really think about the organisation – beggars cannot be choosers. Indirect measures of participation and community contribution may give some idea, but they require honest interpretation and hence can, again, become distorted by self-interest, compounded by an NGDO belief that 'doing good' is itself a proxy for positive reputation. However, as so often seen in development work, the road to hell is paved

with good intentions.[4] Consequently, a bigger burden rests on the NGDO to self-assess its reputation and to know that it is maintaining high quality in its practice. Typical project and programme evaluations do not answer the vital question 'what do people think of you as an organisation and why?' How do they compare you with others? Social audits and similar methods are one way of finding out, but are not, yet, applied widely enough.

Learning

Few, if any, NGDOs would deny the merits of a learning approach to what they do and what they are. Much effort is currently being put into understanding what it means to be a learning organisation. Nevertheless, obstacles to NGDOs making a shift from understanding to practice lie deep. A significant part of the problem lies in a moral history of welfarism and practice of subsidy. The first feeds an assumption that any output must be useful. The second fosters paternalism and a parent-child relationship where, by deep psychological imprint if not in practice, the outsider already knows better, if not best.

Learning which does not question welfarism and paternalism may bring about adaptation in terms of technical improvements. But it does not reach the heart of problems affecting the aid system. These problems have been described as the pathologies of hidden agendas, abiding nationalism in donor behaviour, a culture that values and equates disbursement of funds with development performance, the creation of aid dependency and disempowerment of recipients.[5] The deep challenge for NGDOs is to learn lessons which ensure that their role and position in society do not perpetuate such illnesses. In other words, learning must lead to a more critical self-awareness. This depth of insight is required if organisational agility is to remain principled and not oppor-tunistic.

Adaptation

Adaptation is the name of the sustainabil-ity game. It has many facets: from the simple to the complex elements of doing – via attention to relevance and quality; and from the superficial to the structural aspects of being – via critical awareness and honest self-questioning. In both cases, responsiveness must be directed and prin-cipled, not simply reactive – not a clutch-ing at straws, but shaping and grasping a desired, viable future. Success at both requires many things, but above all, it calls for regeneration through sound leaders and leadership.

Striking a Balance ended with a call for 'NGDO leaders and governors to generate a vision of the future they want beyond aid.'[6] This volume concludes with a parallel appeal. The invocation is that the men and women carrying the burden, and enjoying the privilege, of leading NGDOs should be at the forefront of creating virtuous spirals for sustainability. It will be their most important legacy

Appendix

Levels in Sustainability Systems

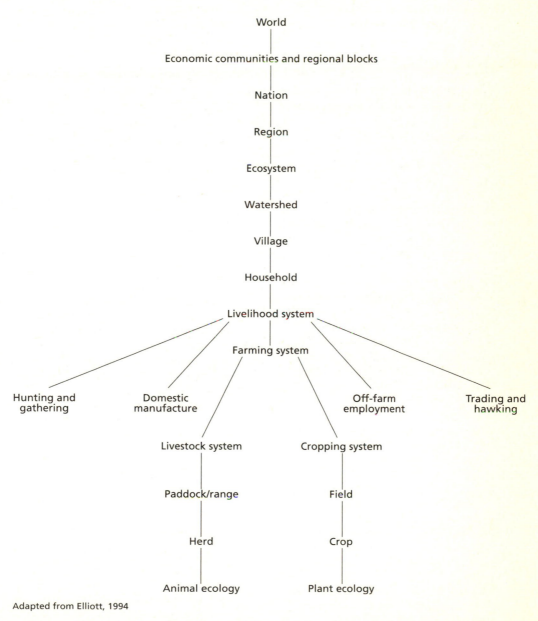

World

Economic communities and regional blocks

Nation

Region

Ecosystem

Watershed

Village

Household

Livelihood system

Farming system

Hunting and gathering

Domestic manufacture

Off-farm employment

Trading and hawking

Livestock system

Cropping system

Paddock/range

Field

Herd

Crop

Animal ecology

Plant ecology

Adapted from Elliott, 1994

Figure A.1 *Levels in Sustainability Systems – A Rural Environment*

Notes

Introduction

1 Workshop on the Enhancement of DMC Participation in the Bank's Business Processes, Manila, 10–12 February, 1999.

2 There is no universally accepted definition of NGDOs or of CBOs. This book follows the criteria for NGDOs set out in *Striking a Balance*, pp. 38–39. Legitimised by the presence and condition of the world's poor, they are formally registereded not-for-profit organisations, established to serve third parties, typically but not solely as intermediaries in the international aid system, employing principles and values associated with voluntarism. They do not distribute an economic surplus to owners. They are not part of or formally controlled by a public body. They are self-governing within the terms set by existing legislation. Formal registration means acceptance of social accountability.

CBOs are member-based, mutual benefit organisations that may be formal or informal in nature. Their members are usually the intended beneficiaries of NDGO work.

3 Elkington, 1997.

4 For example, the International Institute for Sustainable Development in Canada maintains an Indicators Compendium <http://www.iisd.ca>

5 *Striking a Balance* appears to be very useful. It is in its third reprint, has been translated into Russian and Spanish and will soon be translated into French. It is also required reading or core material on a number of NGDO training and degree courses.

6 *Striking a Balance* has been described as a '…manual for the [NGDO] community', Townsend, 1999:615.

7 There are three distinct bodies of literature and experience brought together in this volume. Part I draws on participatory (project) monitoring, evaluation, impact assessment and organisational review. Part II draws on the expanding literature on income generation, fund-raising and social entrepreneurship. Part III relies on organisational studies: leadership, learning behaviour and change processes.

8 Schearer, de Oliveira and Tandon, in Fox and Schearer, 1997:15. Richard Holloway points out that it is equally important for NGDOs to actively communicate with stakeholders about good programmes and results.

9 Other than alluding to the importance of impact and organisational capacity for resource mobilisation, the CIVICUS volume does not substantively address them. This is also the case with many similar volumes. See Further Reading.

10 The term 'principled mobility' was used by one NGDO leader to express this organisational behaviour. Interview with Allan Kaplan of CDRA.

11 A similar distinction between these three types of sustainability can be found in Jordan, 1996 and Cannon, 1999a.

Chapter 1

1 For a summary of evidence from NGDO impact studies, see Fowler 1999b. The most recent study of the impact of Danish NGDOs reaches a similar, economic, conclusion. See Oakley, 1999b.

2 Cox and Healey, 1998.

3 Oakley, 1999b:53.

4 *The Independent*, 16 September, 1999, p6. *Global Environmental Outloook 2000*, UNEP, Nairobi.

5   'More precisely, there is a region (or hyper-region) within which the entire range of systems on which humans are dependent can survive. In other words, this region is the intersection of the sustainable or survival regions of all systems necessary to continued human existence': Clayton and Radcliffe, 1996:43.

6   See note 4.

7   Sutton, 1999.

8   On dependency, see SIDA, 1995; on fungibility, World Bank, 1998.

9   See, for example, Burkey, 1993; Edwards and Hulme, 1992, 1996; Hulme and Edwards, 1996; Fisher, 1993, 1997; Meyer, 1999; Smillie, 1995; Sogge, 1996.

10 Secure, aggregate data on those 'touched' by NGDOs do not exist. Using country cases and extrapolating from previous estimates, a 1993 estimate (UNDP, 1993:93) was an outreach to 250 million people, at that time about 20 per cent of the world's poor. The number of NGDOs has increased rapidly since then and others have expanded (Salamon, 1994). However, since 1993, population growth, the Asian crisis and widening wealth gaps have contributed to the number of the world's poor. Depending on the measures used (US$1 or 2 per day), the 'poor' are between 1.3 and 3 billion individuals. A direct NGDO outreach to some 15–20 per cent of people who are poor (as opposed to poorest) is still probably a fair 'guesti-mate' – some 450–600 million people across the globe.

11 See CDRA, 1999:4.

12 Interview with James Sarpei of CENCOSAD, Ghana.

13 Term used by James Taylor of CDRA.

14 For a highly technical treatment of sustainability from a systems perspective, see Clayton and Radcliffe, 1996.

15 Complexity theory would also say that our actions, like the flapping of a butter-fly's wings, can have climatic effects on the other side of the world as well.

16 For an elaboration on 'reading develop-ment' see CDRA, 1998.

17 David Korten, *The Post Corporate World*, Kumerian Press, 1999.

18 More definitions can be found in Elliott, 1994:3. Some are not definitions as such, but descriptions of what sustainable change would encompass and for whom.

19 Clayton and Radcliffe, 1996:11.

20 Some eminent ecologists argue that sustainability is in fact an illusion: the problems of resource management in conditions of complex uncertainty are insurmountable. The focus of policy must therefore shift to the management of human demands and behaviour. A summary of this debate can be found in Roe, 1995.

21 Clayton and Radcliffe, 1996.

22 Elkington, 1997.

23 Thurow, 1996, Chapter 11.

24 Coupland, 1992.

25 Edwards, 1999a:9.

26 Huntington, 1993.

27 For discussion on positive and negative social capital see Woolcock, 1997.

28 Organisations are purposeful, role-bound social units. Institutions are stable, valued patterns of relationships in society. For more detailed definition see, Fowler, Pratt and Campbell, 1992.

29 Edwards, 1999a:9

30 Over 50 per cent of the estimated US$12–15 billion per year used by NGDOs comes, directly or indirectly, from official overseas development assistance. Randell and German, 1998; OECD, 1999.

31 For a detailed explanation of aid quality see Fowler 1997:pp129–134. For an analysis of why NGDO performance is hampered, see Fowler, 1999b.

Chapter 2

1   *Reasons for Success*, p19.

2   For detailed references, see Fowler, 1997, Chapter 1.

3   For a discussion of a rights-based approach to development see ODI, 1999.

4   Many empowerment approaches are based on a psychosocial model, itself founded on (neo-Frierian) forms of critical social analysis. A good example is *Training for Transformation*, by Anne Hope and Sally Timmel. For details of a

'regenerated' Frierian approach to adult literacy and social change see Archer and Cottingham, 1996 and 1997.

5   The methodology known as Appreciative Inquiry is founded on this principle: see Cooperrider et al, 1995.

6   See, for example, Esman and Uphoff, 1984; Eade, 1997.

7   Kaplan, 1999.

8   For a detailed look at the relationship between output, outcome, impact and results, see Fowler 1997, Chapter 7.

9   Though dated, Esman and Uphoff's work on local institutional development (1984) still reflects the core of what CBO capacity is all about. It is still 'the' book to read.

10 Fowler, 1997:166.

11 In today's development terminology, the underpinning is the social capital available to the group. Trust and shared aspirations are constituents of 'binding' social capital.

12 Kaplan, 1996.

13 For this conclusion in relation to governments and people, see World Bank, 1998.

14 ODI, 1996; Fowler, 1999a.

15 For 'tyrannical' perspectives on participation see Cleaver, 1999; Hailey, 1998, Musse, 1998.

16 It is not the case, however, that NGDOs are, by definition, good at participation or that the official system is necessarily bad at it either. The point is that standardisation is not the same as applying best practice.

17 The need to become more client-centred and tailor products to individual consumer specification is now the prevailing truth in the business world.

18 Fowler, 2000.

19 Howes, 1999:28.

20 Fowler, 1997:94.

21 Bhat and Cheria, 1997:70.

22 This 'illness' also holds true for many governments where aid is a significant proportion of their budgets. For a detailed look at the dependency affects of aid, see SIDA, 1996.

23 Smith, 1997; Holloway, 1977.

24 Interviews with Dinky Solomon in the Philippines and Mariano Valderrama in Peru.

25 A similar dynamic is to be seen between international NGDOs and their local 'partners'.

26 Rao and Hashemi, 1999.

27 Howes, 1999.

Chapter 3

1   Harding, 1991:297.

2   For macro-economic issues the Bretton Woods Project is a good source www.brettonwoodsproject.org or bwref@gn.apc.org.

3   See, for example, Holland and Henriot, 1983; Brown and Tandon, 1983.

4   Howes, 1999:15–16.

5   Wood and Sharif, 1996; Dawson and Jeans, 1997.

6   Oakley, 1999a, 1999b.

7   Two examples are the World Bank's promotion of a Comprehensive Development Framework; and UNDAF that brings together and rationalises the strategies and efforts of all UN agencies.

8   Sterkenburg and van der Wiel, 1999.

9   Soares and Caccia-Bava, 1998.

10 For scaling up of NGDO impact, see Edwards and Hulme, 1992.

11 Personal communication. One respondent in Argentina even went so far as to state that '... the state should take NGDOs as its research and development department'.

12 For a detailed study in relation to agricultural innovation, see Farrington and Bebbington, 1993.

13 SIAD, 1995.

14 CO-TRAIN, 1998.

15 Interview with Dinky Solomon of CO-TRAIN.

16 Brown, 1994; Dass, 1999.

17 Schearer and Tomlinson, 1995.

18 Jordan and van Tuijl, 1993.

19 Key texts are Mohammed, 1997; Nelson, 1997. See also Further Reading.

20 Fox and Brown, 1998.

21 Bain, 1999.

22 She notes that: 'Representation is not the only form of NGO legitimacy and it is understood that NGOs are not organised to play the representative role of political parties. However, if NGO legitimacy rests

partially on their role as intermediary organisations for the poor – a role that political parties seem to find more and more difficult to play – they cannot be perceived to be serving as false interlocutors, divorced from grassroots' realities and failing in their role as bridging organizations to the poor.'

23 Bain, 1999:6.

24 Ibid, p20.

25 Treakle, in Fox and Brown, 1998:220.

26 Obviously, mass mobilisation can be used for political ends – a common excuse for insecure governments to react excessively and clamp down on NGDOs.

27 Blauert and Zadek, 1998:4. See also Brown, 1990.

28 See Further Reading for Part 1 for useful references.

29 For internet access to these, the address is: <http://www.oecd.org/dac/indicators>

30 Frankenberger, 1993.

31 Krishna and Shrader, 1999.

32 For a discussion of these problems see, for example, Harding, 1991; Oakley, Pratt and Clayton, 1998.

33 A different set of 12 areas of sustainability criteria for CBOs can be found in Lanzet, 1997.

34 NGDO credit programmes seldom know the ecological dimensions of the enterprises they support.

35 Useful indicator references – economics: Barbier, 1987b; empowerment: Shetty, 1991; environment: Barbier, 1997b, Karas and Coates, 1994, O'Connor, 1994; human well-being: Alkire, 1997; local capacity: Uphoff, 1992; Fowler, 1997, chapters 3 and 8; social development: UNDP annual reports since 1990. Depending on the type of initiative, more detailed indicators can be and should be selected. See also Further Reading for Part I.

36 Duran, 1999.

37 Uphoff, 1991.

38 Provided by Mariano Valderrama.

39 Interview with Alberto Patiño.

40 Eade, 1997c.

Chapter 4

1 For example, see Smillie and Helmich, 1993, 1999 and Further Reading.

2 This does not necessarily hold true for self-financing foundations whose endowments generate revenue irrespective of whether or not they bring any benefit to society.

3 Kanter, 1979.

4 Vincent and Campbell, 1989.

5 Following on from Vincent and Campbell are a number of important studies that are required reading for anyone interested in the resource dimension of sustainability. See Bennett and Gibbs, 1996; Norton, 1996; Fox and Schearer, 1997; Cannon, 1999; and Holloway, 1999a, 1999b.

6 Brown, 1998.

7 For a critical analysis of corporate power, see Korten, 1995.

8 Salamon and Anheier, 1999.

9 Informed observers suggest that international aid accounts for some 95 per cent of the funds employed by Southern NGDOs.

10 For a detailed analysis of paths for aid flows, see Fowler, 1997:135–148.

11 This question is also being posed by Northern NGDOs. See Smillie, Douxchamps and Sholes/Covey, 1996; INTRAC, 1998; and Further Reading.

12 *Development Information Update*, no 1, Development Initiatives, Evercreech, July 1999.

13 Raffer, 1999, abstracted in <http:/www.ids.ac.uk/id21/static/9ckr1.html> 23 October.

14 For official aid and civil society, see van Rooy, 1998. For examples of poverty focus see DFID, 1997, a White Paper produced by the UK Department for International Development, London,

15 Firm figures on NGDO funding levels and distribution of sources are notoriously difficult to find. For attempts, see Fowler, 1992a, 1999; OECD, 1999.

16 For details of trends in aid allocations, see *Geographical Distribution of Financial Flows to Aid Recipients*, OECD, 1999 <http:www.oecd.org>

17 Valderrama, 1999, Aldaba, 1999.
18 For the situation of non-profit-making organisations in Vietnam, see Sidel, 1997. The Netherlands has just gone through a review designed to reduce aid concentration countries from about 60 to 20.
19 INTRAC, 1998.
20 Data supplied by Development Initiatives, derived from DAC data sheets. With thanks to Judith Randell.
21 UNHCR, 1994.
22 Public support to religious institutions and orders is typical, as are contributions to funds established by a royal family, as in Thailand. Development per se is seldom the intention.
23 Hyden, 1980, 1983.
24 This debate has been a significant feature of NGO-ANC relations pre- and post-apartheid.
25 Ge Yunsong, 1999. The issue of legislative frameworks is receiving significant attention. See for example, ICNPL, 1997; CIVICUS, 1997b.
26 Zhu Youhong, 1999; Young and Woo, 1999.
27 One example is the Chinese Youth Development Foundation (CYDF) – with roots in the Communist Youth League – that has successfully mobilised non-governmental resources from affluent Chinese in Hong Kong, to improve access to primary schools.
28 Gao Bingzhong, 1999.
29 To counter this public image, the Charities Aid Foundation (CAF) will be training journalists on the work of NGOs so that '...they may overcome their instinctive distrust of charities as covers for organised crime'. *CAF Bulletin*, September 1999.
30 Bretton Woods Project, 1999.
31 Fowler, 1994; Kendall, 1999; Salamon et al, 1999.
32 Such a compromise has been characterised as 'creeping self-censorship': Edwards, 1993.
33 Kapur, 1997.
34 In some countries, the situation is said to be deteriorating, exemplified by more stringent and disempowering laws for non-profit-making organisations: van Tuijl, 1999.

35 Bourdeau, 1999.
36 There is also the tactical issue of overcoming government 'ego' and an historically conditioned view in many developing countries that government always knows best about everything all the time.
37 International Federation of Red Cross and Red Crescent Societies, 1998.
38 Weiss, 1998.
39 See Pfeffer and Salancik, 1978. For an application to NGDOs, see Hudock, 1995.
40 For a case study, see Holloway, 1997; Sobhan, 1997.
41 There are ways of establishing a diversification index to assess present conditions and compare future options; Chang and Tuckman, 1994.
42 Ibid, p273.
43 Schmidt and Marc, 1994.
44 Gibbs, Fumo and Kilby, 1999, pxii.
45 This does not mean that businesses do not have a developmental impact. They do and it is quite profound. The point is that the perspective of their support is not social development or equity as such.
46 A common proxy for autonomy is the proportion of tax money in an NGDO's budget. However, this is too simplistic because the degree of influence a state exerts through its funds depends on the nature of the political system. Unlike two-party majority rule, proportional representation seems to exert a tempering influence on the propensity of states to interfere with the non-profit-making organisations they fund. The development foundations in Germany and the Netherlands enjoy substantial autonomy despite significant government funding that can amount to 95 per cent of their total. Transitions in political regime do not, unlike in Britain and America, lead to significant directionality being exerted by the incoming party. For example, in the case of Britain, the Labour government treats NGDOs as a particular type of development contractor, rather than civic entities with autonomous agendas. Reform to donor funding 'windows' for NGDOs – the Civil Society Challenge Fund and Participatory Partnership Agreements – are premised on

applicants having a sufficiently similar agenda to DIFD itself.

47 Salamon, et al, 1999.

48 This self-perception is not as applicable as many would imagine. In terms of money volume, NGDOs are providers of social services, increasingly drawing on a subsidy provided by international aid.

49 Fowler, 1999:5.

Chapter 5

1 A relative inattention to non-financial resources is also to be found in *Striking a Balance*. For a very modest treatment of the issue, see Fowler, 1997:152–155.

2 A special case are economically active CBOs – for example in cooperatives and credit unions – where financial resources are generated that can pay for NGDO services. This is a financial source dealt with in Chapter 7.

3 For example, in its seminal work, of the 11 strategies described in the CIVICUS volume on resource mobilisation (Fox and Schearer, 1997), only one explicitly deals with non-financial resources. The very useful volume by Lisa Cannon does not include this as an explicit strategy in the 20 she describes.

4 Chambre, 1989.

5 Etzioni, 1993; Turniansky and Cwikel, 1996.

6 Even this simple distinction is weak to the extent that staff accepting remuneration below the market rate for their skills also make a 'voluntary' contribution. However, their vested interests in terms of organisational viability are certainly stronger as is their claim to 'co-ownership' of decision-making as compensation for forgone financial reward. See Fowler, 1997.

7 Gill and Snyder, 1990.

8 Fukuyama, 1999.

9 See Further Reading.

10 In the West, solutions are seen to lie in variations on the theme of social contracts; Group of Lisbon, 1995.

11 For a more detailed treatment of volunteers, see Norton, 1996, chapter 7. They can also introduce problems of poor skill, dislike of formal structures, own agendas, confusing organisational mission, etc.

12 Salamon et al, 1999:4–5.

13 Interview with Clotilde Fonseca, chief executive of the foundation. The quotation contains an implicit assumption that 'volunteers' are non-professionals and that to label a professional 'a volunteer' is retrograde. There is no standard international definition for volunteers or what constitutes volunteering. Consequently, terminologies will inevitably have their local sensitivities.

14 Interview with the director of CRY; and Davis, 1997:A30–35.

15 In Kenya, rates of 10 to 15 per cent are common. For example, creation of an NGDO liaison function in World Bank country offices absorbed some 30 people from NGDOs.

16 For example, in Kenya a company agreed to print HIV/AIDS educational messages on its milk cartons.

17 Obviously, this is also a desirable and important function of board members.

18 See Fox and Schearer, 1997:124–125; and SIAD, 1995.

19 From an economist's perspective of social capital as an 'externality', a major investment area to increase social capital's effects on reducing poverty is in communication; Collier, 1999.

20 *The Guardian Weekly*, 6 June 1999, p20.

21 Fox and Schearer, 1997:34.

22 From a presentation by Sam Joseph, country director, ActionAid Somaliland, Kathmandu, 11 August 1998.

23 This is one reason to employ appropriate technologies: to expand the resource base in ways that reduce both investment costs and recurrent demands.

24 The possibilities of other types of non-financial resource are very broad. No sensible summary is possible for this option.

Chapter 6

1 Aldaba, 1999.

2 Conclusions of a study of NGOs in Costa Rica. Personal communication from Mariano Valderrama.

3   The importance of individual identification of beneficiaries in fund-raising is exemplified by NGDOs raising funds through child sponsorship. This remains the most successful model for generating private support for development work. The rate of growth of the largest child sponsorship agencies has approached 40 per cent per annum. Current estimates suggest that there are more than 5 million internationally sponsored children generating cumulative NGDO incomes of over US$1 billion annually (Smillie and Helmich, 1999:19–20).

4   As a co-founder of an NGDO, INTRAC, the first 18 months was supported by voluntary effort alone. Out-of-pocket expenses were also covered by the founders.

5   Bendell, 1998. He points out that community action against pollution from local industries signals the emergence of citizens as a force alongside government exacting compliance at and beyond general statutory requirements. In order to maintain good local relations, companies do take notice – a case of citizen compliance.

6   This is a gross oversimplification. Nevertheless, it does reflect the basic political messages being broadcast in the North and through the aid chain to the South and East.

7   Part of the rejection of old categories is the tendency of politicians to talk only of 'markets' and not of capitalism as the prevailing form of market operation. As JK Galbraith observed, this is done to neutralise debate and cloud the reality of the winners and losers the system creates: BBC interview, 25 November 1999.

8   This section draws on Fowler, 1999a; and Hordijk, 1999.

9   Transcript of telephone interview with Bill Drayton by Caroline Hartnell, editor of *Alliance*, 18 September 1999.

10 Entrepreneurship is seen to be an appropriate term to describe a wide variety of interpretations across diverse organisations without questioning its merits – a conceptual imposition again from North to South. See for example, *CIVICUS World*, July–August, 1998.

11 For example, Boschee; 1998; Dees, 1998.

12 Drawn from Badelt, 1997.

13 This is an important point made by Richard Holloway. Non-profit means 'prohibition of distributing a profit, or surplus for private gain', not 'not making one'; 1999b:25.

14 Anderson, 1998.

15 Actually, the expectation that non-profit-making organisations will benefit less from government subsidy may be a useful 'Third Way' myth of social liberalism. Recent data in the UK suggest that domestic charities are becoming more reliant on state subsidy than before – a continuing product of the Thatcher era that sought to take service provision away from local authorities, *Guardian Weekly*, 30 September, 1999, p24. A similar story has been told for the USA (Wolfe, 1989). Both trends are confirmed by the comparative study of Salamon, Anheier and Associates, 1999.

16 The pioneering work of the Ashoka Foundation is an example of the former concept.

17 The conceptual roots of civic entrepreneurs can be found in the ethics and theories of social action; Dower, 1999. The link with social entrepreneurship lies in the economics of social problem solving. The latter concept focuses on how citizens understand and finance initiatives to address their social problems and not, for example, on how best to deliver social services. Social enterprise is accorded a 'triple bottom line' of social value, economic viability and environmental soundness.

18 The emphasis on partnership across the aid system rests on a questionable premise and neglects donor countries' own history. The idea is to establish in the South and East a 'social contract' model of development prevailing in most Northern countries. In this model, state, market and non-profit sector actors perform in consort and are aligned to overcome the social and environmental dysfunctions created by the limits to competition in a

capitalist market economy (Lisbon Group, 1995). This approach rests on the assumption that the long, differentiated evolutionary processes and struggles between social forces the North has undergone to reach social contract arrangements can be circumvented by judicious application of foreign funds within a uniform framework. Historical analysis of development offers no confirmation that this assumption holds true. In fact, the opposite appears to be the case, namely, that development models, policies and approaches need to be tailored '... *to a country's moment in history. Situational relativism must be accepted by academic development economists as well as by policy makers, both within developing countries and in the international development policy community*' (Adleman and Morris, 1997:840).

Partnership as pursued by donors may apply in some contexts but not in many others. In short, one size does not fit all.

19 'It is far too early, of course, to proclaim [that] social capital research amounts to a coherent theory or new "paradigm" for development studies. Nevertheless, there is good reason to believe that viable alternatives to prevailing orthodoxies are in the wind and that the social dimension of economic development is finally being given the serious attention it deserves.' (Woolcock and Narayan, 1999:21). For social capital in relation to conflict management and resolution, see Abdulai, 1999.

20 For further explanation of these perspectives on civil society, see van Rooy, 1998.

21 Woolcock, 1997.

22 ibid; Hordijk, 1999:44.

23 Hordijk, 1999:45

24 Lee Davis (1997) provides useful detailed information and analysis of the NGO-Business Hybrid. This section follows his usage of the term.

25 Bratton, 1989.

26 Interview with Eduardo Ballon, president of DESCO.

27 van Tuijl, 1999 and discussion with Amil Kandi, president of the Arab NGO Network.

28 Interviews in Cambodia and Kyrgistan in 1996.

29 The variety of unflattering acronyms used to label NGDOs is one example of this mistrust. For a sample of pejorative descriptions, see Fowler, 1997:32.

30 Personal observations and discussions with the members of the Tanzania Association of Non-governmental Organisations (TANGO).

31 Sandar, 1990.

32 See studies by the Asia Pacific Philanthropy Consortium (APPC).

33 Wood and Sharif, 1997.

34 For country studies of the legal conditions under which NGDOs operate, see publications of the International Centre for Non-profit Law (ICNL), Washington, DC. <http:www.icnl.org>

35 Davis, 1997:46.

36 Personal communication, Babar Sobhan.

37 Interview with Jorge Restrepo of Fundaçion FES (FFES).

38 Valderrama, 1999.

39 Ibid, p52.

40 See Davis, 1997:25, for examples.

41 Morales, in Fox and Schearer, 1997:36–37.

42 Interview with Allan Kaplan, director of CDRA.

43 For foundations financed totally from endowments, the challenge to stay agile and not become complacent is tackled in a number of ways. Typical is the approach of the Ford Foundation that relies on a structural turnover of highly professional staff to continuously reinvigorate its thinking and insights.

44 For explanation of a soulful NGDO approach to development, see Westoby, 1997.

45 For details, see Gugler and Jesperson in Fox and Schearer, 1997:249.

46 Draimin and Smillie, 1999.

47 For examples of FLOs, see Schearer in Fox and Schearer, 1997:305.

48 Salamon et al, 1999.

49 PACT, 1993.

50 In the case of the Ford Foundation, this is two years.

Chapter 7

1 The political 'far right' associate subsidy with laziness and undeserved reward. It is used as a pejorative stick with which to beat social democrats and the political 'left'. Hence the danger of using the term here.

2 Bonbright, 1999.

3 The argument that poverty is a destabilising, anti-developmental force in society is now commonly used by Northern politicians to justify aid. Instability is not good for market expansion or attractive for investors. This makes the replacement of aid with foreign direct investment less easy. Poverty is also seen as a source of pressure leading to migration and illegal immigration – an unwelcome vector for transmission of communicable diseases, such as tuberculosis, to the North. Consequently, stability and improvement of living conditions and opportunities in the South and East is in the North's best interest.

4 For a very useful 'balance sheet' of NGDO and government perceptions of each other, see de la Manza, Holloway and N'Diame, in Fox and Schearer, 1997:153.

5 As Anil Najam (1999) shrewdly observes, what NGDOs actually want to do is to co-opt government into their own agenda. The term 'critical engagement' is used by Jane Covey, a member of the NGO-World Bank Committee.

6 Madeley, 1998; Jenkins, 1998.

7 Riddell et al, 1995.

8 Najam, 1995.

9 Tandon, 1989a.

10 For an overview of state–voluntary sector relations, see Clark, 1993, and for Asia, Tandon, 1989b.

11 The Ethiopian system of NGDO regulation exacts a very detailed compliance. NGDOs are registered for one year at a time. Their projects must be approved by local authorities and regional governments carry out periodic evaluations of their work. There are also moves to require them to use particular auditors – contested because this creates havoc with the audit requirements of other donors or of the NGDO itself.

12 Najam, 1995:11.

13 Munishi, 1995:147.

14 Ibid, p148.

15 Hawley, 1993.

16 Korten, 1990.

17 Wallace, Crowther, and Shephard, 1998; Fowler, 1999b.

18 Blackburn, 1996.

19 From a presentation by Tim Brodhead at an NGDO conference in 1987.

20 GrandMet, 1997.

21 Dr Carvedo gained a public reputation as a member of Lima's municipal council, director of a psychiatric hospital and newspaper columnist.

22 Quoted in Heap and Fowler, 1998:4.

23 Regelbrugge, in Fox and Schearer, 1997:211–248.

24 Interview with Rory Tarantino, former chief executive of PBSB.

25 Heap, 1998.

26 Hayday, 1999.

27 Murphy and Bendell, 1997; Heap, 1998; Heap and Fowler, 1999.

28 Holloway, 1999b:81.

29 Fowler, 1988.

30 Henriques, 1998. This is a natural outflow of NEF's work on social auditing (New Economics Foundation, 1995).

31 Nelson, 1997.

32 Norton, 1997:50–56; Kelly and Garcia-Robles, in Fox and Schearer, 1997:79–112; Holloway, 1999b:44–51.

33 In the late 1980s, in response to famine in Ethiopia, Catholic Relief Services (CRS) launched an urgent fund-raising appeal. Knowing the dangers of over-hasty action and food dumping, donations were put into an investment account. Once known by the media, CRS faced accusations of misleading the public about the urgency of the situation and capitalising on the backs of famine victims. Personal conversations with CRS staff.

34 For elaboration on the overheads 'game', see Fowler, 1997:155–159.

35 Quoted in Smillie, 1999.

36 Wheatley and Kellner-Rogers, 1999.

37 Complexity theory offers much new insight into self-organisation as a property of natural systems. See Anderson, Arrow and Pines, 1988; Bak and Chen, 1991.

38 The catchy term 'social venture capitalists' is in vogue for some types of funders of non-profit-making organisations.

39 The Synergos Institute has been particularly active in promoting and understanding FLOs. See Schearer, Winder and Tomlinson, 1995. For a detailed study of Southern foundations, see Draimin and Smillie, 1999.

40 NOVIB, 1996.

41 Communication from Bob Bothwell of the National Council for Responsive Philanthropy based on US research by Craig Jenkins of Ohio State University.

42 For example, Hallowes, 1995; Eade, 1977b; Malhotra, 1997; Fowler, 1998; Knight, 1998; Schearer, 1999; Draimin and Smillie, 1999.

43 Personal interviews with DFID, the European Union (EU), CIDA and the Aga Khan Foundation (AKF).

44 Bonbright, 1999.

45 Schearer, 1999.

46 Quarles van Ufford, Kruit and Downing, 1988.

47 Observations from a previous vantage point as a programme officer in the Ford Foundation.

48 Norton, 1996:111.

49 For trust in relation to non-profit-making organisations, see Anheier, 1995.

Chapter 8

1 Michael Korda, author, quoted in Steckel, 1989:9.

2 Fowler, 1994.

3 Taylor, Marais and Heyns, 1998. This is a particularly useful publication and training resource. See also Avina, 1993.

4 Ibid, p75.

5 Lovell, 1992.

6 The ten principles are as follows: 1 No matter how illiterate or poor, if given an opportunity, people can rise to the occasion and deal with problems. 2 A development organisation should never become a patron. 3 Conscientisation is necessary to empowerment. 4 Self-reliance is essential. 5 Participation and people centredness are essential. 6 Sustainability is essential. 7

There is no one 'fix all' approach. 8 Going to scale is essential. 9 A market perspective and entrepreneurial spirit are useful. 10 The importance of women in development is primary. (Lovell, 1992:24).

7 There are numerous difficulties in managing a very complex organisation like BRAC. Lovell deals with some of them. There have been legal and financial reasons for keeping everything within the BRAC framework.

8 This is also a reflection of BRAC's reading of the political situation and intention not to be associated with any particular party or faction – a charge made against a number of NGDOs during the last election. This does not mean that BRAC is apolitical. For example, its new strategy towards the evolution of village organisations is based on a political reading of opportunities for participation made possible by reform in local governance (Chapter 3).

Chapter 9

1 For example, Hailey and James, 1994; Cumming and Singleton, 1995; Brown, 1998.

2 Although survival without adaptation is not unknown for organisations with substantial endowments. Many of the thousands of British charities fall into this category.

3 Interview with James Taylor of CDRA.

4 Interviews with Laurie Nathan of CCR.

5 For codes of conduct in the Commonwealth, see Ball and Dunn, 1995. For articles on accreditation of non-profit-making organisations, see *Alliance*, vol 4, no 4, CAF, London, December 1999.

6 Personal observation and discussions with leaders of NGDO councils responsible for codes of conduct.

7 See *Alliance*, no 4, vol 3, CAF, September 1999.

8 Johnson and Wilson, 1999.

9 See Further Reading.

10 Smillie, 1999:21–34.

11 Edwards, 1997.

12 Senge, 1990. Peter Senge is probably

known as a leading exponent of the learning philosophy

13 For summaries see Fowler, 1997:64–65; Smillie, 1999; Britton, 1998.

14 Fowler and Biekart, 1996; Fowler, 2000.

15 Hulme and Edwards, 1996.

16 Carlsson, Kohlin and Ekbom, 1994.

17 Meyer, 1997.

18 World Vision, 1997a, 1997b.

19 Taylor, 1997; Johnson and Wilson, 1999.

20 Suzuki, 1998.

21 Edwards, 1997:237; Britton, 1998:4.

22 The World Bank participatory poverty assessment process in Uganda provided cameras to communities so that they could create their images of poverty. Presentation on use of participatory video by Su Braden of Reading University at the Development Studies Association (DSA) NGO study group meeting, London, 2 November 1999.

23 For a still salient critique of projects, see LeCompte, 1985.

24 For elaboration on organisational reading, see Thaw, 1997 and Chapter 11.

25 For an example of an information pyramid, see Fowler, 1997: 177.

26 For a case example of a team approach to include 'those that stay at the office', see Reddy, 1999.

27 BRAC, 1996.

28 They are grappling with issues such as how to respond to donor policies of direct in-country funding in the South, and changing their role from operations to providing support to local NGDOs.

29 This section draws on Pascale, Milleman and Gioja, 1996.

30 Gibbs, 2000.

31 Fowler, 1997:69–74.

32 'Finally, a worrying conclusion is the noticeable absence of a significant "culture of inquiry" into project performance among many Danish NGOs – outside of formal reporting requirements' (emphasis in original): so concluded a recent evaluation of Danish NGDOs (Oakley, 1999).

33 Britton, 1998 and Further Reading.

34 Cannon, 1999:8–13. One observer notes that despite recognition of the three aspects or types of sustainability used in this book, 'the reader is left with a sense that the financial paradigm ends up dominating' (Randell, 1999:10).

Chapter 10

1 For example, Kelleher and McLaren, 1996;Thaw and Petersen, 1997; Fowler, 1997, chapter 8; James, 1998. See also Further Reading.

2 Thaw and Petersen, 1997.

3 See, for example, PACT, 1998; Fowler, Goold and James, 1995; and Further Reading.

4 For more detail on inside-out and outside-in approaches, see Fowler, 1997:197–199.

5 To complement its financial accounts, TTO publishes social accounts. See Further Reading for details of social audit approaches and tool kits.

6 Fowler, 1997:192–195.

7 Kelleher and McLaren, 1995:114.

8 Circular letter from Lady Wood to life members of the Flying Doctor Service, July 1999.

9 Grint, 1997:33.

10 Kotter, 1996; and Further Reading.

11 Srivasta and Cooperrider, 1999.

12 There are obvious parallels with total quality learning and management. See Lessem, 1991.

13 Interviews with Allan Kaplan and James Taylor, CDRA directors.

14 CDRA, 1999:28.

15 Interview with James Thomas, TTO executive director.

16 BEST has been translated into Russian, French and German.

17 Interviews with Khem Raj Sapkota and Kesas Sapkota, VDRC president and secretary.

18 The virtual explosion of NGDOs in Nepal has been opportunistic and fed by aid policies. See Maskay, 1998.

19 Covey and Shah, 1998.

20 The five are for Participation and Governance; Institutional Development; Global Alliance; Occupational and Environmental Health; and Information Resources.

21 Covey and Shah, 1998:13.
22 Interview with Hernando Monge, director-general of CECADE.
23 Echevarria, 1997.
24 The five programmes were indigenous Indian people; education for youth and adults; agrarian reform; worker's movement and Protestant evangelism.
25 Later the Protestant and agrarian reform organisations joined together.
26 Interview with the president, Eduardo Ballon.
27 Patron, 1998.
28 It remains to be seen if the transition to entrepreneur and investor will generate income as expected. The general experience of NGDOs entering the business world has not been very encouraging (García, 1998).
29 Consultancy fees are split between DESCO and the consultant (60:40 or 40:60) depending on who brings in the work.
30 CDRA, 1999:4.

Chapter 11

1 Drucker, 1990b:193.
2 There appears to be a dominance of evidence concerning for-profit organisations which by default is applied to non-profit-making organisations.
3 Sampson, 1999.
4 James, 1994.
5 Salamon and Anheier, 1998.
6 Woolcock, 1997; Fukuyama, 1999.
7 Observers have cast doubts about the categories underpinning the data published by Salamon and Anheier. Their reservations are expressed in relation to the function of non-profit-making organisations and their proportional contribution to a society's social capital (Edwards, 1999b; Fukuyama 1999:57–58). A common critique is the inability to adequately count informal associations, for example those that are ascribed by tradition in many non-Western societies. For a reply to Edwards, see Salamon and Anheier, 1999.
8 See Further Reading.

9 For example, Cyert, 1990.
10 PRIA, 1998b.
11 de Board, 1978; Dartington, 1994.
12 Interview with Bill Drayton, founder of the Ashoka Foundation, by Caroline Hartnell, editor of *Alliance*.
13 Drucker, 1990.
14 From a psychological perspective, the Third Sector attracts individuals that require fulfilment through 'pairing' and the ideal relationship; government attracts people who need security and find comfort in dependency within authoritarian systems; while business offers a psychological home for those driven by fight or flight.
15 Goleman, 1996.
16 Hall, 1991:152–15.
17 See, for example, Handy, 1988.
18 Quarles van Ufford, Kruit and Downing, 1988.
19 In relation to aid policy and practice towards civil society, see van Rooy, 1998.
20 This is not to say that attempts are not made to bring management of non-profit-making organisations into the theoretical frame (Drucker, 1989) and into practical and comparative analysis (Leat, 1993). But one swallow does not make a summer. It is business that teaches non-profit-making organisations, not the other way round. In addition, these analyses suffer from sample biases and limitations that make conclusions highly questionable in relation to the South, East and to NGDOs. This is a particular limitation of the Leat study comparing management of for-profit and non-profit-making organisations in the UK.
21 Drucker, 1990:xv.
22 IFCB, 1998:9.
23 PRIA, 1998b:66.
24 Adair, 1990; Bennis, 1994; Drucker, 1990; Fiedler, 1967; Grint, 1997; Kouzes and Posner, 1995; Mant, 1997; Wheatley, 1994; Vaill, 1996.
25 After Burns, 1978.
26 Mant, 1997:23.
27 Broad-band intelligence allied to psychological damage can also produce effective leaders, but with malign agendas and many followers. Hitler is but one example.

28 Despite the supposedly porous boundaries of corporations, business leadership is typically a quality expressed and researched within – another limitation of business-led theory.

29 Hailey, 1999:6.

30 Grint, 1997:140.

31 Uphoff et al, 1998:45.

32 Fowler, 1997.

33 Uphoff, op cit: 50.

34 Burns, 1999:1.

35 Scott, 1987.

36 Hofstede, 1991; Lessem and Nussbaum, 1996; Trompenaars, 1993.

37 Fowler, 1997.

38 Donnelly, quoted in James, 1999.

39 Hudson, 1995:242.

40 Lessem in Graham, 1991:xvi.

41 Fowler, 1997.

42 Wheatley, 1994.

43 A recent analogy sees individual development akin to the art of cooking, rather than the selection and technical bolting together of a set of behaviour-determining genes. Cooking ingredients are a chance-based mix of potentials provided by parents whose subsequent expression depends on the external processes applied to them. It is a complex, subtle story, not reducible to a linear equation.

44 Senge: 1990:359.

45 Drucker, 1990:21.

46 Uphoff, et al, 1998:50.

47 There is also the consideration that a leader may not want a too strong, younger generation because of the threat it might pose to his or her own leadership. Such insecurity would be a *prima facie* indicator of insecurity and hence of possible psychological 'damage'.

48 Coleman, 1991; Tannen, 1996.

49 Moser, 1993; Macdonald et al, 1997. Relative neglect of gender dimension is partly attributed to the fact that, until relatively recently, men have been the researchers and interpreters of organisational behaviour.

50 Boserup, 1965; Angier, 1999.

51 Fowler, 1997:76–81.

52 Rao, Stuart and Kelleher, 1999. This book contains very useful organisational development strategies derived from practical cases.

53 Ibid:3.

54 Quoted in Hailey, 1999:7.

55 For example, Fowler, Campbell and Pratt, 1993.

56 'Successor Generation Programme Proposal', CODE-NGO, Manila.

57 Bonbright, 1997.

58 See, Hallowes, 1998; van Schalkwjk, 1999.

59 Fowler, 1997:207; Schein, 1999.

60 For a more detailed proposal for NGDO leadership development, see Fowler, 1992b.

61 In the mid-1990s GTZ ran an organisational development consultants' programme for Africa. Over a two-year period, participants underwent four one-month periods of formal training, interposed by periods of on-the-job exposure and case reflection. CDRA operates a non-certificate fellowship programme involving six formal training sessions of eight days, plus a two-week orientation and one week closure spread over two years. The intervening practice periods can be mentored and accompanied.

62 Cases in *Reasons for Success* include development programmes that may be within an NGDO or government. They shed some light on the transition issue, but nowhere near enough to recommend how it can best proceed and under what conditions.

63 This study was not designed to fill the gap. With hindsight, this may have been a shortcoming. I hope to do something about it through a dedicated study on NGDO leadership.

64 Different authors suggest a different number of stages. The number is less important than the principle behind them. NGDOs have life stages to go through. See, Avina, 1993; Kaplan, 1996; Taylor et al, 1998.

65 White water is the term associated with fast-flowing rivers that crash through rocks and rapids. It will always be so; Vaill, 1996.

66 Drucker, 1990:xv.

67 Smillie and Hailey, 2000: a study by the AKF of nine NGDOs in South Asia is one of the few to look specifically at their leadership.

68 Interview with Isagani Serrano, vice-president of PRRM.

69 For example, in Ethiopia, by refusing a work permit the government vetoed the selection of the proposed expatriate successor to the departing leader of the Christian Relief and Development Association. In Zimbabwe, the government has exercised its legal right to remove an NGDO leader.

70 Examples are Plan International and Oxfam UK.

71 This is reported by Hailey (2000) for the AKRSP and for AKF in east Africa in relation to the Kenya Community Development Foundation (personal communication with board members).

Chapter 12

1 Wheatley, 1994:133.

2 For a detailed look at accountability, see Edwards and Hulme, 1996.

3 *Economist*, 11–17 December 1999, p18. The question hinges on the extent to which international governance will be 'hijacked' by special interest groups. What happens when this occurs is highlighted in the US by the back-payment of UN arrears with conditions demanded by anti-abortion groups.

4 Hancock, 1989; Maren, 1997; Porter, Allen and Thompson, 1991.

5 Fowler, 2000.

6 Fowler, 1997:234.

References

Abdulai, N (1999) 'Negotiations and Conflict',
paper presented at a conference on
Democratization, Development
Management and Conflicts in Africa,
23–26 November, Economic Commission
for Africa, Addis Ababa

Adair, J (1990) *Great Leaders*, Talbot Adair,
Brookwood

Adelman, I and Morris, C (1997) 'Editorial:
Development History and its Implications
for Development Theory', *World
Development*, 25(6): pp831–840

Adirondack, S (1992) *Just about managing?
Effective management for voluntary
organisations and community groups,*
London Voluntary Service Council,
London

Aldaba, F (1999) 'The Future of Philippine
NGOs: No Escape from the Market in a
World with Declining Aid', paper
presented at a conference on NGOs in a
Global Future, 8–11 January, Birmingham

Aldrich, H and Pfeffer, J (1976) 'Environments
of Organizations', *Annual Review of
Sociology*, 2: pp79–105

Alianza (1995) *Progression Indicators*, Alianza
Para Desarrollo Juvenil Comunitario,
Guatemala City

AKRSP (1992) 'Institutional Maturity Index:
A Process Approach for Participatory
Monitoring and Evaluation of Village
Organisations in Gilgit', Aga Khan Rural
Support Programme, Gilgit

Alkire, S (1997) 'Dimension of Human
Development: Towards a Synthesis of
Lists', paper presented at the Development
Studies Association Meeting, 11–13
September, University of East Anglia,
Norwich

Anderson, P (1998) *The Origins of
Postmodernity*, Verso, London

Anderson, P, Arrow, J and Pines, D (eds)
(1988) *The Economy as an Evolving
Complex System*, Addison-Wesley,
Redwood, California

Angier, N (1999) *Women: An Intimate
Geography*, Virago, London

Anheier, H (1995) 'Theories of the Nonprofit
Sector: Three Issues', *Nonprofit and
Voluntary Sector Quarterly*, 24(1):
pp15–23

Archer, D and Cottingham, S (1997)
'REFLECT: A new approach to literacy
and social change', *Development in
Practice*, 7(2): pp199–202

Archer, D and Cottingham, S (1996) *Action
Research Report on 'REFLECT':
Regenerated Frierian Literacy Through
Empowering Community Techniques*,
Serial No 17, Overseas Development
Administration, London

Ashman, D, Brown, D and Zwick, E (1997)
*Formation and Governance: Experience
from Eight Organisations in Africa, Asia
and Latin America*, Synergos Institute,
New York

Avina, J (1993) 'The Evolutionary Life Cycles
of Non-Governmental Development
Organisations', *Public Administration and
Development*, Vol 13, No 5

Badelt, C (1997) 'Entrepreneurship theories of
the non-profit sector', *Voluntas*, 8(2):
pp162–178

Bain, K (1999) 'Building or Burning Bridges:
The Accountability of Trans-National
NGO Networks in Policy Alliances with
the World Bank', paper presented at the
Conference on NGOs in a Global Future,
Birmingham

Bak, P and Chen, K (1991) 'Self-Organised
Criticality', *Scientific American*, pp46–53,
January

Ball, C and Dunn, L (1995) *Non-Governmental Organisations: Guidelines for Good Policy and Practice*, Consultative Draft, The Commonwealth Foundation, London

Banuri, T, Hyden, G, Juma, C and Rivera, M, 1994, *Sustainable Human Development From Concept to Operation: A Guide for the Practitioner*, UNDP, New York

Barbier, E (1987a) 'Cash crops, food crops and agricultural sustainability', *Gatekeeper Series* No SA2, International Institute for Environment and Development, London

Barbier, E (1987b) 'The Concept of Sustainable Economic Development', *Environmental Conservation*, 14(2): pp101–110

Beatty, J (1998) *The World According to Peter Drucker*, Free Press, New York

Beishon, J (1999) 'Keeping tabs on multinational NGOs', *Alliance*, l 4(3):pp11–13, Charities Aid Foundation, London

Bendall, J (1998) 'Citizens' Cane? Relations between business and civil society' paper presented at the Third Biennial Conference of the International Society for International Development, Geneva, 8–12 July

Bennett, J and Gibbs, S (1996) *NGO Funding Strategies: An Introduction for Southern and Eastern NGOs*, International NGO Training and Research Centre, Oxford

Bennis, W (1994), *On Becoming a Leader*, Perseus Books, Reading, Mass

Bennis, W (1989) *Why Leaders Can't Lead: The Unconscious Conspiracy*, Jossey-Bass, San Francisco

Bhat, M and Cheria, A (1997) 'Sustainability of Interventions: Withdrawal – The Concept, Need and Practice', *SEARCH Bulletin*, XII(2): pp 68–77, SEARCH, Bangalore

Blackburn, J (1996) *The Institutionalisation of Participatory Approaches, PRA Topic Pack*, Institute of Development Studies, University of Sussex, Brighton

Blauert, J and Zadek, S (eds) (1998) *Mediating Sustainability: Growing Policy from the Grassroots*, Kumerian, West Hartford

Bonbright, D (1999) 'The Grantmakers' Paradox', *Alliance*, 4(4): pp11–13, Charities Aid Foundation, London

Bonbright, D, (ed) (1997) *Leading Public Entrepreneurs*, Ashoka Foundation, San Francisco

Booij, D and ole Sena, S (1998) 'Capacity Building Using The Appreciative Inquiry Approach; The Experience of World Vision in Tanzania', *Working Paper*, 2, World Vision, Arusha

Boschee, J (1998) 'What does it take to be a Social Entrepreneur?', National Centre for Social Entrepreneurs, Minneapolis

Boserup, E (1965) *The Conditions of Agricultural Growth: The Economics of Agrarian Change under Population Pressure*, George Allen and Unwin, London

BRAC (1996) *Beacons of Hope: an impact assessment study of BRAC's Rural Development Programme*, Bangladesh Rural Advancement Committee, Dhaka, February

Bratton, M (1989) 'The Politics of NGO–Government Relations in Africa', *World Development*, 17(4): pp 569–587, April

Bretton Wood Project (1999) *Questioning the IMF, World Bank Growth Model*, The Bretton Woods Project, London

Britton, B (1998) 'The Learning NGO', *Occasional Paper Series*, No 17, International NGO Training and Research Centre, Oxford

Brown, D (1990) 'Bridging Organizations and Sustainable Development', *Working Paper*, 8, Institute of Development Research, Boston

Brown, D and Korte, C (1996) 'Farmer Led Extension and Institutional Development: The Case of Mag'uumad Foundation, Cebu, The Philippines', Institute of Development Studies, Brighton, mimeo

Brown, D and Tandon, R (1983) 'Ideology and political economy in inquiry: action research and participatory research', *The Journal of Applied Behavioural Science*, 19(3):pp277–294

Brown, D R (1998) 'Evaluating Institutional Sustainability in Development Programmes: Beyond the Dollars and Cents', *Journal of International Development*, 10(1):pp55–70

Brown, L (1994) 'Creating Social Capital: Nongovernmental Development

Organizations and Intersectoral Problem Solving', *IDR Reports*, 11(3), Boston

Brudney, J (1990) 'Volunteering in the Public Sector: Emerging Issues', in Independent Sector, 1990, *The Nonprofit Sector (NGOs) in the United States and Abroad: Cross-Cultural Perspectives,* pp65–78, Spring Research Forum Working Papers, Independent Sector and United Way, Washington, DC

Burkey, S (1993) *People First: A Guide to Self-Reliant, Participatory Development*, Zed Books, London

Burns, J (1998) 'Empowerment for Change: A Conceptual Working Paper', paper prepared for the Kellogg Leadership Studies Project, The James MacGregor Burns Academy of Leadership, Washington, DC

Burns, J (1978) *Leadership*, Harper and Row, New York

CAF, 1994, *International Giving and Volunteering*, Charities Aid Foundation, London

Cannon, L (1999a) 'Defining Sustainability', *OD Debate*, 6(1):pp12–13, Glenwood, SA, February

Cannon, L (1999b) *Life Beyond Aid: Twenty Strategies to Help Make NGOs Sustainable*, Interfund, Johannesburg

Carlsson, J , Kohlin, G and Ekbom, A (1994) *The Political Economy of Evaluation: International Aid Agencies and the Effectiveness of Aid*, St Martins Press, London

Carney, D (1999) 'Approaches to Sustainable Livelihoods for the Rural Poor', *Poverty Briefing*: 2, Overseas Development Institute, London

CDRA (1999) *Development Practitioners – Artists of the Invisible*, Annual Report 1998/1999, Community Development Resource Association, Cape Town

CDRA (1998) *Crossroads: A Development Reading*, Annual Report 1997/1998, Community Development Resource Association, Cape Town

Chambers, R (1997) *Whose Reality Counts?: putting the first last*, Intermediate Technology, London

Chambers, R (1993) *Challenging the Professions: Frontiers for rural development*, Intermediate Technology, London

Chambers, R (1987) 'Sustainable livelihoods, environment and development: putting poor rural people first', *Discussion Paper* 240, Institute of Development Studies, University of Sussex, Brighton

Chambers, R (1983) *Rural Development: Putting the Last First*, Longman, Harlow

Chambers, R, Longhurst R and Pacey, A (eds) (1981) *Seasonal Dimensions to Rural Poverty*, Frances Pinter, London

Chambre, S (1989) 'Responding to Uncertainty by Bearing Witness: Volunteering as Collective Behaviour in the AIDS Epidemic, 1981–1989', Centre for the Study of Philanthropy, City University of New York, New York

Chang, C and Tuckman, H (1994) 'Revenue diversification among non-profits', *Voluntas*, 5(3):pp273–290

CIVICUS (1997) *Legal Principles for Citizen Participation: Towards a Legal Framework for Civil Society Organisations*, CIVICUS, Washington, DC

Clark, J (1993) 'The State and the Voluntary Sector', *HRO Working Paper*, 12, The World Bank, Washington, DC, October

Cleaver, F (1999) 'Paradoxes of Participation: Questioning Participatory Approaches to Development', *Journal of International Development*, 11(4): pp597–612

Coleman, G (1991) 'Investigating Organisations: A Feminist Approach', *Occasional Paper*, 37, School for Advanced Urban Studies, University of Bath, Bath

Collier, P (1999) 'Social Capital and Poverty', *Social Capital Initiative Working Paper,* 4, Social Development Family, Environmentally and Socially Sustainable Development Network, The World Bank, Washington, DC

Cooke, B (1998) 'The Social-Psychological Limits of Participation?', paper presented at a conference on Participation – The New Tyranny?, 3–4 November, Institute of Development Policy Management, Manchester

Cooperrider, D, Ludema, J, Srivstva, S and Wishart, C (1995) *Appreciative Inquiry: A*

Constructive Approach to Organizational Capacity Building, Weatherhead School of Management, Case Western Reserve University, Cleveland

CO-TRAIN (1998) *Promotion of a Common Rural Community Organizing Standard in the Philippines*, Community Organization Training and Research Advocacy Institute, Manila

Covey, J and Shah, T (1998) *Participatory Research in Asia (PRIA) – Report of an Organisational and Strategic Review*, Society For Participatory Research in Asia, October

Cox, A and Healey, J (1998) 'Promises to the Poor: the Record of European Development Agencies', *Poverty Briefing*, 1, Overseas Development Institute, London

Craig, G and Mayo, M (eds) (1995) *Community Empowerment: A Reader in Participation and Development*, Zed Books, London

Cumming, L and Singleton, B (1995) 'Organizational Sustainability – An End of the Century Challenge for Canadian Voluntary International Development Organizations', paper presented at the Eleventh Annual Conference for the Study of International Development, Montreal, June 6

Cyert, R (1990) 'Defining Leadership and Explicating the Process', *NonProfit Management and Leadership*, 1(1): pp29–38

Dartington, T (1994) 'Leadership and Voluntary Organisations', The Management Unit, National Council for Voluntary Organisations, London

Dass, P (1999) 'Intersectoral Partnership in Sustainable Development: The need for the 21st Century', *Institutional Development*, VI(1): pp13–28, Society for Participatory Research in Asia, New Delhi

Davis, L (1997) *The NGO-Business Hybrid: Is the Private Sector the Answer?*, Johns Hopkins University, Baltimore

Davis, R (1998) *Order and Diversity: Representing and Assisting Organisational Learning in Non-Government Aid Organisations*, PhD Thesis, University of Swansea, Cardiff

Dawson, E (1997) 'The Relevance of Social Audit for Oxfam UK', paper presented at the First Euroconference on Social and Ethical Auditing and Accounting, 15–16 September, Nijenrode

Dawson, J and Jeans, A (1997) *Looking Beyond Credit: Business development services and the promotion of innovation among small producers*, IT Publications, London

de Board, R (1993) *The Psychoanalysis of Organizations: A psychoanalytic Approach to Behaviour in Groups and Organizations*, Routledge, London

Dees, J (1998) 'Enterprising Nonprofits', *Harvard Business Review*, pp 55–67, January–February

DFID (1997) *Eliminating World Poverty: A Challenge for the 21st Century*, White Paper on International Development, Department for International Development, London

Donnelly Roark, P (1995) 'Donor Organiz-ations and Participatory Development', *Issues Paper*, 1, United Nations Development Programme, New York

Dower, N (1997) 'Global Ethics: Theory and Social Reality', paper presented at the Development Studies Association Meeting, 11–13 September, University of East Anglia, Norwich

Draimin, T and Smillie, I (1999) *Strengthening Civil Society: The Role of Southern Foundations*, A Report for the Synergos Institute, New York, April

Drucker, P (1990a) 'Lessons for Successful Nonprofit Governance', *Nonprofit Management And Leadership*, 1(1): pp 7–14, Jossey-Bass, San Francisco, Fall

Drucker, P (1990b) *Managing the Nonprofit Organization: Principles and Practices*, HarperCollins, New York

Drucker, P (1989) 'What Business Can Learn From Nonprofits', *Harvard Business Review*, pp88–93, July–August, Boston

Duran, R (1999) 'Measures of Empowerment and Sustainability', in *Capability, Participation and Impact: The Planning and Measurement of Sustainable Area Development: A casebook of designs and experiences*, Philippine Rural Reconstruction Movement, Manila

Eade, D (1997a) *Capacity-Building: An Approach to People–Centred Development*, Oxfam, Oxford

Eade, D (1997b) 'Partnership: casual affairs, marriages of convenience, or lasting relationships?', *Development In Practice*, 7(1): pp189–191, Oxfam, Oxford

Eade, D (ed) (1997c) *Development and Patronage*, Oxfam, Oxford

Echeverria, L (ed) (1997) *Desarrollo Rural Sostenible en Costa Rica: Advances y persepectivas* (Sustainable Rural Development in Costa Rica: Progress and perspectives), Cecade/Porvenir, San José

Eckman, K (1993) 'Use of Indicators of Unsustainability in Development Programs', *Impact Assessment*, 11, Fall

Edwards, M (1999a) *Future Positive: International Cooperation in the 21st Century*, Earthscan, London

Edwards, M (1999b) 'Enthusiasts, Tacticians and Sceptics: The World Bank, Civil Society and Social Capital', paper prepared for a review by the Kettering Foundation, New York, mimeo

Edwards, M (1997) 'Organisational learning in non-governmental organizations: what have we learned?', *Public Administration and Development*, 17, pp235–250

Edwards, M (1993) 'Does the doormat influence the boot?: critical thoughts on UK NGOs and international advocacy', *Development In Practice*, 3(3): pp163–175, Oxfam, Oxford

Edwards, M and Hulme, D (1996) *Beyond the Magic Bullet: NGO Performance and Accountability in the Post-Cold War World*, Earthscan, London

Edwards, M and Hulme, D (eds) (1992) *Making a Difference: NGOs and development in a changing world*, Earthscan

Elkington, J (1997) *Cannibals with Forks: The Triple Bottom Line of 21st Century Business*, Capstone, Oxford

Enderle, G and Peters, G (1998) *A Strange Affair? The Emerging Relationship Between NGOs and Transnational Companies*, Price Waterhouse Coopers, London

Esman, M, and Uphoff, N (1984) *Local Organisations: Intermediaries in Rural Development*, Cornell University Press, Ithaca, NY

Etzioni, A (1993) *The Spirit of Community: Rights, Responsibilities and the Communitarian Agenda,* Crown, New York

Farrington, J and Bebbington, A (1993) *Reluctant Partners?: Non-Governmental Organizations, the State and Agricultural Development*, Routledge, London

Favis, M (1998) 'Creatively managing the donor environment', *OD Debate*, 5(4): pp10–12, Glenwood, SA, October

Fiedler, F (1967) *The Theory of Leadership Effectiveness*, McGraw-Hill, London

Fisher, J (1997) *Nongovernments: NGOs and the Political Development of the Third World*, Kumerian Press, West Hartford

Fisher, J (1993) *The Road to Rio: Sustainable Development and the Nongovernmental Movement in the Third World*, Praeger, New York

Fowler, A (1999) 'NGDOs as a Moment in History: Beyond Aid to Civic Entrepreneurship?' paper presented at a conference on NGOs in a Global Future, 8–11 January, Birmingham

Fowler, A (2000) 'NGOs, Civil Society and Social Development: Changing the Rules of the Game', *Geneva 2000 Occasional Paper,* 1, United Nations Research Institute for Social Development, Geneva

Fowler, A (1998) 'Authentic Partnerships in the New Policy Agenda for International Aid: Dead End or Light Ahead?' *Development and Change*, 29(1): pp137–159

Fowler, A (1997) *Striking a Balance: A Guide to Enhancing the Effectiveness of Non-Governmental Organisations in International Development*, Earthscan, London

Fowler, A (1994) 'Capacity Building and NGOs: A Case of Strengthening Ladles for the Global Soup Kitchen?', *Institutional Development*, 1(1): pp18–24, PRIA, Delhi

Fowler, A (1992a) 'Distant Obligations: Speculations on NGO Funding and the Global Market', *Review of African Political Economy*, 55: pp9–29, Sheffield, November

Fowler, A (1992b) 'Some Thoughts on a Human Resource Development Strategy for Potential Leaders and Senior Cadres of Non-Governmental Development Organisations in Africa', in Fowler, A, Campbell, P and Pratt, B , *Institutional Development and NGOs in Africa: Policy Perspectives for European Development Agencies*, pp47–51, International NGO Training and Research Centre, Oxford

Fowler, A (1988) 'Non-Governmental Organizations in Africa: Achieving Comparative Advantage in Micro-Development', *Discussion Paper*, 249, University of Sussex, Institute of Development Studies, August

Fowler, A and Biekart, K (1996) 'Do Private Aid Agencies Really Make a Difference?', in Sogge, D (ed), *Compassion and Calculation*, pp107–128, Pluto Press, London

Fowler, A and Young, R (1998) *Perspectives on Sustainability for Non-Governmental Organisations and Their Donors: A guide drawing on work in progress of the Bangladesh Rural Advancement Committee,* BRAC, Dakar, March

Fowler, A, Campbell, P and Pratt, B (1992) *Institutional Development and NGOs in Africa: Policy Perspectives for European Development Agencies*, NGO Management Series, 1, International NGO Training and Research Centre and NOVIB, Oxford/The Hague, October

Fowler, A, Goold, L and James, R (1995) 'Practical Guidelines for Self-Assessment of NGO Capacity', *Occasional Paper*, 10, INTRAC, Oxford, December

Fox, J and Brown, L D (1998) *The Struggle for Accountability: The World Bank, NGOs and Grassroots Movements*, MIT Press, Cambridge, Mass

Fox, L and Schearer, B (eds) (1997) *Sustaining Civil Society: Strategies for Resource Mobilization*, CIVICUS, Washington, DC

Fox, L (1995) 'Strengthening Third Sector Financing in Development; The Role of Official Development Assistance', Synergos Institute, New York

Fox, L and Schearer, B (eds) (1997) *Sustaining Civil Society: Strategies for Resource Mobilisation*, CIVICUS, Washington, DC

Frankenberger, T (1993) 'Indicators and Data Collection Methods for Assessing Household Food Security', *Household Food Security: Concepts, Indicators Measurements*, UNICEF/IFAD, New York/Rome

Friere, P (1973) *Education for Critical Consciousness*, Seabury Press, New York

Fukuyama, F (1999) *The Great Disruption: Human Nature and the Reconstitution of Social Order*, Profile Books, London

Gao Bingzhong (1999) 'The Rise of Associations and their Legitimation Problems', paper presented at an International Conference of the Development of Non-profit Organisations and the China Project Hope, Beijing, November

García, G (1998) 'Notas para un balance de las experiencias de incursión empresarial de las organizaciones no gubermentales en el Peru', in Valderamma, M (ed), *Cambios en las Organizaciones de Promoción del Desarollo Peruanas*, Lima, ALOP–CEPES–Sos Faim

Gardner, H (1993) *Frames of Mind: The Theory of Multiple Intelligences*, Basic Books, New York

Gardner, J (1991) *On Leadership*, Independent Sector, Washington, DC

Ge Yunsong (1999) 'On the Establishment of Social Organisations Under Chinese Law', paper presented at an International Conference of the Development of Non-profit Organisations and the China Project Hope, Beijing, November

Gibbs, C, Fumo, C and Kuby, T (1999) *Nongovernmental Organizations in Bank-Supported Projects: A Review*, Evaluation Department, World Bank, Washington, DC

Gibbs, S (2000) 'Decentralised NGO Management', *Occasional Paper*, No 19, International NGO Training and Research Centre, Oxford, February

Gill, E and Snyder, M (1990) 'A Functional Analysis of Volunteers' Motivations', *The Nonprofit Sector (NGOs) in the United States and Abroad: Cross-Cultural Perspectives*, Spring Research Forum Working Papers, Independent Sector and United Way, Washington, DC, pp79–96

Goleman, D (1996) *Emotional Intelligence: Why it Can Matter More than IQ,*

Bloomsbury Press, London

Graham, P (1991) *Integrative Management: Creating Unity From Diversity*, Blackwell, London

GrandMet (1997) *Report on Corporate Citizenship*, Grand Metropolitan Corporation, London

Grint, K (1997) *Fuzzy Management: Contemporary Ideas and Practices at Work*, OUP, Oxford

Grønbjerg, K (1993) *Understanding Nonprofit Funding*, Jossey-Bass, San Francisco

Group of Lisbon (1995) *Limits to Competition*, MIT Press, Cambridge, Mass

Hammond, A, Adriaanse, A, Rodenburg, E, Bryant, D and Woodward, R (1995) *Environmental Indicators: a systematic approach to measuring and reporting on environmental policy performance in the context of sustainable development*, World Resources Institute, Washington, DC

Hailey, J (1999) 'Charismatic Autocrats or Development Leaders: Characteristics of First Generation NGO Leadership', paper presented at the Development Studies Association Conference, University of Bath, 11–13 September

Hailey, J (1998) 'Beyond the Formulaic: Process and Practice in South Asian NGOs', paper presented at a conference on Participation – The New Tyranny? 3–4 November, Institute of Development Policy Management, Manchester

Hailey, J and James, R (1994) 'Developing the Sustainable NGO: Strengthening the Capacity of Southern NGOs', paper presented at the Development Studies Association Conference, University of Lancaster, September

Hailey, J and James, R (1994) 'Developing the Sustainable NGO: Strengthening the Capacity of Southern NGOs', paper presented at the Development Studies Association Conference, University of Lancaster, September

Hall, R (1991) *Organizations: Structures, Processes and Outcomes*, Prentice Hall, Englewood Cliffs

Hallowes, D (1998) 'Learning about Leadership from Leaders', *OD Debate,*

5(4): pp7–9, Glenwood, SA, October

Hallowes, D (1995) 'Of Partners and Patrons: NGO Perceptions of Funders', *AVOCADO Series*, 5, Olive Information Services, Durban

Hancock, G (1989) *The Lords of Poverty*, The Atlantic Monthly Press, New York

Harding, P (1991) 'Qualitative indicators and the project framework', *Community Development Journal*, 26(4): pp294–305, Oxford University Press, Oxford, October

Harriss, J (ed) (1997) 'Policy Arena: "Missing Link" or "Analytically Missing": The Concept of Social Capital', *Journal of International Development*, 9(7): pp919–972

Hatch, M-J (1997) *Organization Theory*, Oxford University Press, Oxford

Hawley, K (1993) *From Grants to Contracts; A Practical Guide for Voluntary Organisations*, NCVO/Directory of Social Change, London

Hayday, M (1999) 'New finanthropists offer a hand up', *Alliance*, 4(4): p18, Charities Aid Foundation, London

Heap, S (1998) 'NGOs and the Private Sector: Potential for Partnerships?' *Occasional Paper Series*, 27, International NGO Training and Research Centre, Oxford

Heap, S and Fowler, P (1999) 'NGOs, the Private Sector and their Constituencies', International NGO Training and Research Centre, Oxford, forthcoming

Heimovics, R, Herman, D and Jurkiewicz-Coughlin, C (1993) 'Executive Leadership and Resource Dependence in Nonprofit Organizations: A Frame Analysis', *Public Administration Review*, 53(5), September/October

Hellberg-Phillips, A (1998) 'Finding coherence in the core of our organisation', *OD Debate*, 5(4): pp3–7, Glenwood, SA, October

Henriques, A (1998) 'Social and Ethical Accounting, Auditing and Reporting: Concepts, Terminology and Glossary', a Research Paper, New Economics Foundation, London

Hofstede, G (1991) *Cultures and Organisations: Software of the Mind*, McGraw-Hill, Maidenhead

Holland, J and Henriot, P (1983) *Social analysis, linking faith and justice,* Center of Concern, Washington DC

Holloway, R (1999a) *Towards Financial Self-Reliance: A Handbook of Approaches to Resource Mobilisation for Citizens' Organisations in the South – Trainer's Manual,* Beta Edition, Aga Khan Foundation, Geneva

Holloway, R (1999b) *Towards Financial Self-Reliance: A Handbook of Approaches to Resource Mobilisation for Citizens' Organisations in the South,* Beta Edition, Aga Khan Foundation, Geneva

Holloway, R (1997) *Exit Strategies: Transitioning from International to Local NGO Leadership,* PACT, New York

Honadle, G, and van Sant, J (1975) *Implementation for Sustainability: Lessons from Integrated Rural Development,* Kumerian Press, West Hartford, Connecticut

Hordijk, P-A (1999) 'The State of the Art of the Social Enterprise', Matrix Consultants, Utrecht, mimeo

Howes, M (1999) *NGOs and the Institutional Development of Membership Organisations,* Research Report 36, Institute of Development Studies, University of Sussex

Hudock, A (1995) 'Sustaining Southern NGOs in Resource-Dependent Environments', *Journal of International Development,* 7(4): pp653–668

Hudson, M (1995) *Managing Without Profit,* Penguin, London

Hulme, D and Edwards, M (eds) (1996) *NGOs, States and Donors: Too Close for Comfort?,* Macmillan, London

Huntington, S (1993) 'The Clash of Cultures', *Foreign Affairs,* 72(3)

Hyden, G, 1983, *No Short Cuts to Progress: African Development Management in Perspective,* University of California Press, Berkeley

Hyden, G (1980) *Beyond Ujamaa in Tanzania: Underdevelopment and an Uncaptured Peasantry,* Heinemann, London

ICNPL (1996) *Global Standards and Best Practices for Laws Governing Non-Governmental Organizations,* study commissioned by the World Bank, International Centre for Non-Profit Law, Washington

IFCB (1998) *A Synthesis of Consultation and Surveys,* International Forum on Capacity Building, PRIA, New Delhi

IFRCRCS (1997) *World Disasters Report 1997,* International Federation of Red Cross and Red Crescent Societies, Geneva, Oxford University Press, Oxford

IIED (1995) 'Critical Reflections From Practice', *PLA Notes,* 24, International Institute for Environment and Development, London

INTRAC (1998) *Direct Funding from a Southern Perspective – Strengthening Civil Society?* International NGO Training and Research Centre, Oxford

James, C (1994) *The Black Jacobins: Toussaint L'Ouverture and the San Domingo Rebellion,* Allison and Busby, London

James, R (1999a) 'Making it personal – Leadership and change in NGOs', *OD Debate,* 6(2): pp7–8, Glenwood, SA, October

James, R (1999b) 'Developing NGO leadership: Some Reflections from Malawi', International Training and Research Centre, Oxford, mimeo

James, R (1998) *Demystifying Organisation Development: Practical Capacity Building Experiences of African NGOs,* International NGO Training and Research Centre, Oxford

James, R (1994) 'Strengthening the Capacity of Southern NGO Partners: A Survey of Current Northern NGO Approaches', *Occasional Papers,* 5 , INTRAC, Oxford

Jenkins, H (1998) 'The People's Global Action (PGA) against "free" trade and the WTO 1st International Conference, 23–26 February', Informal Note, Non-Governmental Liaison Service, Geneva

Johnson, H and Wilson, G (1999) 'Institutional sustainability as learning', *Development in Practice,* 9(1&2): pp43–55

Jordan, L and van Tuijl, P (1993) 'Democratizing global power relation: Steps towards a political foundation for a global NGO campaign to reshape the

Bretton Woods Institutions', INGI, The Hague

Jordan, L and van Tuijl, P (1997) 'Political Responsibility in NGO Advocacy: Exploring shapes of global democracy', Bank Information Center/NOVIB, Washington, DC /The Hague

Jordan, P (1996) *Strengthening the Public Private Partners: An Assessment of USAID's Management of PVO and NGO Activities*, Appendix, Centre for Development Information and Evaluation, USAID, Washington, DC

Kanter, R (1993) *Men and Women of the Corporation*, Basic Books

Kanter, R (1979) 'The Measurement of Organizational Effectiveness, Productivity, Performance and Success: Issues and Dilemmas in Service and Non-Profit Organizations', *PONPO Working Paper*, 8, Yale University, Institution for Social and Policy Studies, Institute of Development Research, Boston

Kaplan, A (1999) 'Organisational Capacity: A Different Perspective', *Development Dossiers*, 10, Non-Governmental Liaison Service, Geneva

Kaplan, A (1996) *The Development Practitioner's Handbook*, Pluto Press, London

Kapur, D (1997) 'New Conditionalities of the International Financial Institutions' in *International Monetary and Financial Issues for the 1990s*, pp127–138, Research Papers for the Group of 24, III, United Nations, New York and Geneva

Kelleher, D and McLaren, K (1996) *Grabbing the Tiger by the Tail: NGOs Learning for Organisational Change*, Canadian Council for International Cooperation, Ottawa

Kingman, A (1999) 'Sustaining civil society: why legitimacy matters', *Alliance*, 4(4): pp14–16, Charities Aid Foundation, London

Kingman, A (1999) 'Accreditation – a kitemark for the non-profit sector?', *Alliance*, 4(3): pp8–10, Charities Aid Foundation, London

Knight, B (1998) 'Effective Cooperation between Foundations and NGOs towards Sustainable Societies', paper presented at the International Conference on

Foundations and NGOs as Agents of Change, Evalangelische Akademie, Locum 4–6 December

Korten, D (1995) *When Corporations Rule the World*, Earthscan, London

Korten, D (1990) *Getting to the 21st Century: Voluntary Action and the Global Agenda*, Kumerian Press, West Hartford

Korten, D (1980) 'Community Organisation and Rural Development: a Learning Process Approach', *Public Administration Review*, American Society for Public Administration, September/October, pp480–511

Korten, D (1999) *The Post-Corporate World: Life After Capitalism*, Kumerian Press, West Hartford

Kotter, J (1996) *Leading Change*, Harvard Business School Press, Boston

Kouzes, M and Posner, B (1995) *The Leadership Challenge*, Jossey-Bass, San Francisco

Krishna, A, Uphoff, N and Esman, M (1998) *Reasons for Hope: Instructive Experiences in Rural Development*, Kumerian Press, West Hartford

Krishna, A and Shrader, E (1999) 'Social Capital Assessment Tool', paper prepared for a conference on Social Capital and Poverty Reduction, 22–24 June, World Bank, Washington, DC

Lanzet, P (1997) 'Sustainability Criteria of Peoples' and Community Based Organisations', *SEARCH Bulletin*, XII(2): pp54–67, SEARCH, Bangalore

Leach, M (1994) 'Building Capacity Through Action Learning', *IDR Reports*, 10(5), Institute of Development Research, Boston

Leat, D (1993) *Managing Across Sectors: Similarities and Differences Between For-Profit and Voluntary Non-Profit Organisations*, VOLPROF, City University Business School, London, March

LeCompte, B (1986) *Project Aid: Limitations and Alternatives*, Development Centre, OECD, Paris

Lessem, R (1991) *Total Quality Learning*, Blackwell, Oxford

Lessem, R and Nussbaum, B, 1996, *Sawubona Africa: Embracing four worlds in South African management*, Zebra Press, Stanton

Lopa, M (1995) *Singing the Same Song: Reflections of Two Generations of NGO Workers in the Philippines*, ANGOC and PhilDHRRA, Manila

Lovell, C (1992) *Breaking the Cycle of Poverty: The BRAC Strategy*, Kumerian Press, West Hartford

Macdonald, M, Sprenger, E and Dubel, I (1997) *Gender and Organisational Change: Bridging the Gap Between Policy and Practice*, Royal Tropical Institute, Amsterdam

Madeley, J (1998) 'Globalisation Under Attack...Or Not', PANOS, 30 April

Malhotra, K (1997) 'Something Nothing' Words, Lessons in Partnership from Southern Experience', in Hately, L amd Malhotra, K, *Between Rhetoric and Reality: Essays on Partnership in Development*, pp37–56, North South Institute, Ottawa

Mannan, M (1996) 'Women targeted and women negated: An aspect of the environmental movement in Bangladesh', *Development in Practice*, 6(2): pp113–120

Mant, A (1997) *Intelligent Leadership*, Allen and Unwin, London

Maren, M (1997) *The Road to Hell: The Ravaging Effects of Foreign Aid and International Charity*, Free Press, New York

Maskay, B (1998) *Non-Governmental Organizations in Development: Search for a New Vision*, Centre for Development and Governance, Kathmandu

Maxwell, S (1999) 'The Meaning and Measurement of Poverty', *Poverty Briefing*: 3, Overseas Development Institute, London

Meyer, C (1999) *The Economics and Politics of NGOs in Latin America*, Praeger, New York

Meyer, C (1997) 'The Political Economy of NGOs and Information Sharing', *World Development*, 25(7): pp1127–1140

Mohammed, A (1997) 'Notes on MDB Conditionality on Governance', in *International Monetary and Financial Issues for the 1990s*, pp 139–145, Research Papers for the Group of 24, III, United Nations, New York and Geneva

Mohan, G (1998) 'Beyond Participation: Strategies for Deeper Empowerment', paper presented at a conference on Participation – The New Tyranny? 3–4 November, Institute of Development Policy Management, Manchester

Moingeon, B and Edmonson, A (eds) (1996) *Organizational Learning and Competitive Advantage*, Sage, London

Morehouse, W (1991) 'Grass Roots Power: The Right to Development Northern Style', *Echoes*, pp21–33, International Group on Grass Roots Initiatives, Utrecht

Moser, C (1993) *Gender Planning and Development: Theory, Practice and Training*, Routledge, London

Mosse, D (1998) 'The Making and Marketing of Participatory Development: A Sceptical Note', paper presented at a conference on Participation – The New Tyranny? 3–4 November, Institute of Development Policy Management, Manchester

Munishi, G (1995) 'Social Service Provision in Tanzania: The Relationship between Political Development Strategies and NGO Participation', in *Service Provision Under Stress: States and Voluntary Organisations in Kenya, Tanzania and Uganda*, pp141–152, James Currey, London

Murphy, D and Bendell, J (1997) *In the Company of Partners: Business, environmental groups and sustainable development post-Rio*, Policy Press, Bristol

Myers, B (1999) *Walking With The Poor: Principles and Practices of Transformational Development*, Orbis Books, New York

Myers, B (ed) (1999) *Working with the Poor: New Insights and Learning from Development Practitioners*, World Vision, Monrovia

Najam, A (1999) 'Citizens Organizations as Policy Entrepreneurs', in Lewis, D (ed), *International Perspectives on Voluntary Action*, pp142–181, Earthscan, London

Najam, A (1995) *Nongovernmental Organizations as Policy Entrepreneurs*, Program on Non-Profit Organizations, Institute for Social and Policy Studies, Yale University, New Haven

Narayan, D (1995) 'Designing Community

Based Development', *Participation Series*, No 007, Environment Department, World Bank, Washington, DC

NEF (1996) *Participatory Rapid Appraisal: NEF Experience and Applications*, Near East Foundation, Cairo

Nelson, N and Wright, S (1995) *Power and Participatory Development: Theory and Practice*, Intermediate Technology, London

Nelson, P (1997) 'Conflict, Legitimacy and Effectiveness: Who Speaks for Whom in Transnational NGO Networks Lobbying the World Bank', article submitted to *Nonprofit and Voluntary Sector Quarterly*, mimeo

Nelson P (1995) *The World Bank and Non-Governmental Organisations: The Limits of Apolitical Development*, Macmillan, Basingstoke

Network Cultures (1996) 'Quid pro Quo', *Culture and Development*, 24, South–North Network Cultures and Development, Brussels

New Economics Foundation (1995) *Social Audit Resource Kit*, New Economics Foundation, London

Newstrom, J W, Reif, W and Monczka, R (1975) *A Contingency Approach to Management: Readings*, McGraw-Hill, New York

Norton, M (1996) *The WorldWide Fundraiser's Handbook: A Guide to Fundraising for Southern NGOs and Voluntary Organisations*, Directory of Social Change, London

NOVIB (1996) *Investing in People: The Path to Self-Help ... and Interdependence*, NOVIB Coordinating Office, Manila

O'Leary, M and Simmons, M (1995) *Reflections: A Record of Training from the Evolution of Krom Akphiwat Phum*, Overseas Development Bureau of Australia, Canberra and Krom Akphiwat Phum, Battambang, Cambodia

Oakley, P (1999a) *Danish NGO Impact Study: A Review of Danish NGO Activities in Developing Countries – Synthesis Report*, INTRAC/Bech Distribution, Oxford/Copenhagen

Oakley, P(1999b) *Danish NGO Impact Study: A Review of Danish NGO Activities in Developing Countries – Summary Report*, INTRAC/Bech Distribution, Oxford/Copenhagen

Oakley, P, Pratt, B and Clayton, A (1998) *Outcomes and Impact: Evaluating Change in Social Development*, International Training and Research Centre, Oxford

O'Connor, J (1994) 'Towards Environmentally Sustainable Development: Measuring Progress', paper prepared for the IUCN–World Conservation Union General Assembly, Buenos Aires, January

ODI (1999) 'What Can We Do With A Rights-Based Approach to Development?, *Briefing Paper*, 1999(3), Overseas Development Institute, London

ODI (1996) 'The Impact of NGO Development Projects', Briefing Paper, 2, Overseas Development Institute, London, May

OECD (1999) *The Facts About European NGOs Active in International Development*, Organisation for Economic Cooperation and Development, Paris

Oestergaard, L (ed) (1993) *Gender and Development: A Practical Guide*, Routledge

Oxfam (1995) 'Women and Culture', *Gender and Development*, 3(1), Oxfam, Oxford

PACT (1998) *POAT User's Manual: Participatory Organizational Assessment Tool*, PACT, Washington, DC

PACT (1993) *Options for Sustainability: Reader and Report on Endowments as a Modality for Funding Development Work*, PACT/PRIP, Bangladesh

Paez, C and Noel Elano, J (1993) 'Financial Sustainability: The Philippine NGO Experience, *Transnational Associations*, 5, pp298–291, New York

Pascale, R, Millemann, and Gioja, L (1996) 'The Disciplines of Agility', *Working Paper*, 16, mimeo, draft

Patron, P (1998) 'Peru: Civil Society and the Autocratic Challenge', in van Rooy, (ed) *Civil Society and the Aid Industry*, pp168–196, Earthscan, London

Perkins, J and Sandringham, S (eds) (1998) *Trust, Motivation and Commitment: A Reader*, Strategic Renumeration Research

Centre, Farringdon

Pfeffer, J and Salancik, G (1978) *The External Control of Organizations: A Resource Dependence Perspective*, Harper and Row, New York

Pinzas, T (1997) 'Partners or Contractors? The Relationship Between Official Aid Agencies and NGOs – Peru', *Occasional Paper*, 15, International NGO Training and Research Centre, Oxford

Porter, D, Allen, B and Thompson, G (1991) *Development in Practice: Paved with Good Intentions*, Routledge, London

PRIA (1998a) *Capacity Building on Organisational Management of VDOs in India*, Society for Participatory research in India, New Delhi

PRIA (1998b) 'Politics of Capacity Building: South Asia Consultation of the International Working Group on Capacity Building', 27–28 November, 1997', *Institutional Development*, V(1): pp 65–69, Society for Participatory Research in Asia, New Delhi

Quarles van Ufford, P, Kruit D and Downing (1988) *The Hidden Crisis in Development: Development Bureaucracies*, Free University Press, Amsterdam

Raffer, K (1999) 'More Conditions and Less Money: Shifts in aid policies during the 1990s', paper presented at the Development Studies Association Conference, University of Bath, 11 September

Randell, J and German, T (eds) (1998) *The Reality of Aid: An Independent Review of Poverty Reduction and Development Assistance*, Earthscan, London

Randell, M (1999) 'No Magic Solutions...', *OD Debate*, 6(4): pp 9–10, Glenwood, SA, August

Rao, A and Hashemi, S (1999) 'Institutional Take-Off or Snakes and Ladders: Dynamics of sustainability of Local Level Organisations in Bangladesh', *Occasional Paper Series*, 30, International NGO Training and Research Centre, Oxford

Rao, A, Stuart, R and Kelleher, D (1999) *Gender at Work: Organizational Change for Equality*, Kumarian Press, West Hartford

Reddy, C (1999) 'Developing the other side of organisational life – those that stay "at the office"', *OD Debate*, 6(4): pp16–17, Glenwood, SA, October

Riddell, R, Bebbington, A with Davis, D (1995) *Developing Country NGOs and Donor Governments*, Overseas Development Institute, London

Rossing Feldman, T, and Assaf, S (1999) 'Social Capital: Conceptual Frameworks and Empirical Evidence – An Annotated Bibliography', *Social Capital Initiative Working Paper*, 5, Social Development Family, Environmentally and Socially Sustainable Development Network, The World Bank, Washington, D C

Rowlands, J (1995) 'Empowerment Examined', *Development in Practice*, 5(2): pp101–107, Oxfam, Oxford

Sahley, C (1995) *Strengthening the Capacity of NGOs: Cases of Small Enterprise Development Agencies in Africa*, NGO Management and Policy Series, 4, International NGO Training and Research Centre, Oxford

Said, E (1994) *Culture and Imperialism*, Vantage, London

Salamon, L (1994) 'The Rise of the Nonprofit Sector', *Foreign Affairs*, 73(2): pp109–122, July/August

Salamon, L and Anheier, H (1999) *The Emerging Sector Revisited: A Summary*, Center for Civil Society Studies, Johns Hopkins University, Baltimore

Salamon, L et al (1999) *Global Civil Society: Dimensions of the Nonprofit Sector*, Institute for Policy Studies, Center for Civil Society Studies, Johns Hopkins University, Baltimore

Sampson, A (1999) *Mandela: The Authorised Biography*, HarperCollins, London

Sandar, P (1990) 'A History of Philanthropy in India', Report to the Ford Foundation, New Delhi

Schearer, B, de Oliveira, M and Tandon, R (1997) 'A Strategic Guide to Resource Enhancement', in Fox, L and Schearer, B (eds) *Sustaining Civil Society: Strategies for Resource Mobilisation*, CIVICUS, Washington, DC

Schearer, B (1999) 'Aligning Grantmaking with Partnership', *Institutional*

Development, VI(1): pp29–38, Society for Participatory Research in Asia, New Delhi

Schearer, B, Winder, D and Tomlinson, J (1995) *The Emerging Role of Foundation-Like Organisations in Strengthening Civil Society in Southern Nations: Summary Findings of Case Study Research*, The Synergos Institute, Washington, DC

Schearer, S and Tomlinson, J (1995) *Case Studies of Partnership Efforts to Address Poverty and Development Problems in Africa: Policy Discussion Paper*, Synergos Institute, May

Schein, E (1999) *Process Consultation Revisited*, Addison-Wesley, Reading, Mass

Schein, E (1992) *Organisational Culture and Leadership*, Jossey-Bass, San Francisco

Schmidt, M and Marc, A (1994) 'Participation in Social Funds', *Environment Department Papers*, No 004, The World Bank, Washington, DC

Schoonhoven, C (1981) 'Problems with Contingency Theory', *Administrative Science Quarterly*, Cornell University, Ithaca, 26(3): pp349–337, September

Schutte, L (1995) 'Case Study project on the Process and Techniques of Foundation-Building in the South: The Kagiso Trust South Africa', Witwatersrand University, Johannesburg, mimeo

Scott, W (1987) *Organizations: Rational, Natural and Open Systems*, Prentice-Hall, Englewood Cliffs

Scott, W and Meyer, J (1994) *Institutional Environments and Organizations: Structural Complexity and Individualism*, Sage, London

SEARCH (1997a) 'Gender Training: Conceptual Framework, Process and Critical Issues', *Search Bulletin*, XII(4): October–December, Search Bangalore

SEARCH (1997b) 'Assessing Women's Empowerment: Indicators, Designs and Methods', *Search Bulletin*, XII(3), July–September, Search Bangalore

Selle, P and Strømsnes, K (1998) 'Membership and democracy: Should we take passive support seriously?', paper presented at a conference on Participation – The New Tyranny? 3–4 November, Institute of

Development Policy Management, Manchester

Semboja, J and Therkildsen, O (eds) (1995) *Service Provision Under Stress: States and Voluntary Organisations in Kenya, Tanzania and Uganda*, James Currey, London

Senge, P (1990) *The Fifth Discipline: The Art and Practice of the Learning Organisation*, Doubleday, New York

Shetty, S (1991) *The Assessment of 'Empowerment' in Development Projects – An Enquiry*, Master of Science Thesis in Social Policy and Planning in Developing Countries, London School of Economics and Political Science, London, mimeo

SIAD (1995) *SIAD Tool Box: A Collection of Operational Pointers and Instruments for Sustainable Integrated Area Development*, SIAD Organising Committee, Kaisahan, Manila

SIDA (1996) *Aid dependency: Causes, Symptoms and Remedies*, Swedish International Development Agency, Stockholm

Sidel, M (1997) 'The emergence of the voluntary sector and philanthropy in Vietnam: functions, legal regulation and prospects for the future', *Voluntas*, 8(3): pp283–302

Smillie, I (1995) *The Alms Bazaar: Altruism Under Fire – Non-Profit Organizations and International Development*, IT Publications, London

Smillie, I (1999) 'At Sea in a Sieve? Trends and issues in the relationship between Northern NGOs and Northern Governments', in *Stakeholders: Government–NGO Partnerships for Development*, pp7–38, Earthscan, London

Smillie, I and Helmich, H (eds) (1993) *Non-Governmental Organisations and Governments: Stakeholders for Development*, OECD, Paris

Smillie, I and Helmich H (eds) (1999) *Stakeholders: Government–NGO Partnerships for Development*, Earthscan, London

Smillie, I, Douxchamps, F, Sholes, R and Covey, J (1996) 'Partners or Contractors? Official Donor Agencies and Direct Funding Mechanisms: Three Northern

Case Studies – CIDA, EU and USAID', *Occasional Paper Series*, 11, International NGO Training and Research Centre, Oxford

Smillie, I and Hailey, J (2000) *Management for Change: Myths and Realities in South Asian NGO Management*, Aga Khan Foundation, Geneva

Smith, B (1997) 'Happy Endings? Exit, withdrawal and development relationships', *OD Debate*, 4(3):pp15–17, Glenwood, SA, June

Smith, C (1994) 'The New Corporate Philanthropy', *Harvard Business Review*, pp 05–116, May–June

Soares, J and Caccia-Bava, S (eds) (1998) *Os Desafios da Gestão Municipal Democrática* (The Challenges of Democratic Municipal Government), Cortex, São Paulo

Sobhan, B (1997) 'Partners or Contractors? The Relationship Between Official Aid Agencies and NGOs in Bangladesh', *Occasional Paper Series*, 14, International NGO Training and Research Centre, Oxford

Sogge, D (ed) (1996) *Compassion and Calculation: The Business of Private Aid Agencies*, Pluto Press, London

Srivasta, S and Cooperrider, D (eds) (1999) *Appreciative Management and Leadership: The Power of Positive Thought and Action in Organisations*, Williams, Edison, Ohio

Staudt, K (1990) *Women, International Development and Politics: The Bureaucratic Mire*, Temple University Press

Steckel, R (1989) *Filthy Rich and other Nonprofit Fantasies – Changing the way nonprofits do business in the 90s*, Ten Speed Press, Berkeley

Sterkenburg, J (1987) 'Rural Development and Rural Development Policies: Cases from Africa and Asia', *Nederlands Geographische Studies*, 46, Konikrijk Nederlands Aardrijkskunde Genootschap/Geographische Institute, Rijksuniversiteit, Utrecht

Sterkenburg, J and van der Wiel, (eds) (1999) *Integrated Area Development:*

Experiences with Netherlands Aid in Africa, Netherlands Development Assistance Agency, The Hague

Strachen, P with Peters, C (1997) *Empowering communities: A Casebook from West Sudan*, Oxfam, Oxford

Sutton, R (1999) 'The Policy Process: An Overview', *Working Papers*, No, 118, Overseas Development Institute, London

Swieringa, J and Wierdsma, A (1992) *Becoming a Learning Organization: Beyond the learning curve*, Addison-Wesley

Tandon, R (1994) 'NGO–State Relations in Asia: A Research Agenda', Society for Participatory Research in India, New Delhi

Tandon, R (1989a) *NGO–Government Relations: A Source of Life or A Kiss of Death?*, Society for Participatory Research in Asia, New Delhi

Tannen, D (1996) *You Just Don't Understand: Women and Men in Conversation*, Virago, London

Taylor, J (1998) 'On the road to becoming a learning organisation', *OD Debate*, 5(5): pp3–7, Glenwood, SA, October

Taylor, J, Marais, D and Heyns, S (eds) (1998) *Community Participation and Financial Sustainability*, Community Development Resource Association and Juta Press, Cape Town

Thaw, D (1999) 'Working with Resistance' *Ideas for Change*, Part 4, Olive Publications, Glenwood, SA, June

Thaw, D (1997) 'How well do you "read" your organisation?' *Ideas for Change*, Part 2, Olive Publications, Glenwood, SA, December

Thaw, D and Petersen, R (1997) 'How are you managing organisational change', *Ideas for Change*, Part 1, Olive Publications, Glenwood, SA, July

Thom, G (1999) 'Accreditation and Power: fighting the kitemark', *Alliance*, 4(3): pp17–18, Charities Aid Foundation, London

Thurow, L (1996) *The Future of Capitalism*, William Morrow, New York

Townsend, J (1999) 'Are Non-governmental Organisations Working in Development a Transnational Community?', *Journal of*

International Development, 11(4): pp613–623

Trompenaars, F (1993) *Riding the Waves of Culture: Understanding Cultural Difference in Business*, Nicholas Brealey, London

Turniansky, B and Cwikel, J (1996) 'Volunteering in a voluntary community: Kibbutz members and voluntarism', *Voluntas*, 7(3): pp300–317

UNDP (1993) *Human Development Report*, United Nations Development Programme, Oxford University Press, Oxford

UNHCR (1994) *Partnership in Action (PARINAC): Oslo Declaration and Plan of Action*, UNHCR, Geneva

Uphoff, N (1992) 'Local Institutions and Participation for Sustainable Development', *Gatekeeper Series*, 34, International Institute for Environment and Development, London

Uphoff, N (1991) 'A Field Methodology for Participatory Self-Evaluation, *Community Development Journal*, 26(4): pp271–286, Oxford University Press, Oxford, October

Uphoff, N (1989) 'Field Methodology for Participatory Self-Evaluation of PPP Group and Inter-Group Association Performance', Paper prepared for the People's Participation Programme of the U N Food and Agricultural Organisation, Cornell University, Ithaca, mimeo, May

Uphoff, N, Esman, M and Krishna, A (1998) *Reasons for Success: Learning From Instructive Experiences in Rural Development*, Kumerian Press, West Hartford

Uphoff, N (1992) *Learning from Gal Oya: possibilities for participatory development and post-Newtonian social science*, Cornell University Press, Ithaca, NY

Vaill, P (1996) *Learning as a Way of Being*, Jossey-Bass, San Francisco

Valderrama, M (1999) 'Latin American NGOs in an Age of Scarcity: When Quality Matters', paper presented at a conference on NGOs in a Global Future, 8–11 January, Birmingham

van Rooy, A (ed) (1998) *Civil Society and the Aid Industry*, Earthscan, London

van Schalkwyk, L (1999) 'Mentoring in context', *OD Debate*, 6(3): pp13–15,

Glenwood, SA, June

van Tuijl, P (1999) 'NGOs and Human Rights: Sources of Justice and Democracy', *Journal of International Affairs*, 52(2): pp493–512

Vincent, F and Campbell, P (1989) *Towards Greater Financial Autonomy*, A Manual on Financing Strategies and Techniques for Development NGOs and Community Organisations, IRED, Geneva

von Nostrand, C (1993) *Gender Responsible Leadership: Detecting Bias, Implementing Interventions*, Sage, London

Wallace, T, Crowther, S and Shephard, A (1998) *The Standardisation of Development: Influences on UK NGOs' Policies and Procedures*, Worldview Press, Oxford

WCED (1987) *Our Common Future*, World Commission on Environment and Development, OUP, Oxford

Weiss, T (ed) (1998) *Beyond UN Subcontracting: Task-Sharing with Regional Security Arrangements and Service-Providing NGOs*, Macmillan, Basingstoke

Westoby, P (1997) 'A Soulful Approach to Community Development', *AVOCADO Series*, 2 (97), Olive Publishers, Durban

Wheatley, M (1994) *Leadership and the New Science*, Berrett-Koehler, San Francisco

Wheatley, M and Kellner-Rogers, M (1999) 'Bringing Life to Organisational Change', The Berkana Institute, Provo, Utaha

Whiteside, M (1999) 'Empowering the landless: Case studies in land distribution and tenure security for the poor', *Developing Good Practice Discussion Series*, 2, Christian Aid, London

Wolfe, A (1989) *Whose Keeper?: Social Science and Moral Obligation*, University of California Press, Berkeley

Wood, G and Sharif, I (eds) (1997) *Who Needs Credit?: Poverty and Finance in Bangladesh*, University Press, Dhaka

Wood, S (1979) 'A Reappraisal of the Contingency Approach to Organization', *Journal of Management Studies*, pp335–357, October

Woolcock, M (1997) 'Social Capital and Economic Development: Towards a Theoretical Synthesis and Policy

Framework', paper presented at the 90th Annual Meeting of American Sociological Association, Washington, DC

Woolcock, M and Narayan, D (1999) 'Social Capital: Implications for Development Theory, Research and Policy', paper submitted to the *World Bank Research Observer*, World Bank, Washington DC, February

World Bank (1996) *The World Bank Participation Sourcebook*, Environmentally Sustainable Development Division, World Bank, Washington, DC

World Bank (1998) *Assessing Aid: What Works, What Doesn't and Why*, World Bank, Washington, DC

World Vision (1997) 'African Voices on Advocacy', *Discussion Paper 4*, Spring, World Vision, Milton Keynes

World Vision (1997) 'Transnational NGOs and Advocacy', *Discussion Paper 5*, World Vision, Milton Keynes

Young, G, Samarasinghe, V and Kusterer, K (1993) *Women at the Centre: Development Issues and Practices for the 1990s*, Kumerian Press, West Hartford

Young, N and Woo, A (1999) *An Introduction to the Non-Profit Sector in China*, Charities Aid Foundation, London, draft

Zadek, S and Evans, R (1993) *Auditing the Market: A Practical Approach to Social Auditing*, New Economics Foundation/ Tradecraft, London/Gateshead

Zadek, S and Raynard, P (1994) 'Accounting for Change: The Practice of Social Auditing', New Economics Foundation, London, mimeo

Zand, D (1996) *The Leadership Triad: Knowledge, Trust and Power*, Oxford University Press

Zhu Youhong (1999) 'Social Innovation of China's Third Sector: views on the birth and development of non-profit organisations', paper presented at an International Conference of the Development of Non-profit Organisations and the China Project Hope, Beijing, November

Further Reading

The suggested readings are heuristic. They do not represent a systematic review of available literature, but items that have proven useful for this study.

Part I – Sustainable Impact

Sustainability thinking

In relation to the physical environment and other systems: Anderson et al, 1988; Clayton and Radcliffe, 1996; Daly and Cobb, 1990; Edwards, 1999; Elliott, 1996; Elkington, 1997; Trist, 1980.

In relation to NGDOs: Anheier, 1995; Cannon, 1999; Cumming and Singleton, 1995; Fowler and Young, 1998; Herman and Heimovics, 1994; Randell, 1999; Smillie, 1995.

NGDO Development Approaches and Processes

Participation: Blackburn, 1996; Cleaver, 1999; Donnelly-Roark, 1995; IIED, 1995; Jena, 1995; Mosse, 1998; Narayan, 1995; Oakley, 1991; Schmidt and Marc, 1994; World Bank, 1996.

NGDO micro-development approaches: Archer and Cottingham, 1996, 1999; Burkey, 1993; Chambers, 1983, 1987, 1993, 1997; Carney, 1999; Chambers, Pacey and Longhurst; 1981; Eade, 1997a; Korten, 1980; Myer, 1999, 1997, 1999b; Wallace et al, 1998.

NGDOs, macro-level development and the policy process: Clark, 1991; Edwards, 1993; Fisher, 1993, 1997; Najam, 1999; Sutton, 1999; Townsend, 1999.

Gender and development: Moser, 1993; Oestergaard, 1993; Oxfam, 1995; SEARCH, 1997a, 1997b; Young et al, 1993.

NGDO accountability: Fox and Brown, 1998; Edwards and Hulme, 1992; Jordan and van Tuijl, 1997; Nelson, 1997.

Sustainability and NGDO interventions: Brown, 1990, 1994; Dass, 1999; Taylor et al, 1998.

Withdrawal: Bhat and Cheria, 1997; Fowler, 1997; Holloway, 1997; Smith, 1997.

Community Capacity Building and Empowerment

Local institutional capacity building: AKRSP, 1992; Booij and Ole Sena, 1998; Eade, 1997a; Esman and Uphoff, 1984; Howes, 1999; Rao and Hashemi, 1999; Uphoff, 1991, 1992.

Empowerment: Craig and Mayo, 1995; Friere, 1973; Holland and Heriot, 1983; Nelson and Wright, 1995; Strachen and Peters, 1997; Whiteside, 1999.

Social capital (and development): Collier, 1999; Harriss, 1997; Krishna and Shrader, 1999; Rossing-Feldman and Assaf, 1999; Woolcock, 1997; Woolcock and Narayan, 1999.

Indicators

Sustainable development: Carvalho and White, 1993; Davies and Williamson, 1994; Eckman, 1993; Frankenberger, 1993; Greeley et al, 1992; Hammond et al, 1995; Harding, 1991; Karas and Coates, 1994; OECD, 1998; Oakley, Pratt and Clayton, 1998; O'Connor, 1994.

On CBO *capacity and empowerment*: KRSP,
1992; Alianza, 1995; Duran, 1999; Rowlands,
1995; Shetty, 1991; Uphoff, 1991.

NGDOs: Kanter, 1979; Fowler, 1997; Herman
and Heimovics, 1994; Lawrie, 1993.

Performance – Results, Assessment and Social Audit

Micro-impact: Cox and Healy, 1998; Edwards
and Hulme, 1992; Gibbs, Fumo and Kuby,
1999; Hossain and Myllylä, 1998; Krishna,
Uphoff and Esman, 1998; ODI, 1996; Oakley,
1999; Sogge, 1996; World Bank, 1998.

Policy reform: Fox and Brown, 1998; Miller,
1994; Najam, 1999.

Social Audit: New Economics Foundation,
1995; Zadek and Evans, 1993; Zadek and
Raynard, 1994.

Part II – Sustainability of Resources

Resource dependency

Aldrich and Pfeffer; 1976; Chang and
Tuckman, 1994; Heimovics et al, 1993;
Hudock, 1995; Newstrom et al, 1975; Pfeffer
and Salancik, 1978; Scott, 1987; Scott and
Meyer, 19994; Wood, 1979.

Resource mobilisation

Bennett and Gibbs, 1996; Brudney, 1990; CAF,
1994; Cannon, 1999b; Fox and Schearer,
1997; Holloway, 1999a, 1999b; Norton,
1996; NOVIB, 1996; PACT, 1993.

Social entrepreneurship

Badelt, 1997; Bonbright, 1997; Boschee, 1998;
Davis, 1997; Dees, 1998; Hordijk, 1999;
Steckel, 1989.

NGOs, Donors and the Aid System

Bonbright, 1999; Clark, 1993; Hulme and
Edwards, 1996; INTRAC, 1998; Nelson,
1995; Schearer, 1999; Smillie and Helmich,
1993, 1999; Smillie et al, 1996; Smillie, 1999.

Partnership

In development system: Eade, 1997b; Fowler,
1998, 1999b; Hallowes, 1995; Knight, 1998;
Malhotra, 1997; Muchunguzi and Milne,
1997; PACT, 1990.

With business, including corporate citizenship:
Enderle and Peters, 1998; GrandMet, 1997;
Heap, 1998; Heap and Fowler, 1999; Murphy
and Bendell, 1997; Smith, 1994.

Part III – Sustainability of the Organisation

Organisation and Leadership

General and profit-making organisations:
Adair, 1990; Beatty, 1998; Bennis, 1989, 1994;
Burns, 1998; de Board, 1993; Fiedler, 1967;
Gardner, 1991; Handy, 1985; Hatch, 1997;
Hesselbein et al, 1997; Kouzes and Posner,
1995; Mant, 1997; Schein, 1992; Srivasta and
Cooperrider, 1999; Vaill, 1996; Zand, 1996.

*Non-profit making organisations (and
management)*: Adirondack, 1992; Smillie and
Hailey, 2000; Bonbright, 1997; Drucker,
1990a, 1990b; Fowler, 1997; Hailey, 1999;
Handy, 1998; Leat, 1993.

Gender: Coleman, 1991; Kanter, 1993;
Macdonald et al, 1997; Staudt, 1990; Tannen,
1996; van Nostrand, 1993; Rao, Stuart and
Kelleher, 1999.

Organisational learning and assessment

Learning: Britton, 1998; Davis, 1998;
Edwards, 1997; Johnson and Wilson, 1996;
Kelleher and McLaren, 1996; Moingeon and

Edmonson, 1996; Lessem, 1991; Senge, 1990; Swieringa and Wierdsma, 1992; Vaill, 1996.

Assessment tools for capacity building: Britton, 1998; Fowler, Goold and James, 1995; Leach, 1994; PACT, 1998; Sahley, 1995.

Social audit: see Part I.

NGO accreditation: Bieshon, 1999; Kingman, 1999; Thom, 1999.

Organisational change and leadership regeneration

NGDO capacity building: CDRA, 1998, 1999; Cooperrider et al, 1995; Eade, 1997; Fowler, 1994, 1997; IFCB, 1998; Kaplan, 1996, 1999; PRIA, 1998.

General and NGDOs: Avina, 1993; Fowler, 1997; James, 1994, 1998, 1999a, 1999b; Kelleher and McLaren, 1996; Kotter, 1996; Lopa, 1995; Macdonald et al, 1997; Thaw and Petersen, 1997; Wheatley and Kellner-Rogers, 1999.

Mentoring and accompanying

Fowler, 1997; Hughes, 1998; Hallowes, 1998; van Schalkwyk, 1999.

Index